Un-pre-dict-able™

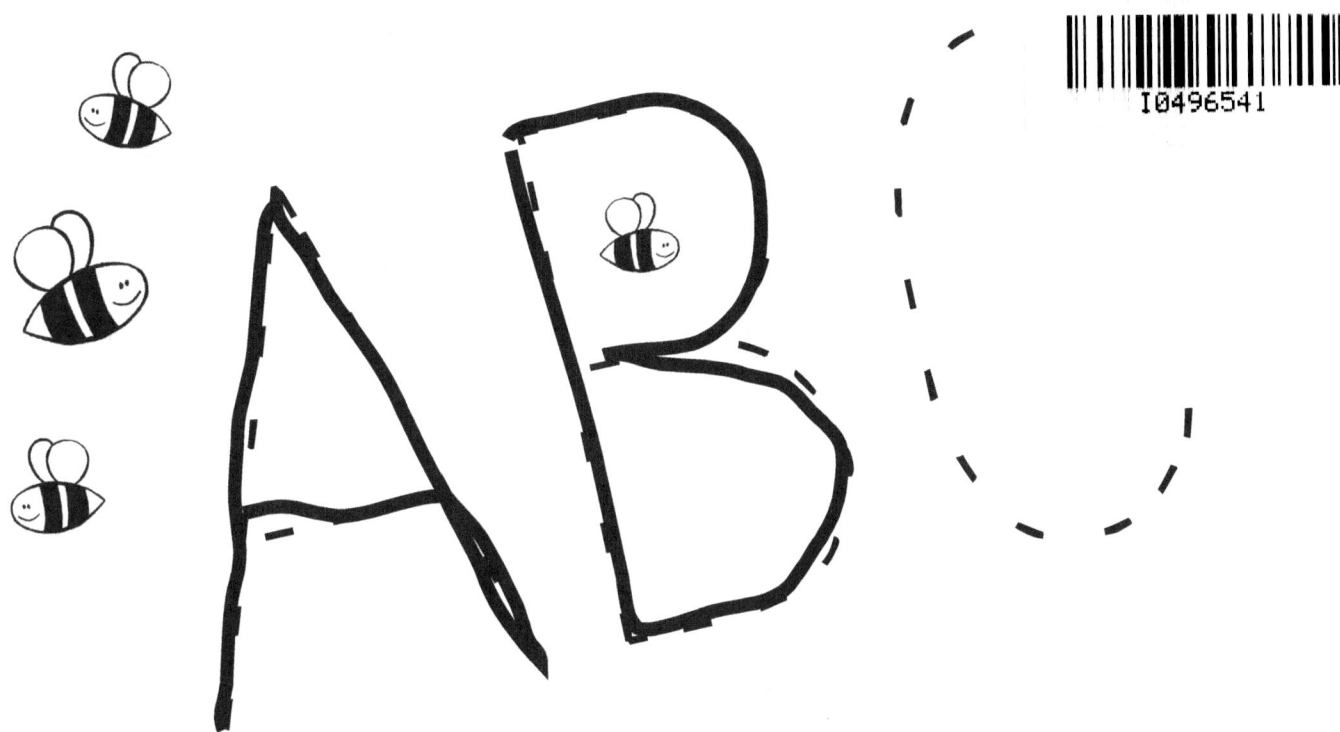

Color, Write and Read

(with some unexpected twists along the way!)

Created by Krysta Bernhardt

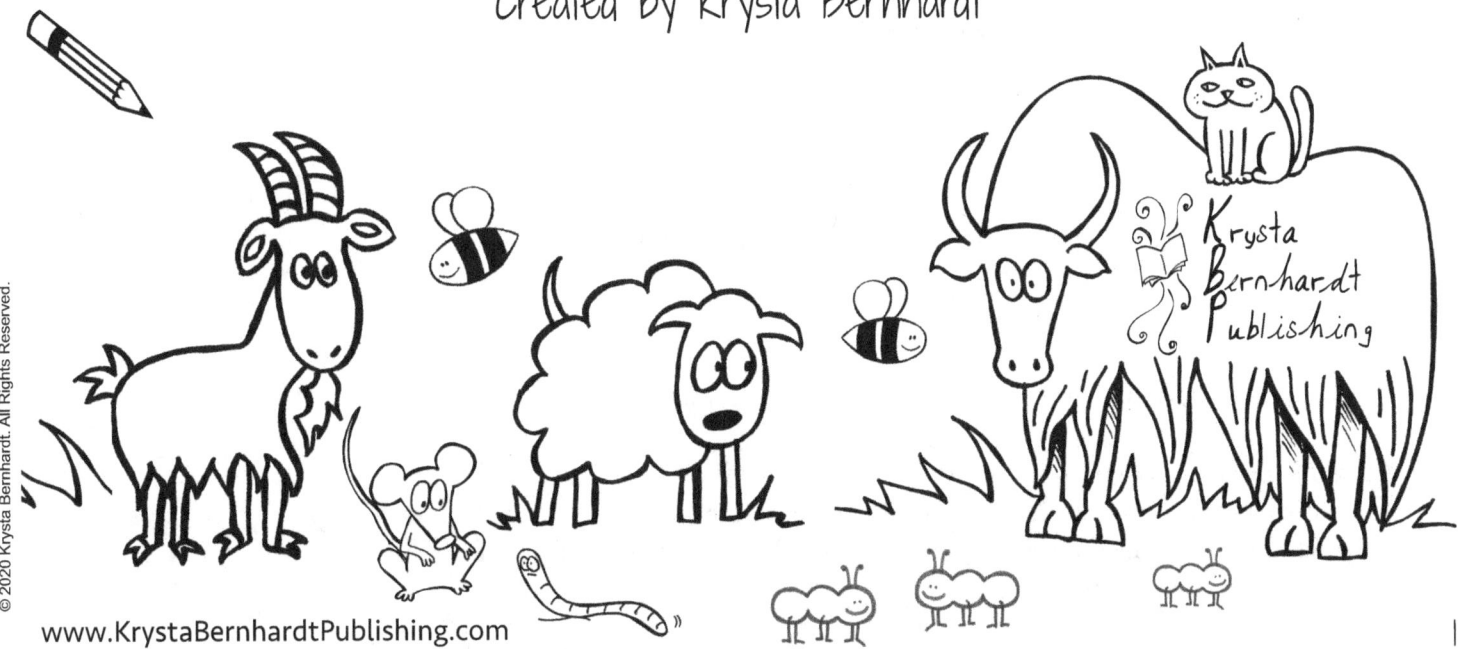

Special thanks to David, Gavyn, Owen, my extended family and my friends who have always supported my creative ideas. This little book is dedicated to my inner child who is always saying "you can do this!" even when the grown up me sometimes has other ideas.

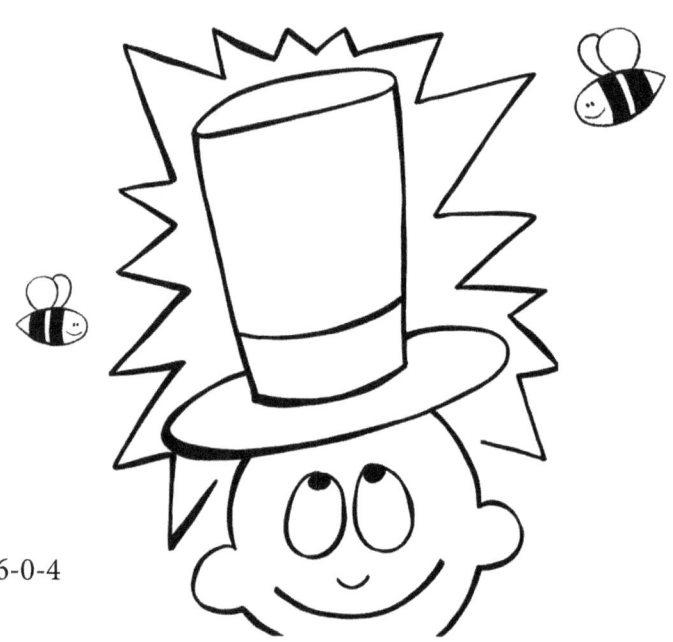

ISBN: 978-1-7355696-0-4

Copyright © 2020 Krysta Bernhardt Publishing, Zieglerville, PA

www.KrystaBernhardtPublishing.com

All contents, text, design and illustrations created by Krysta Bernhardt

All rights reserved. No part of this book may be reproduced or transmitted in any form or by any means, electronic or mechanical, including photocopying, recording, or by any information storage and retrieval system without the written permission of the author, except where permitted by law.

Aa Bb Cc Dd Ee Ff Gg Hh Ii Jj Kk Ll Mm Nn

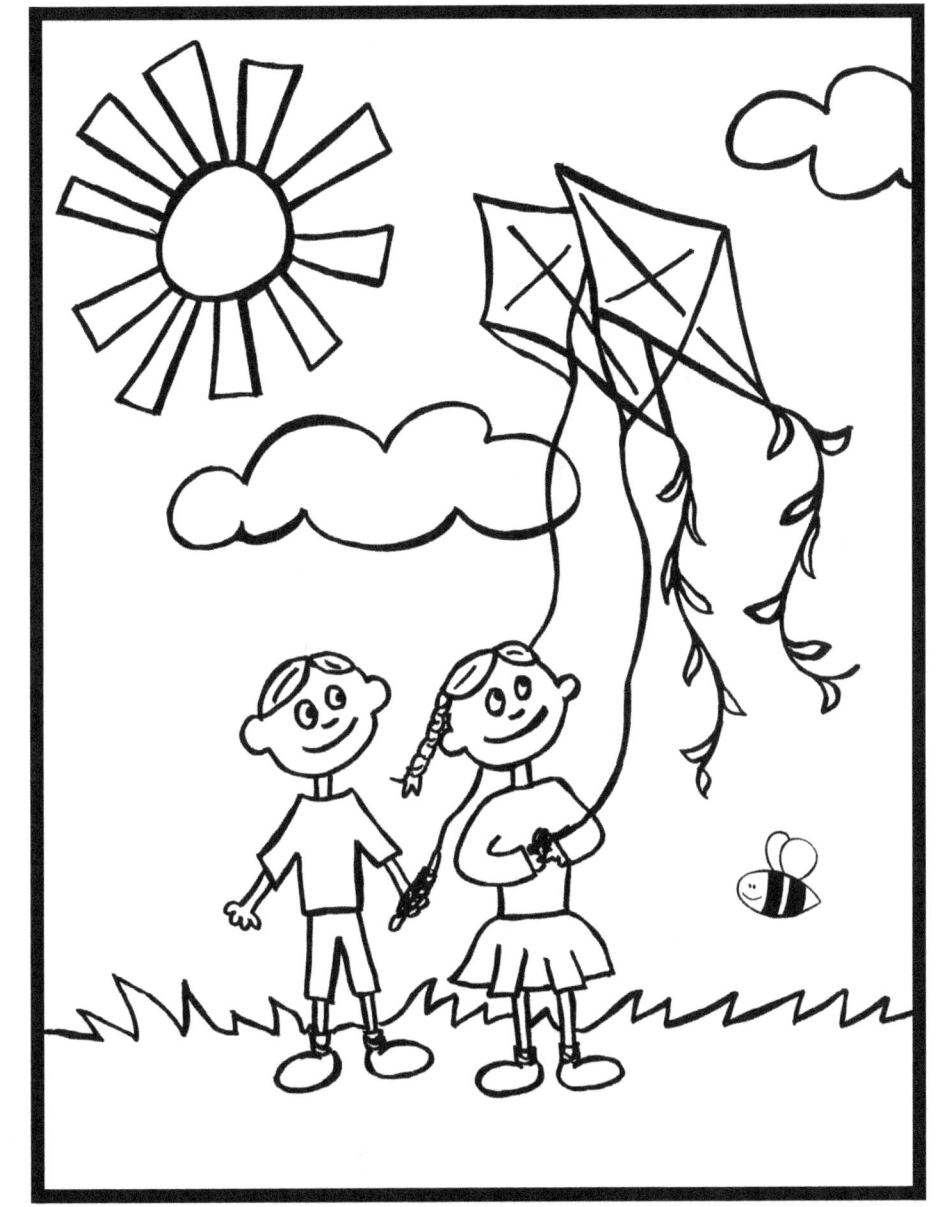

Oo Pp Qq Rr Ss Tt Uu Vv Ww Xx Yy Zz

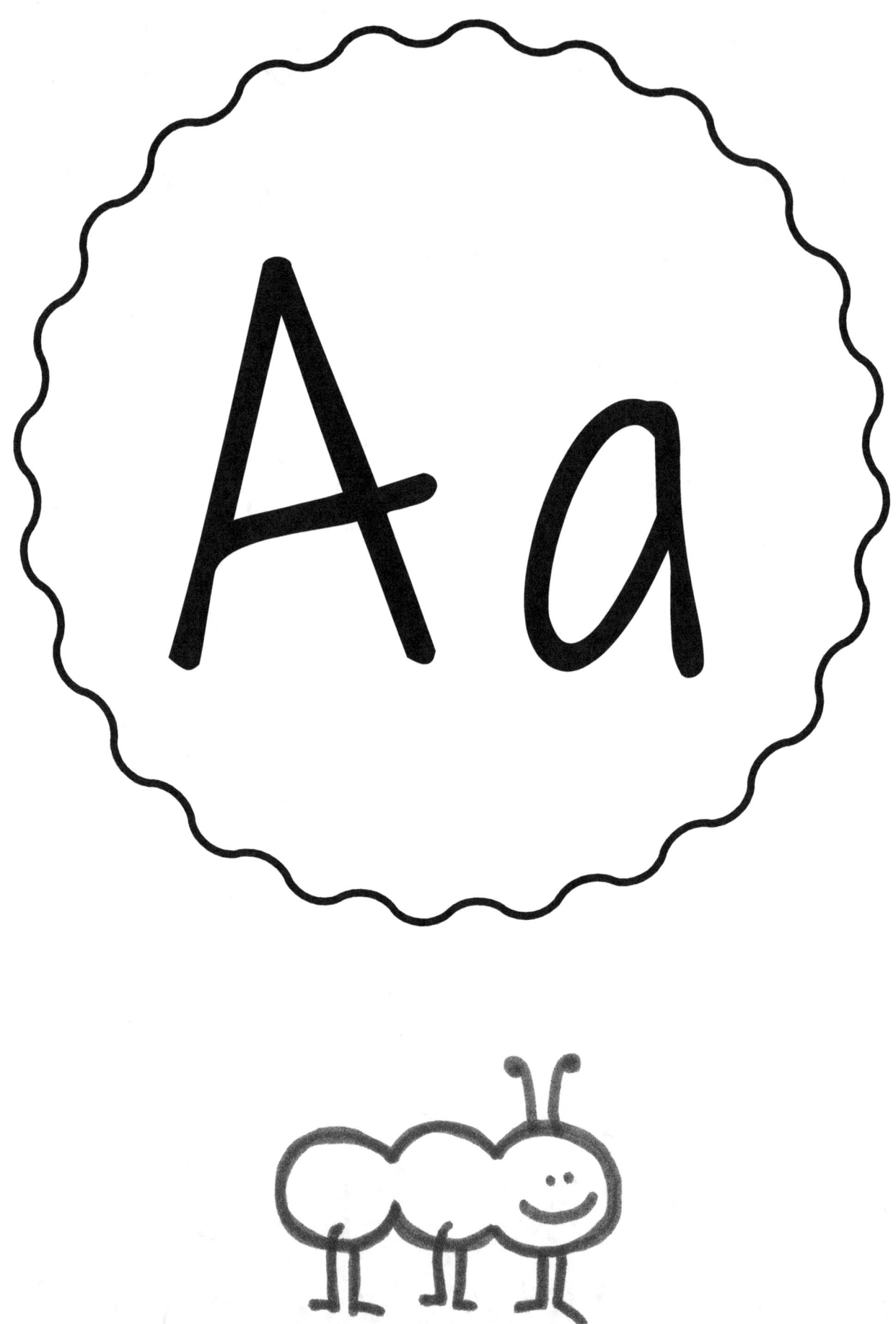

Color the picture, then trace and write the letters below.

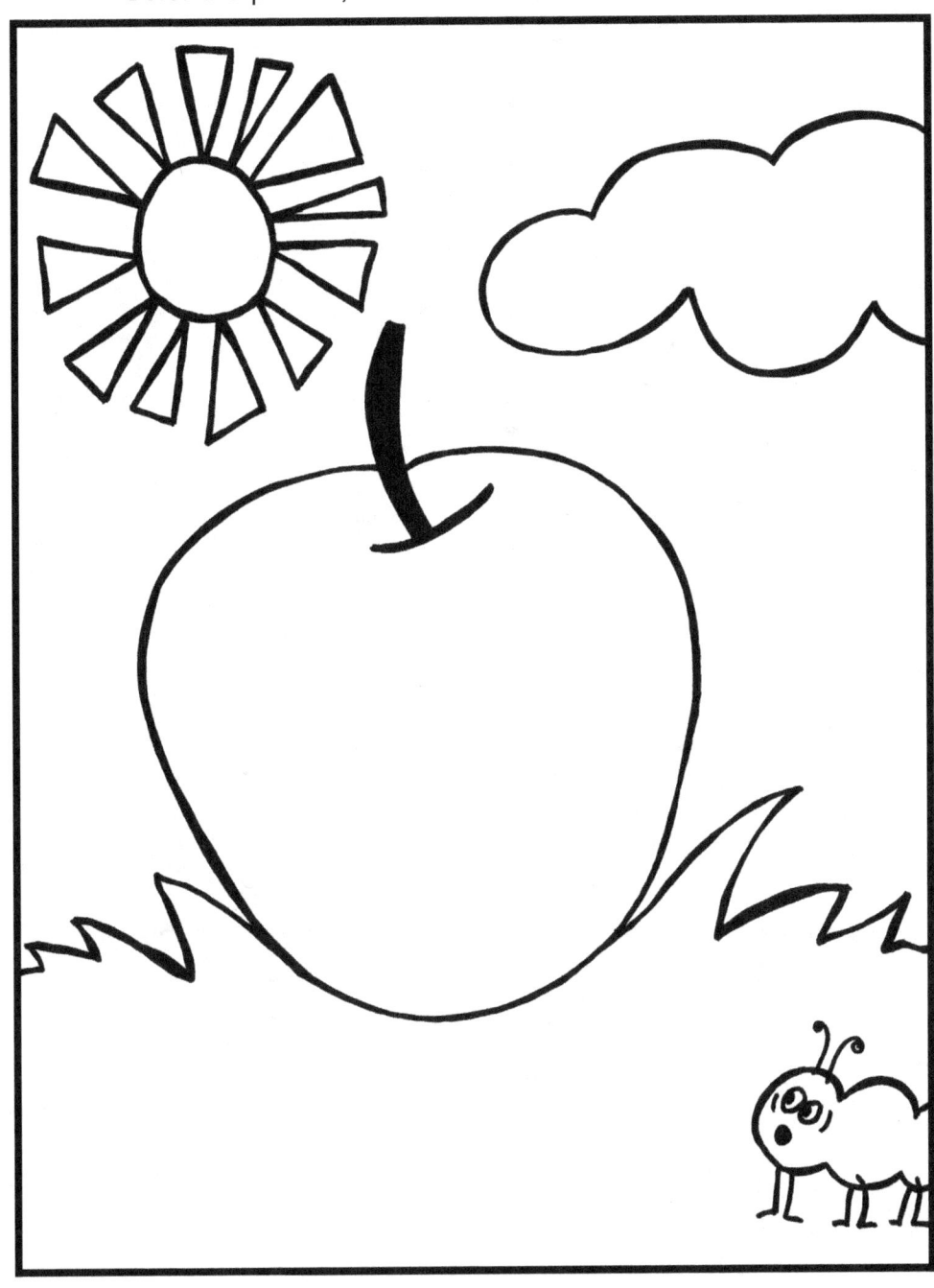

Color the picture, then trace and write the word below.

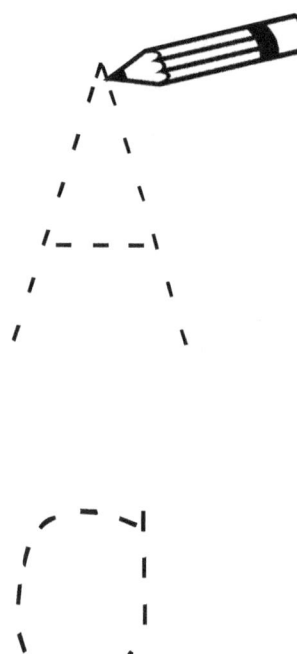

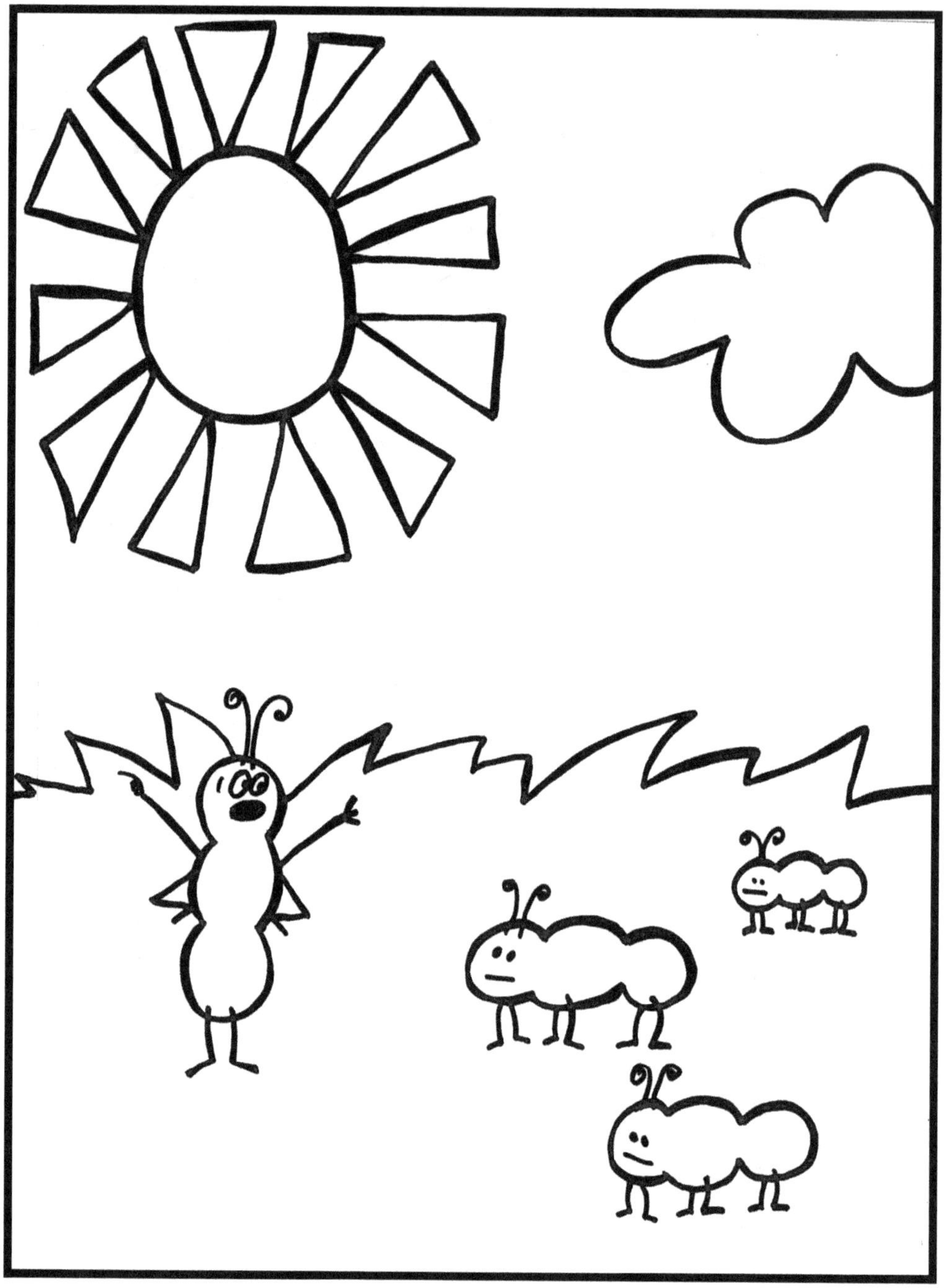

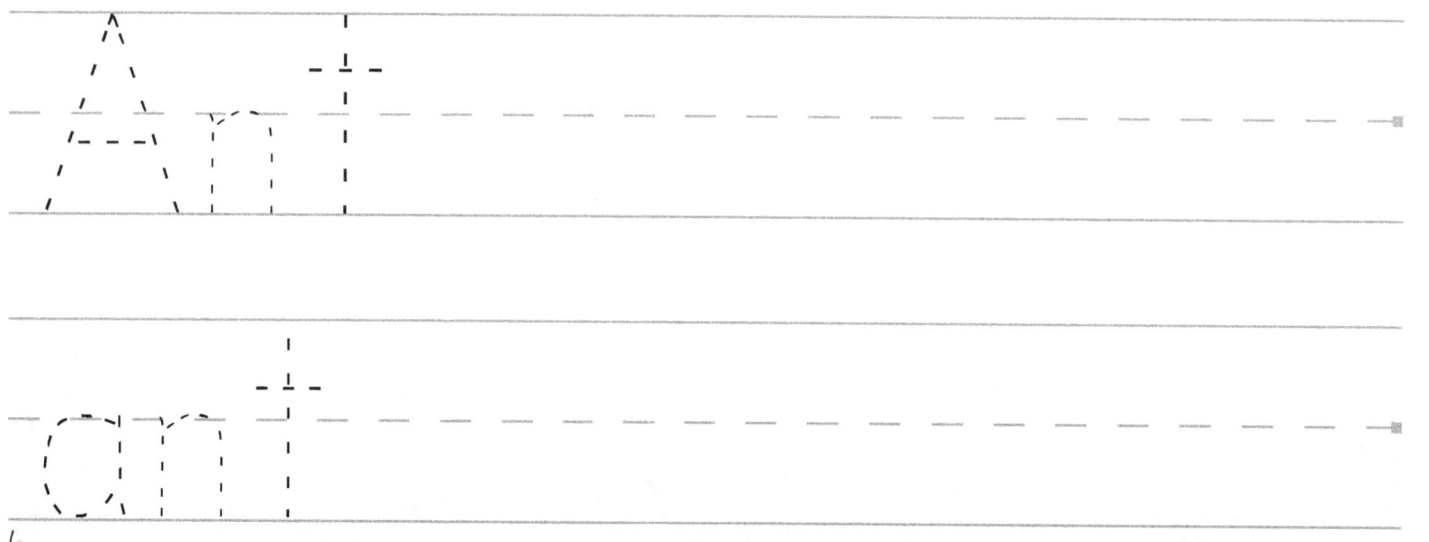

Color the picture, then trace and write the phrase below.

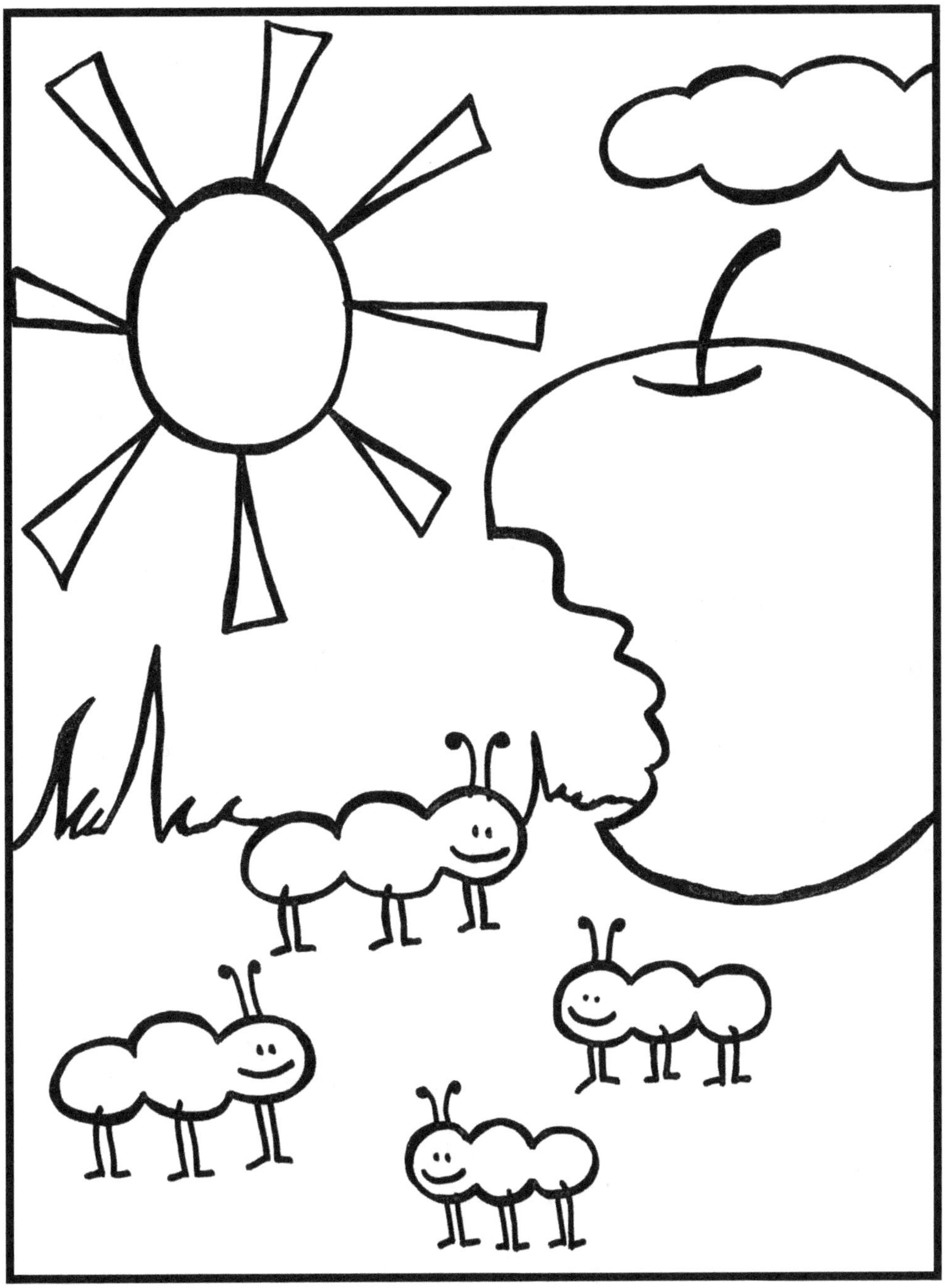

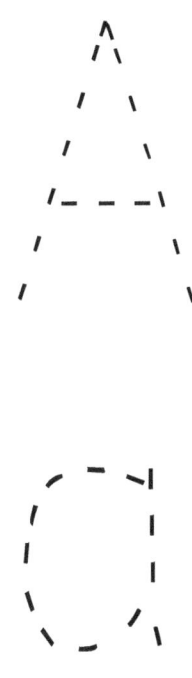

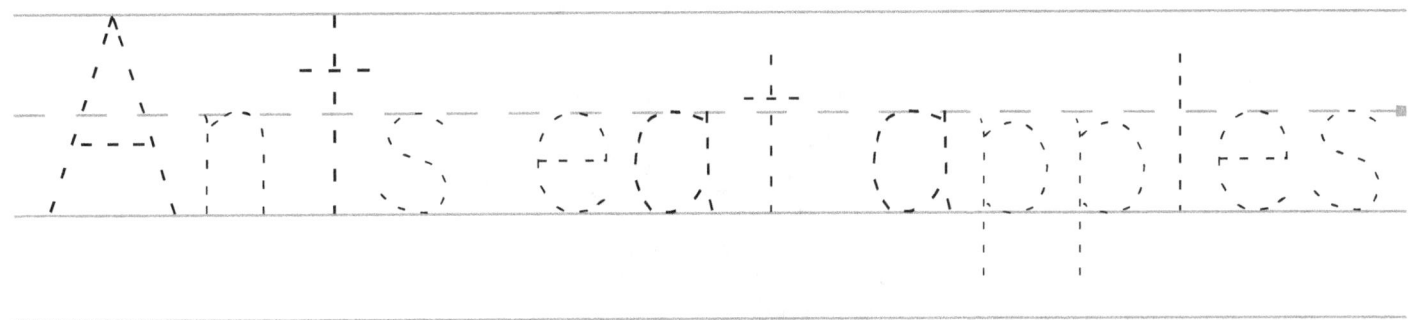

Bb

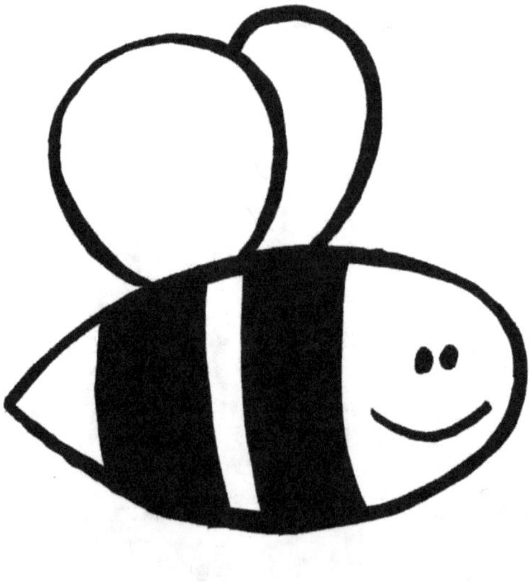

Color the picture, then trace and write the letters below.

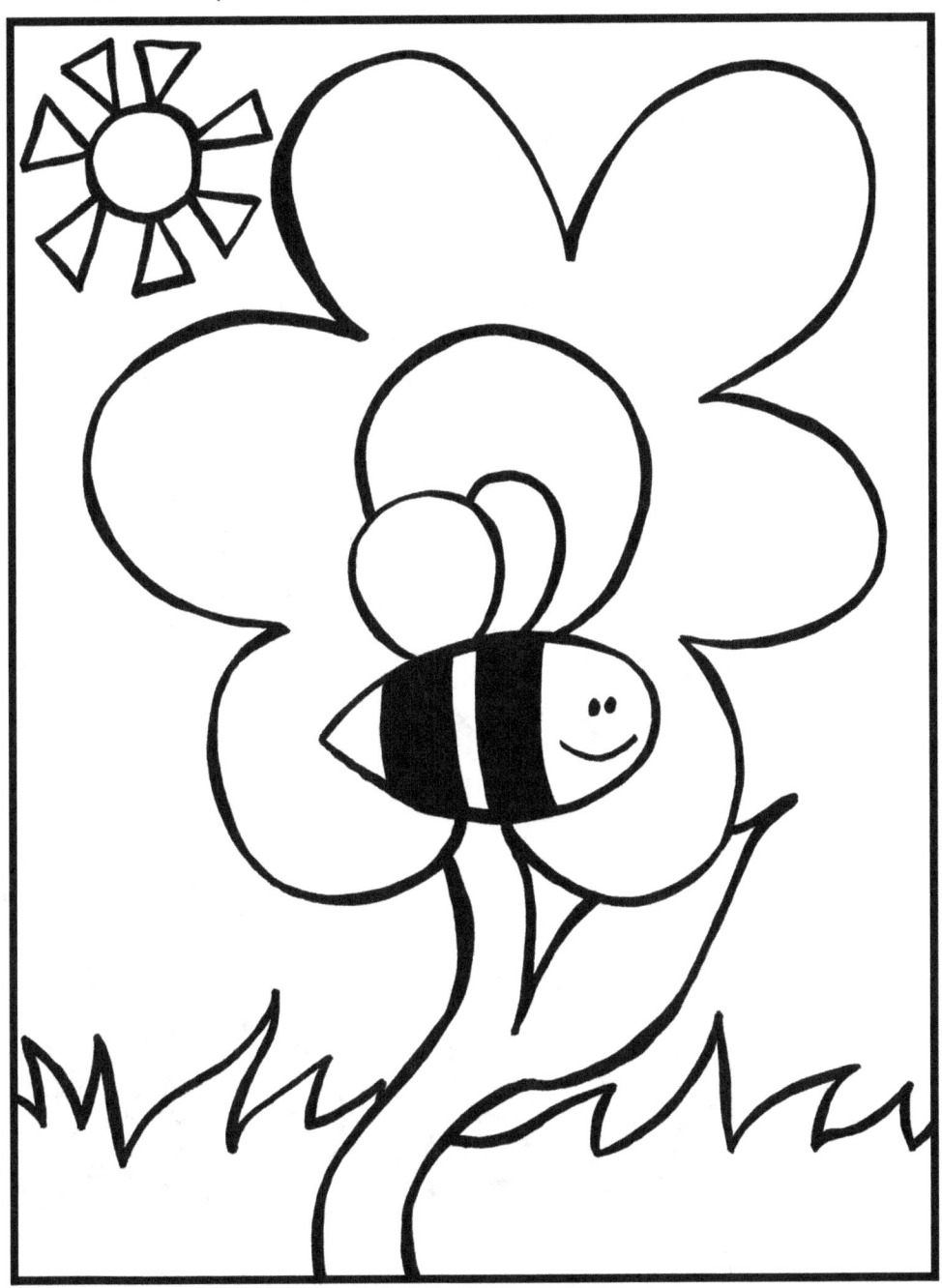

Color in the picture and trace the letters below.

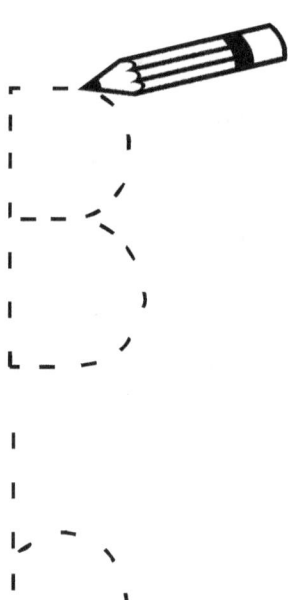

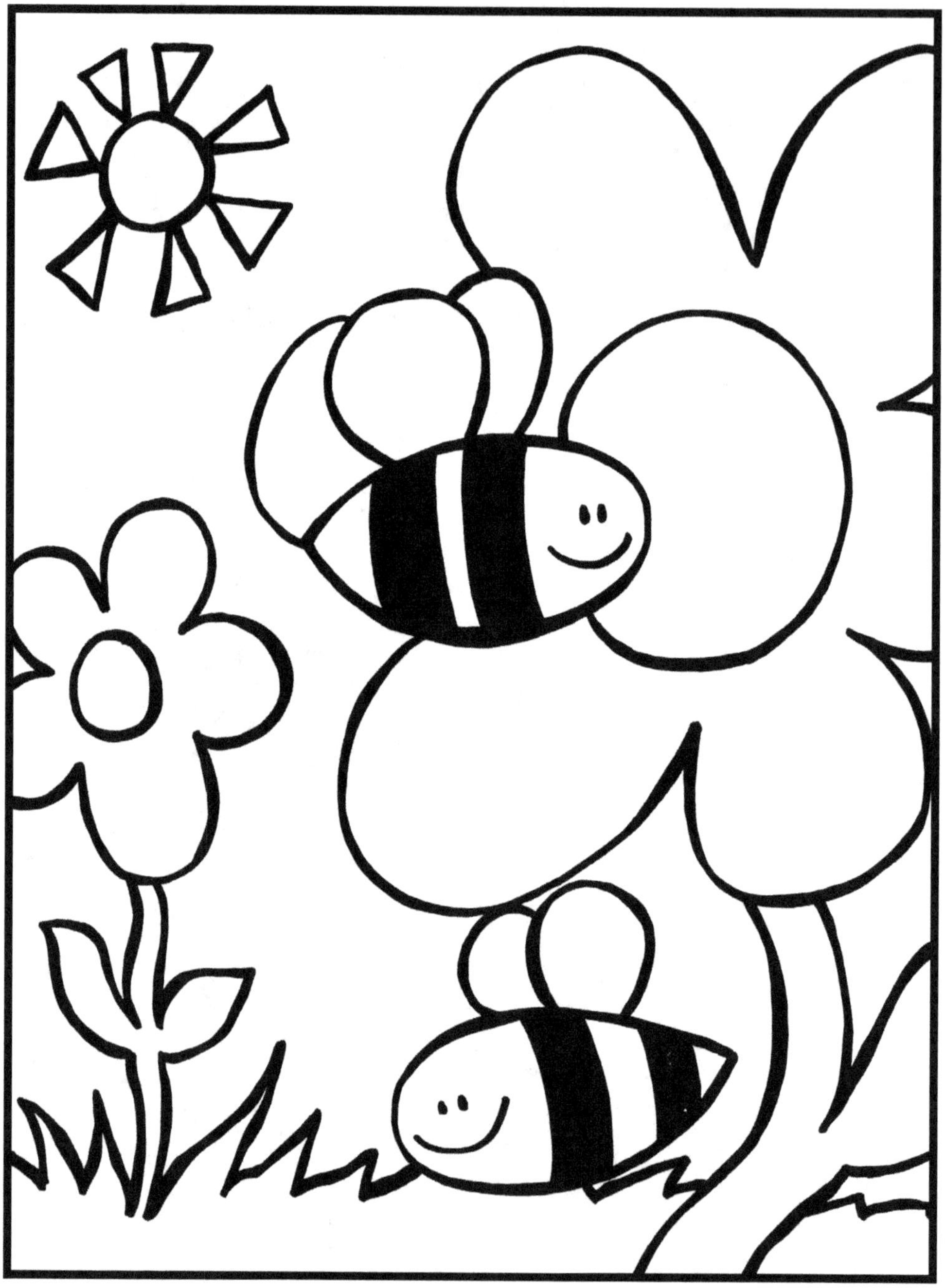

Bee

bee

Color the picture, then trace and write the phrase below.

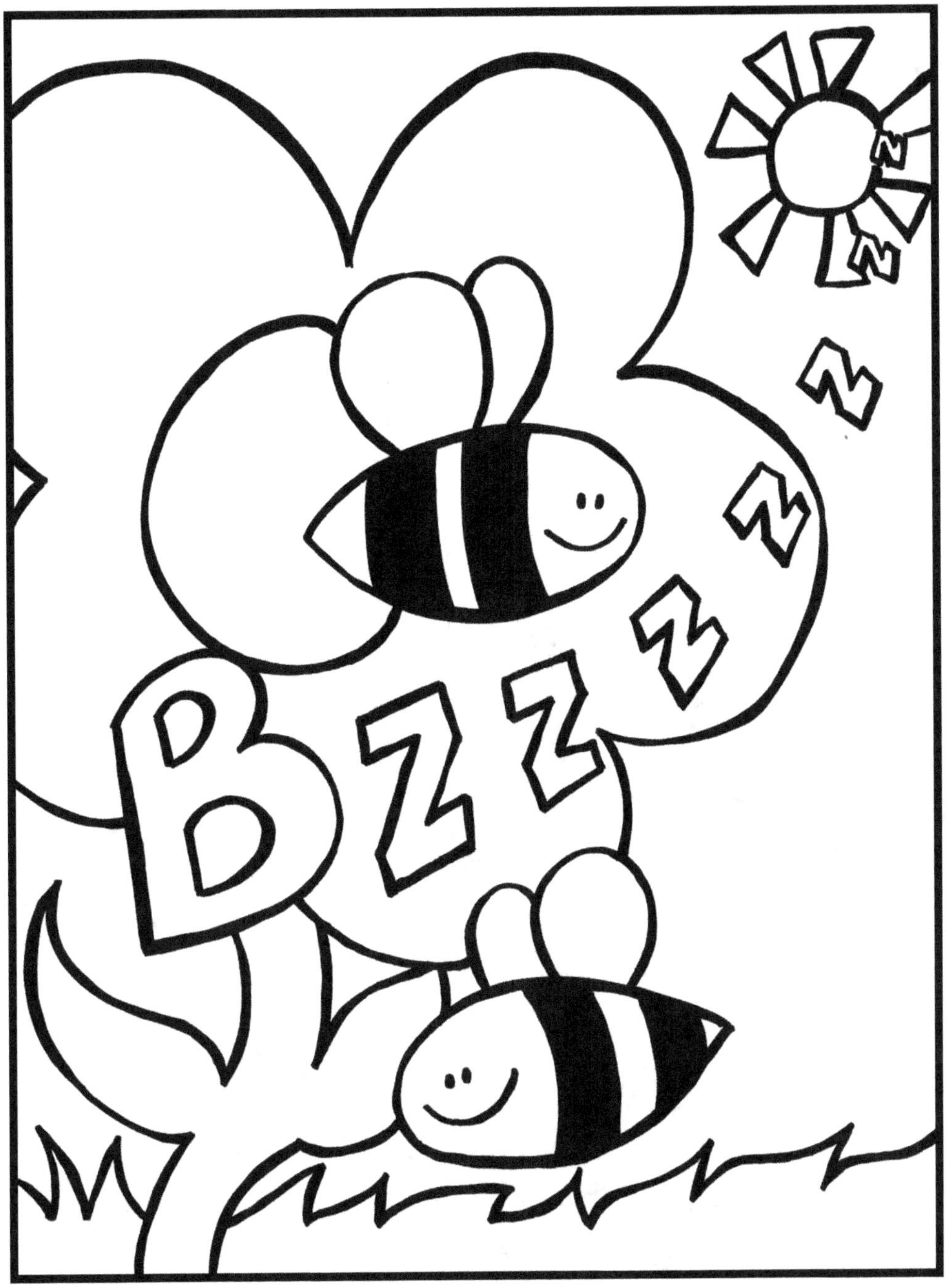

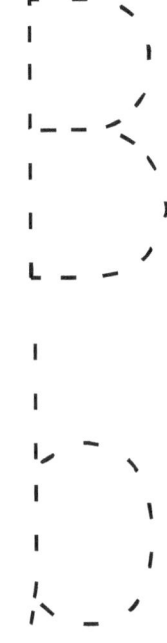

Bees buzz

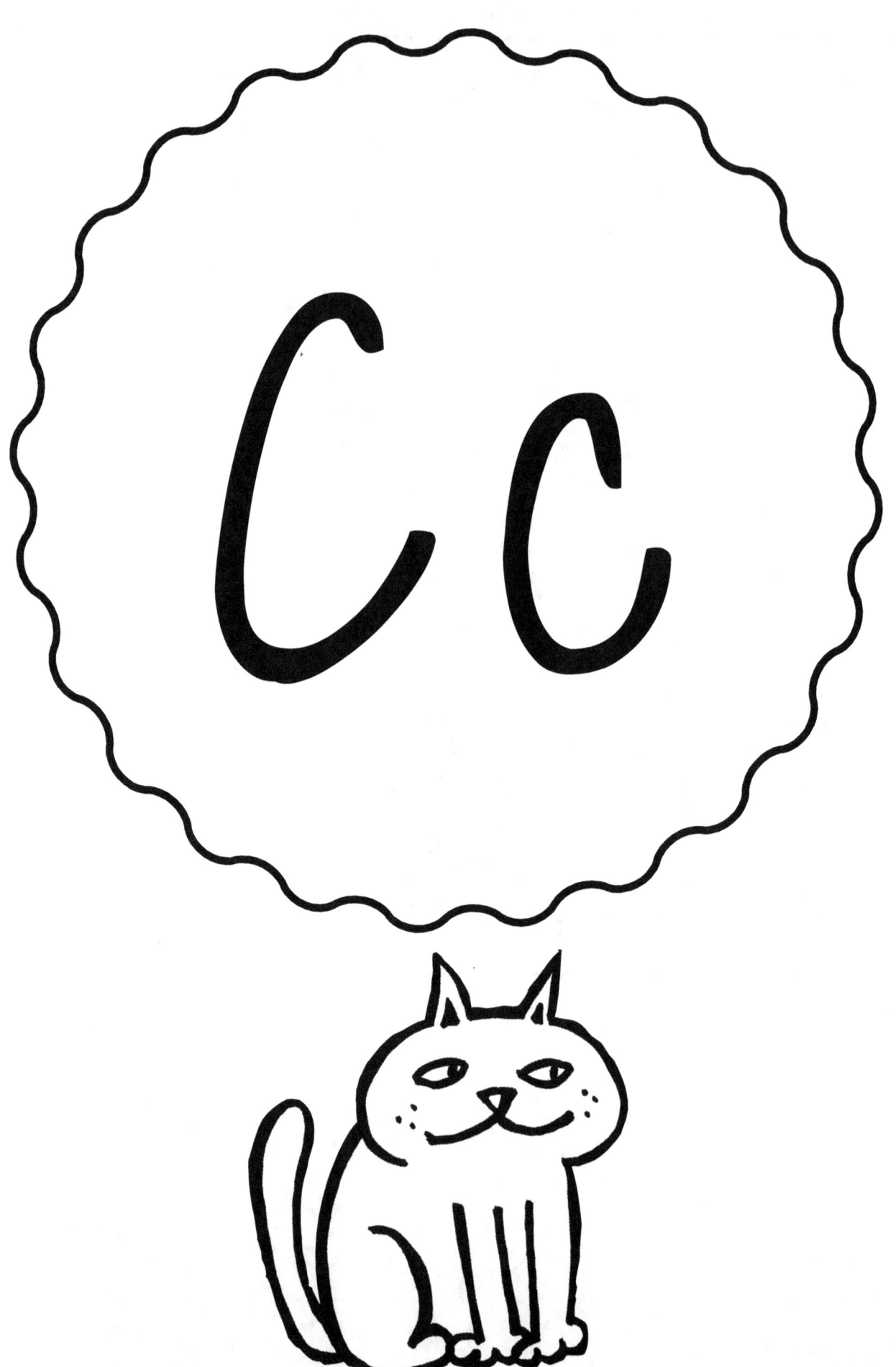

Color the picture, then trace and write the letters below.

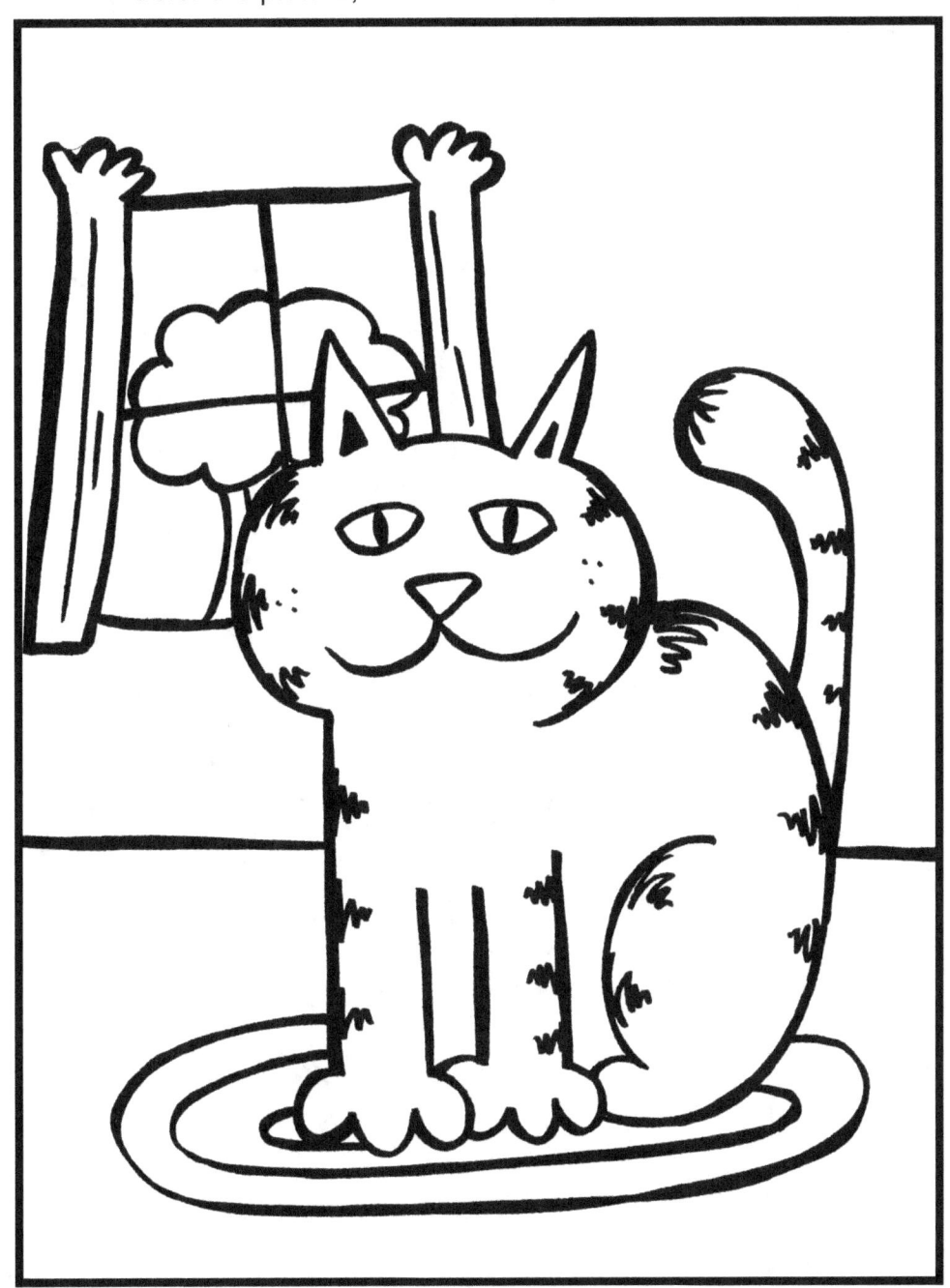

Color in the picture and trace the letters below.

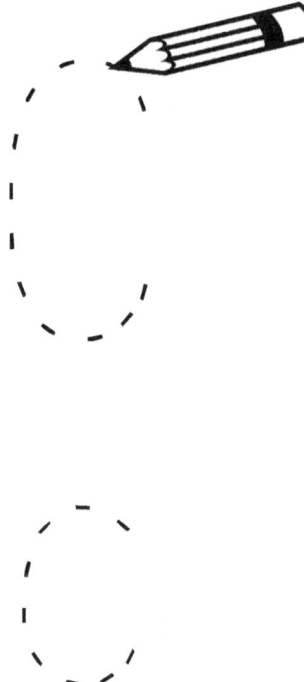

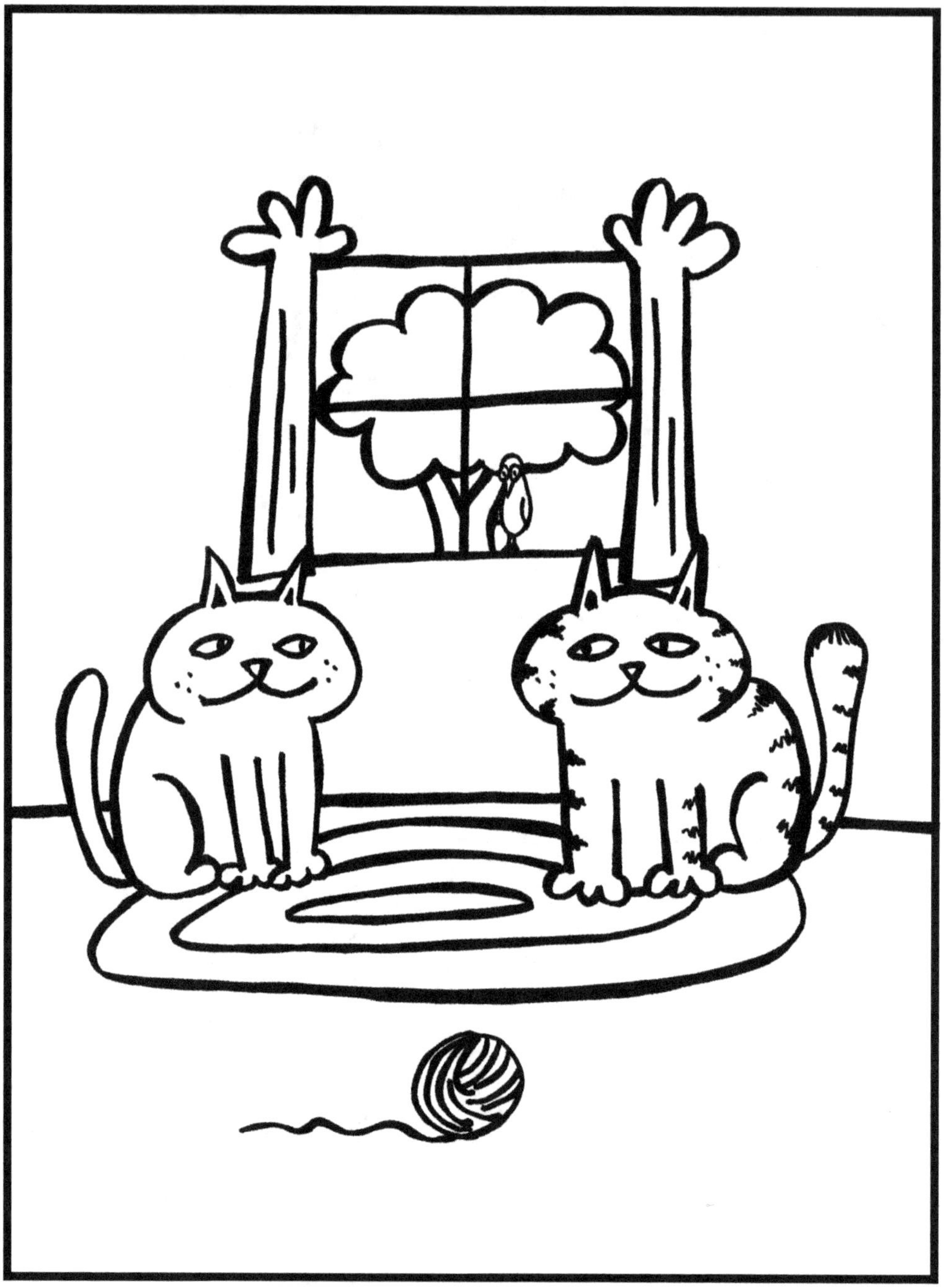

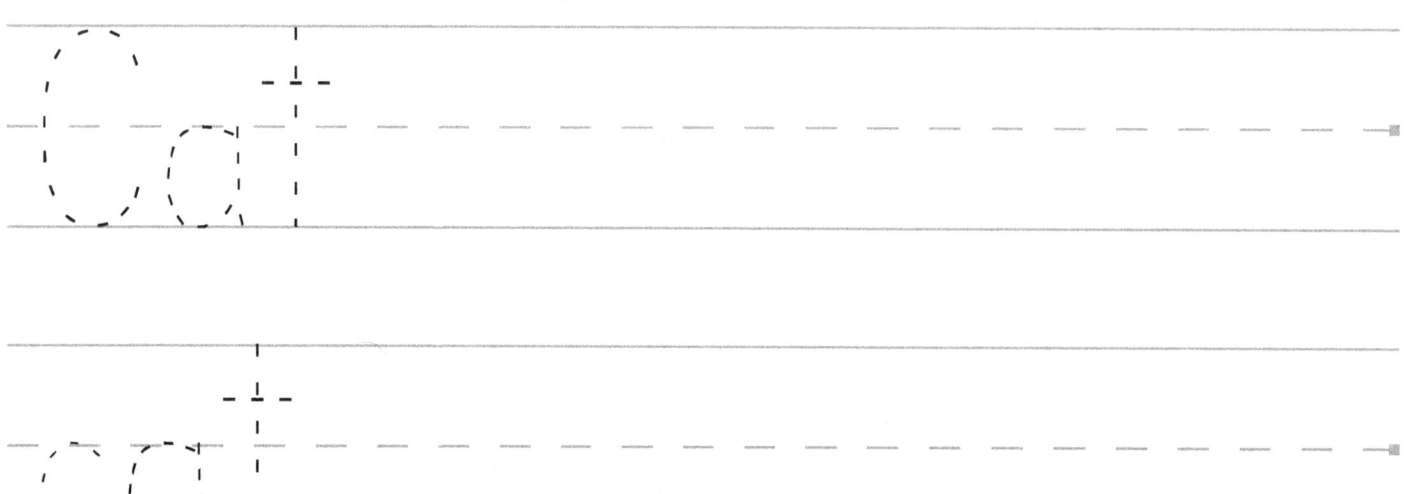

Color the picture, then trace and write the phrase below.

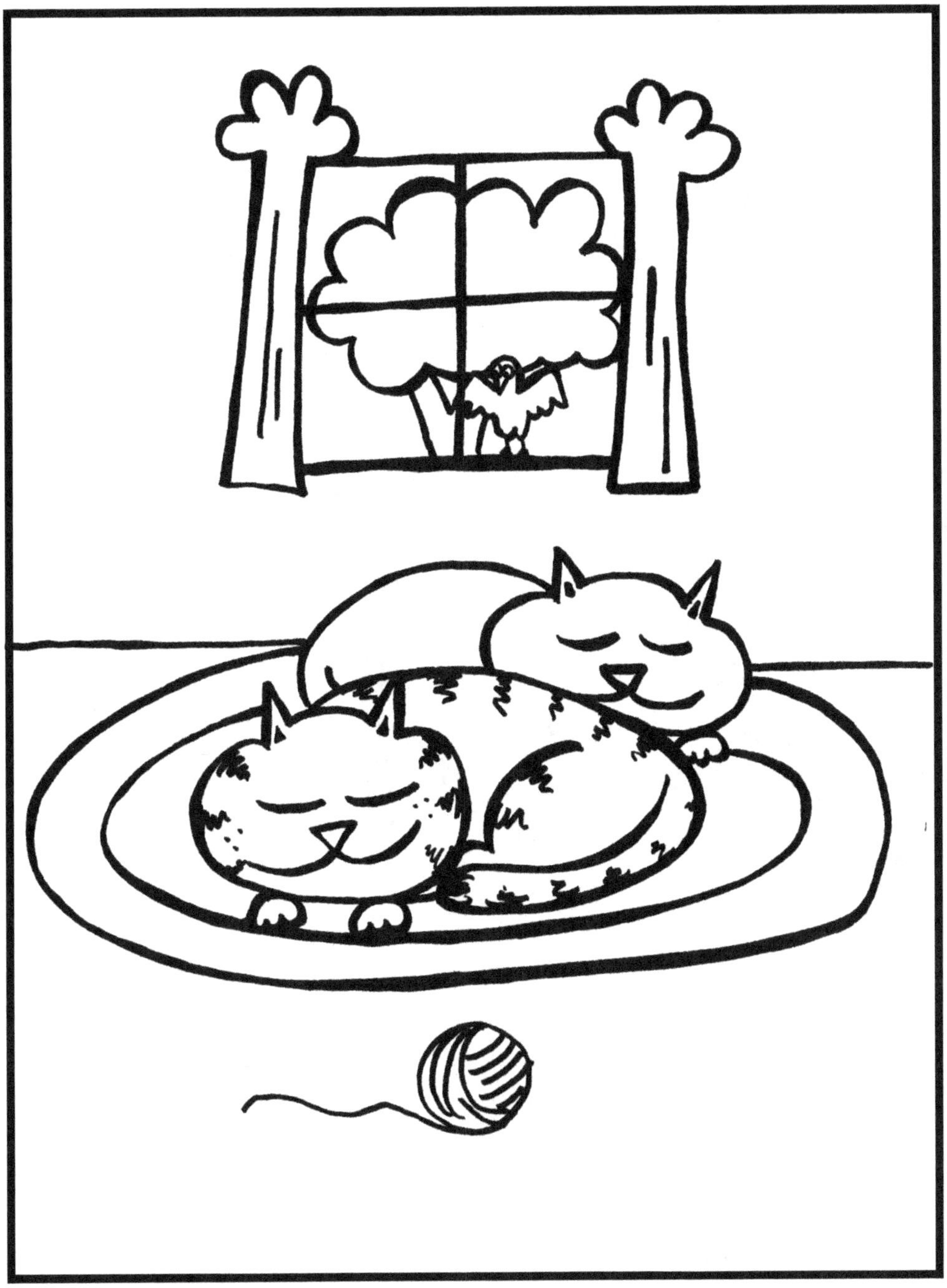

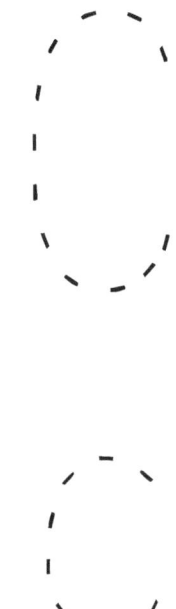

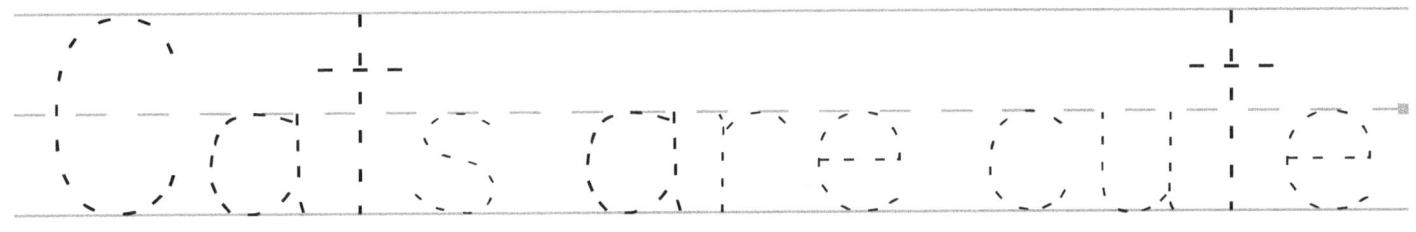

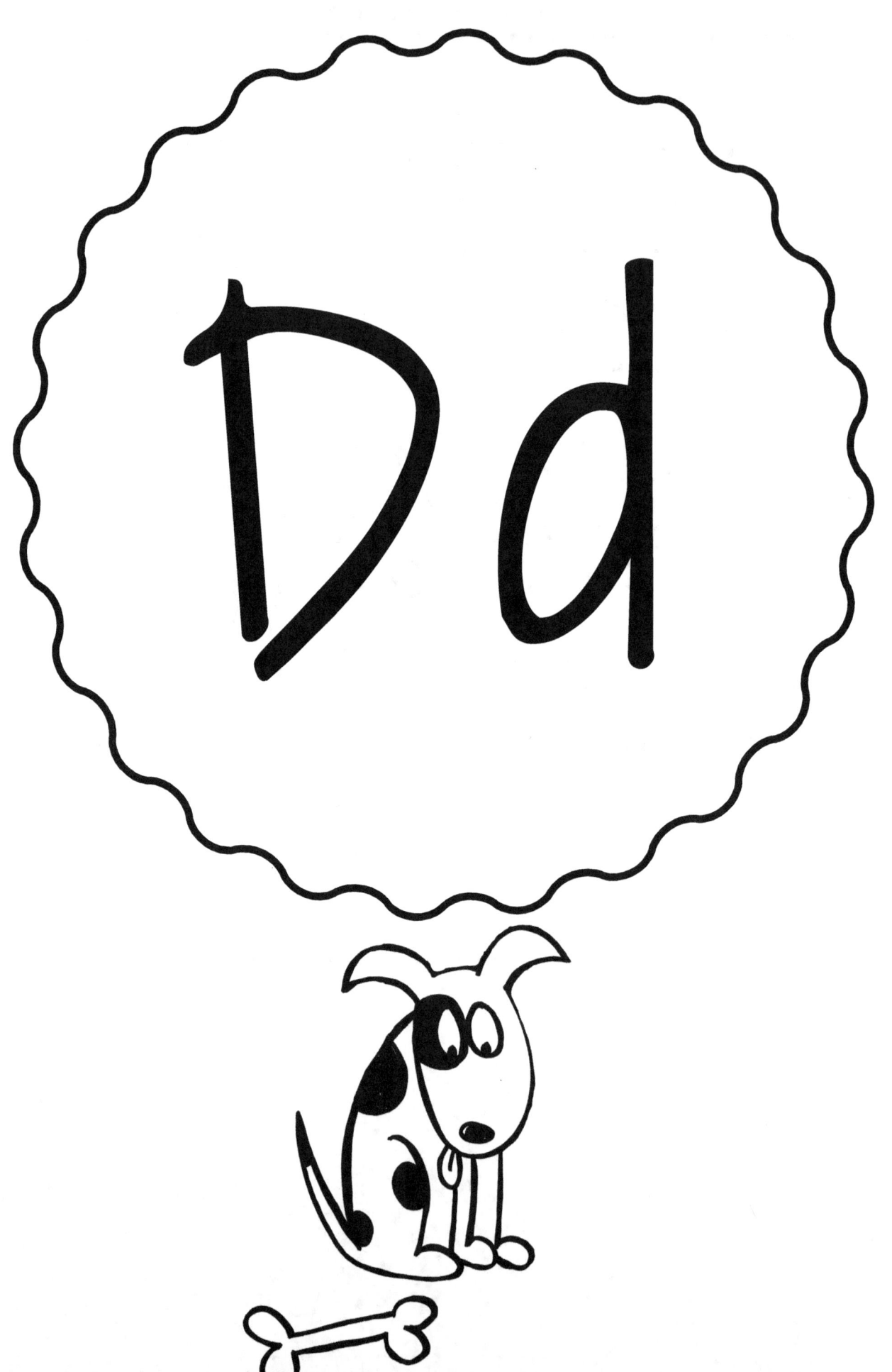

Color the picture, then trace and write the letters below.

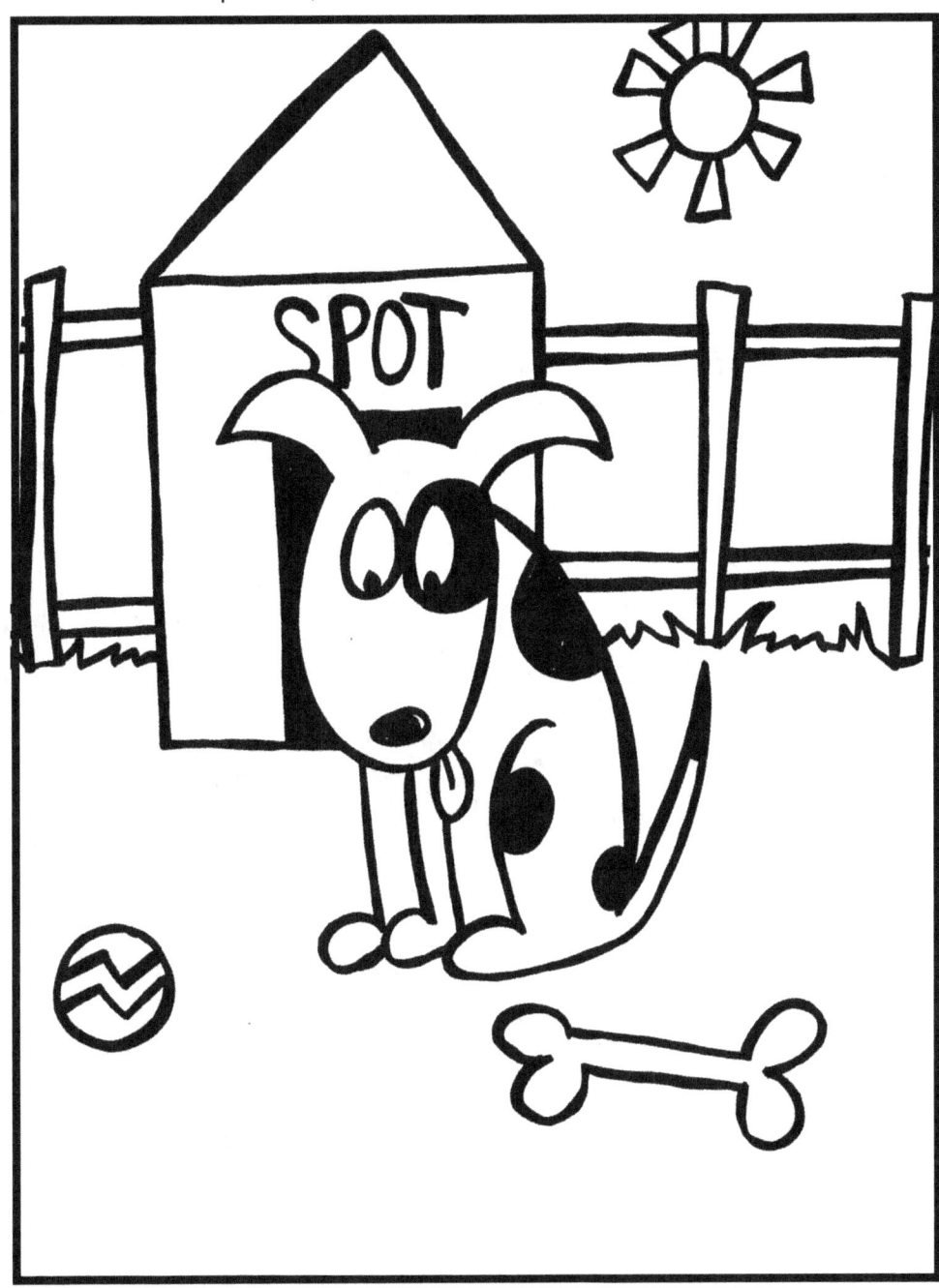

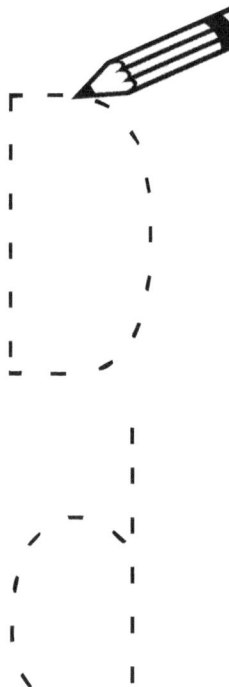

Color the picture, then trace and write the word below.

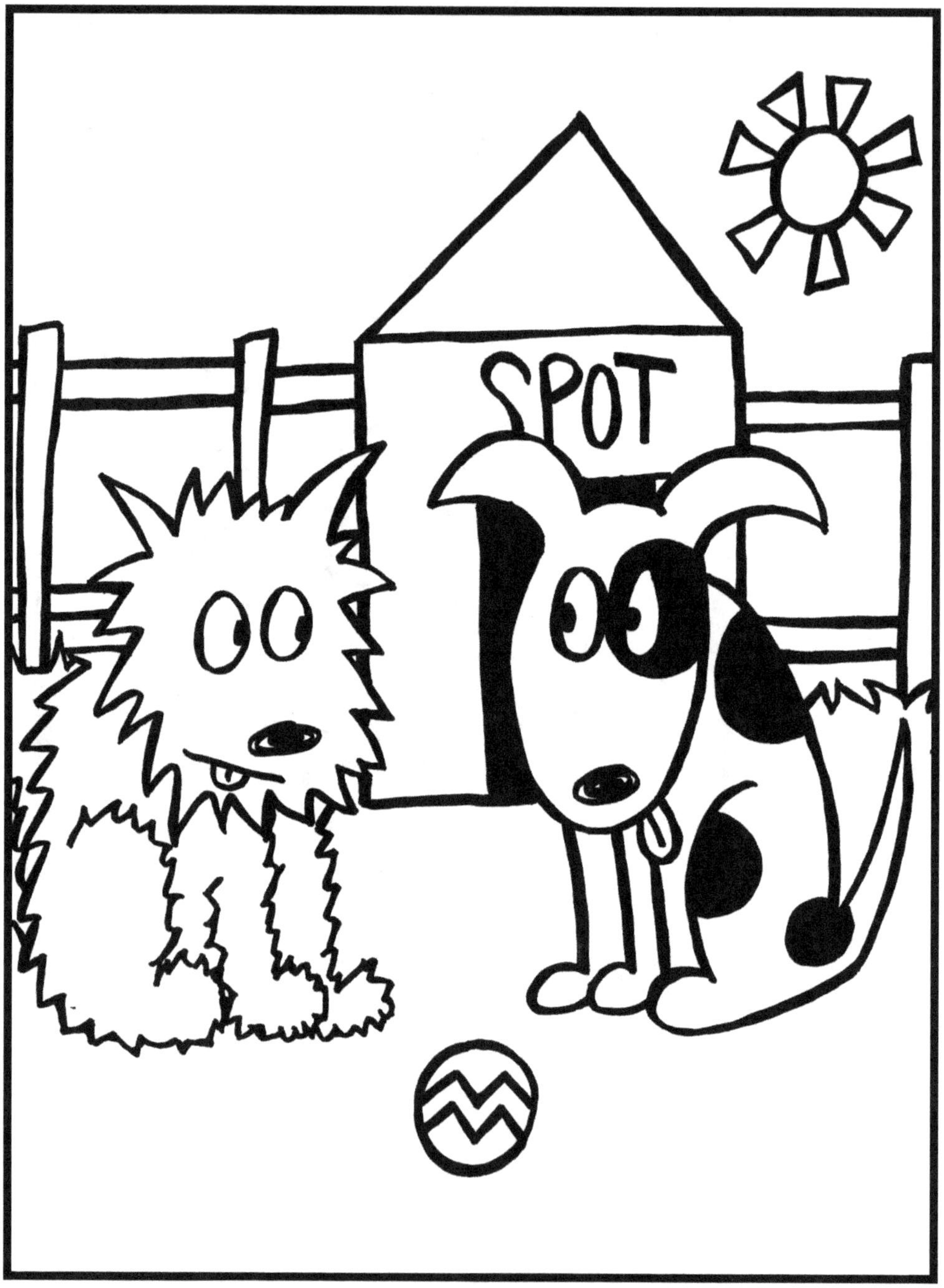

Dd

dog

Color the picture, then trace and write the phrase below.

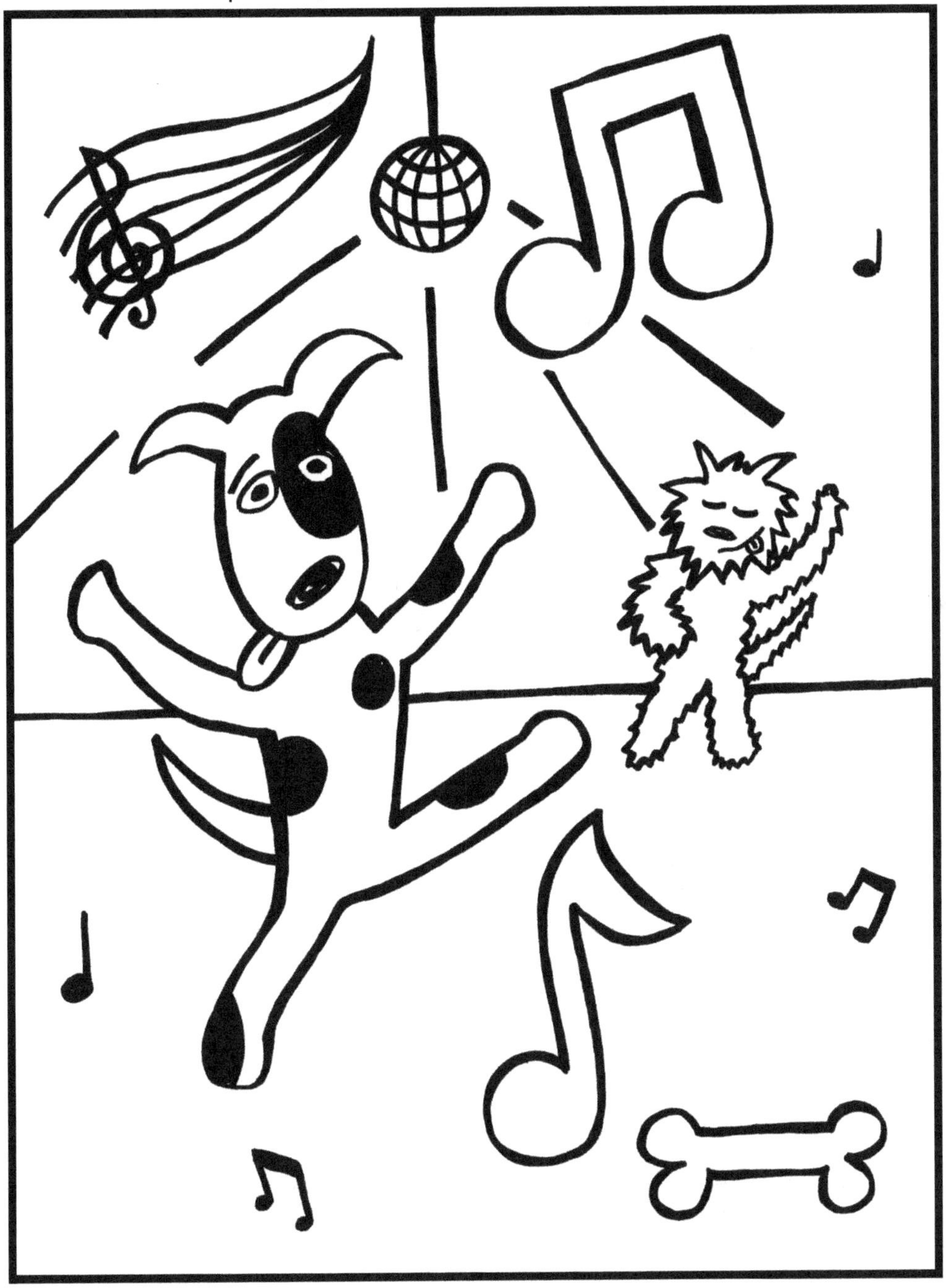

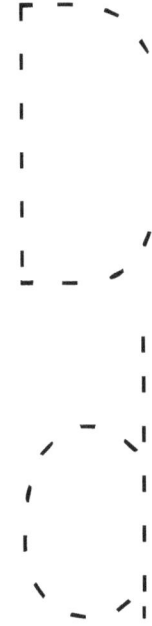

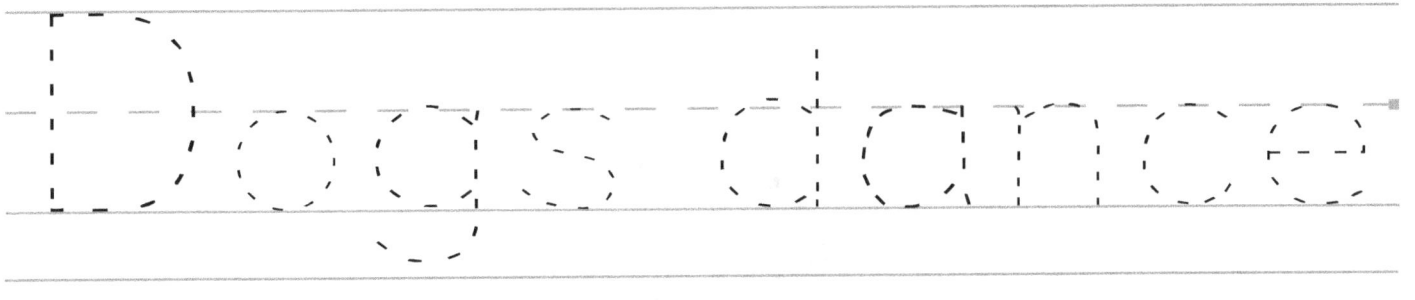

Ee

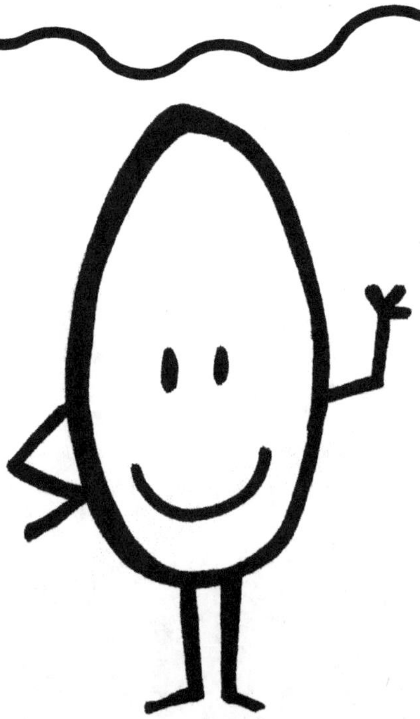

Color the picture, then trace and write the letters below.

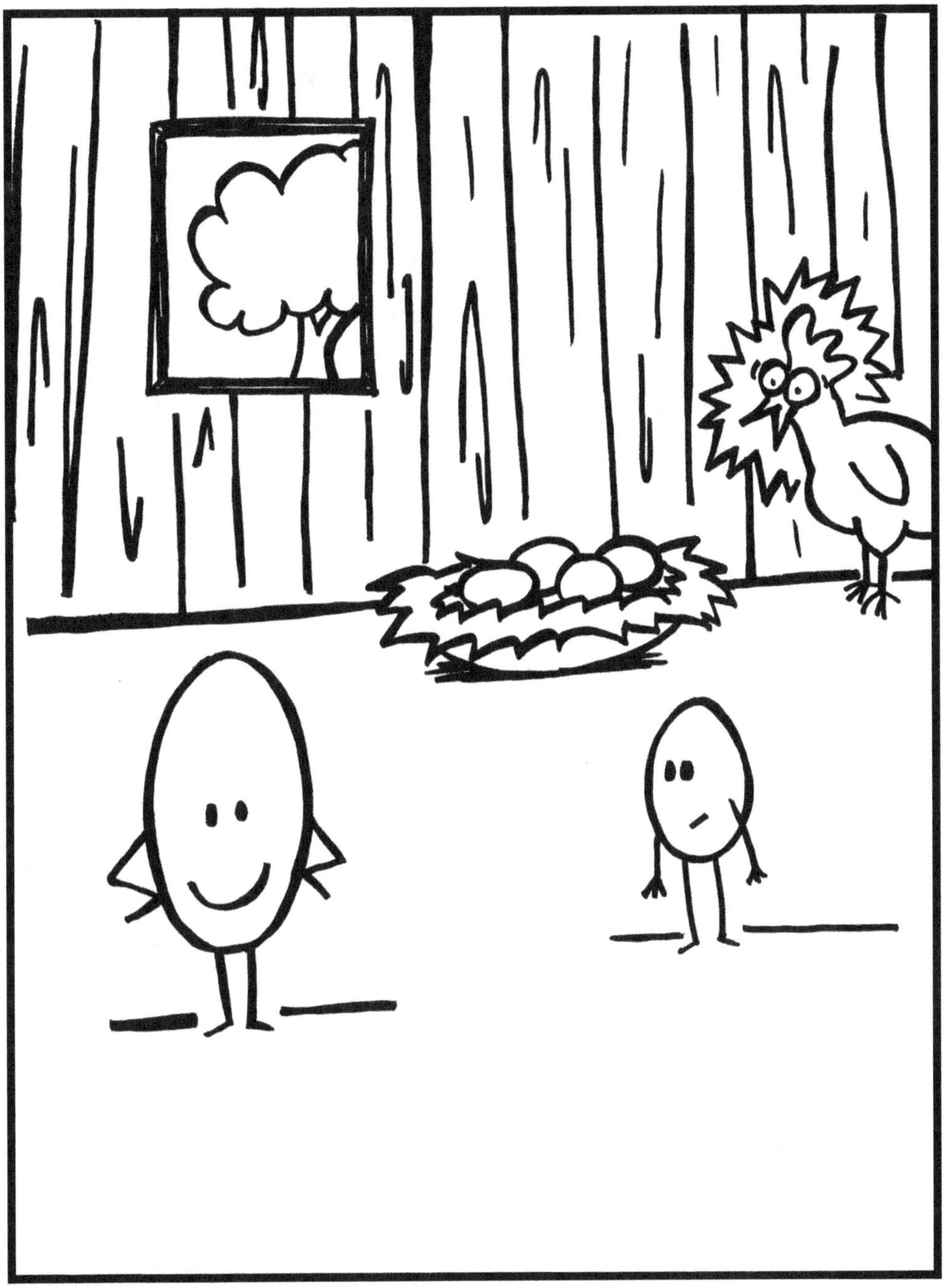

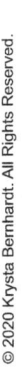

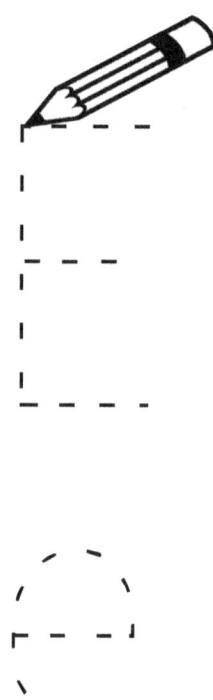

Color the picture, then trace and write the word below.

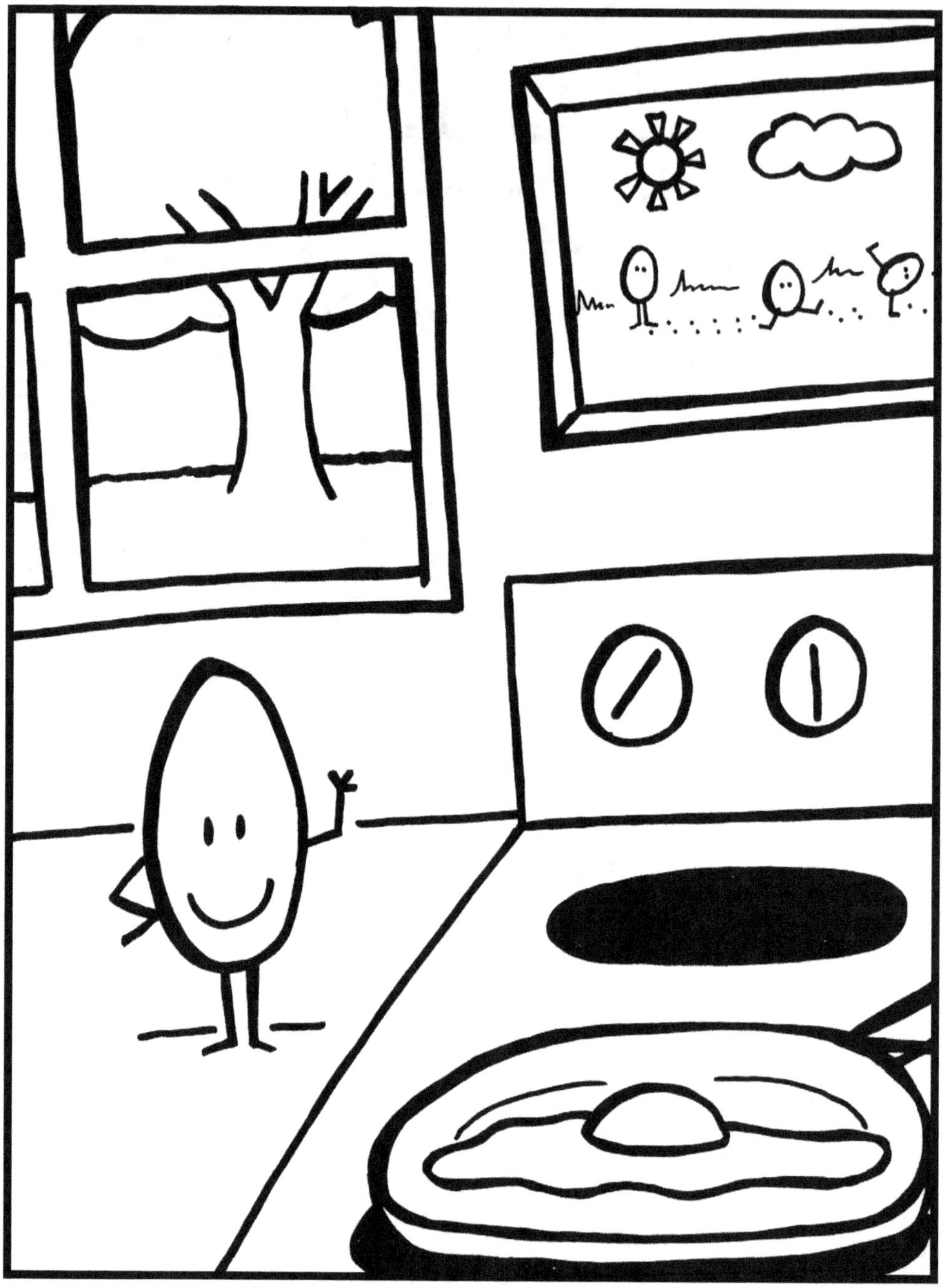

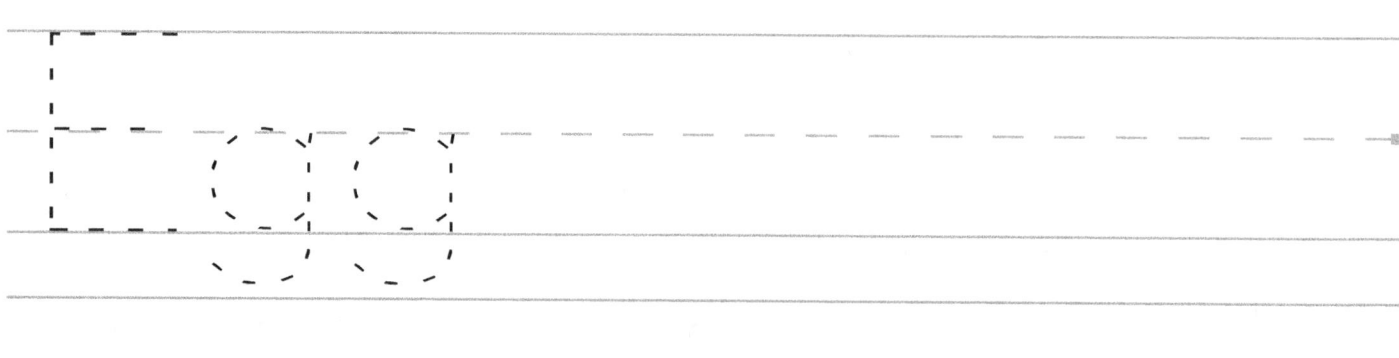

Color the picture, then trace and write the phrase below.

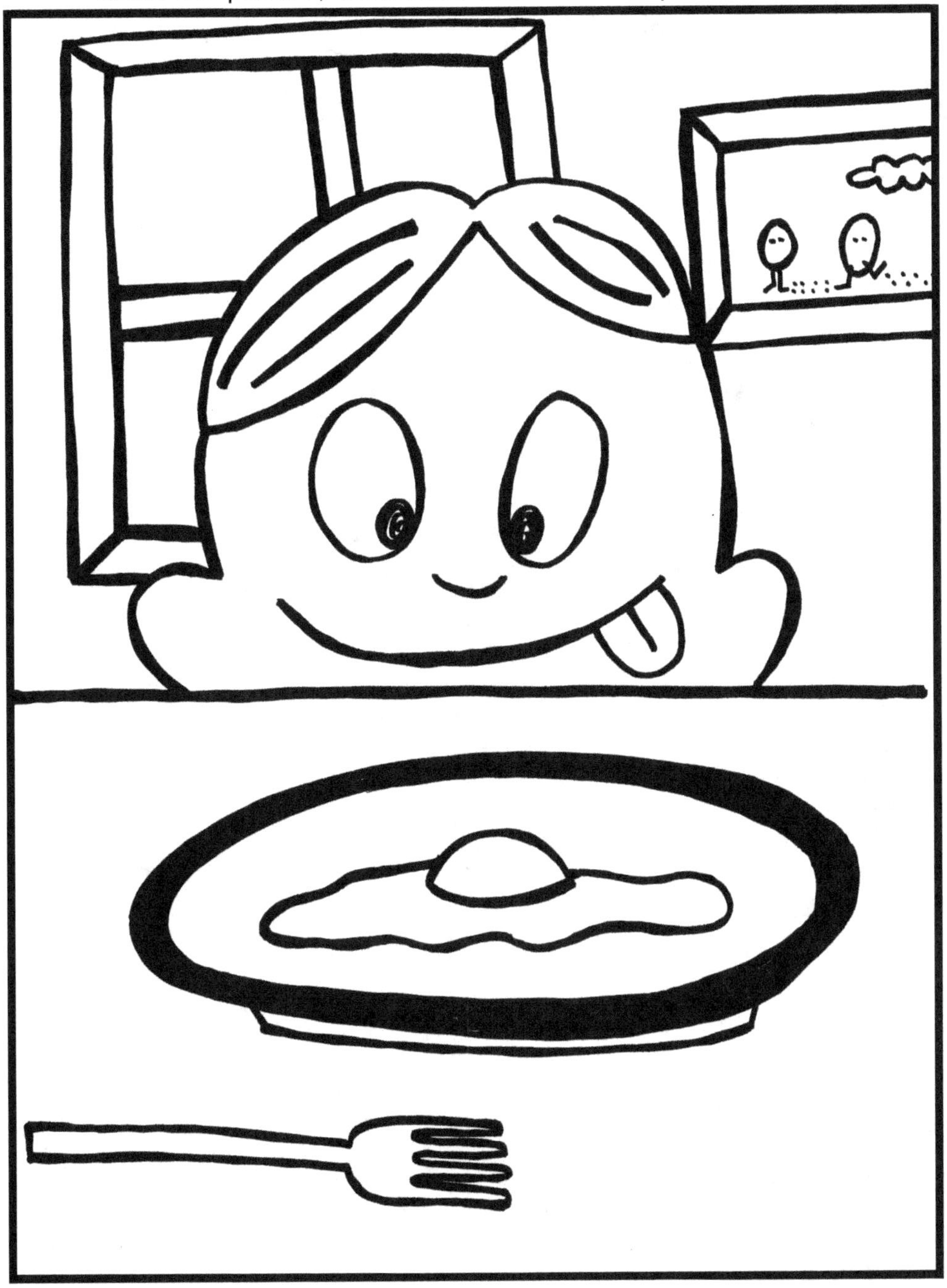

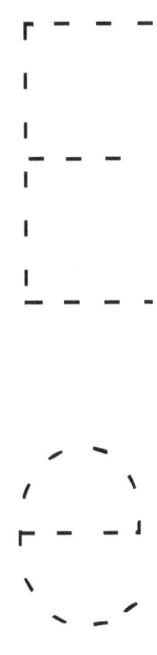

I at eggs

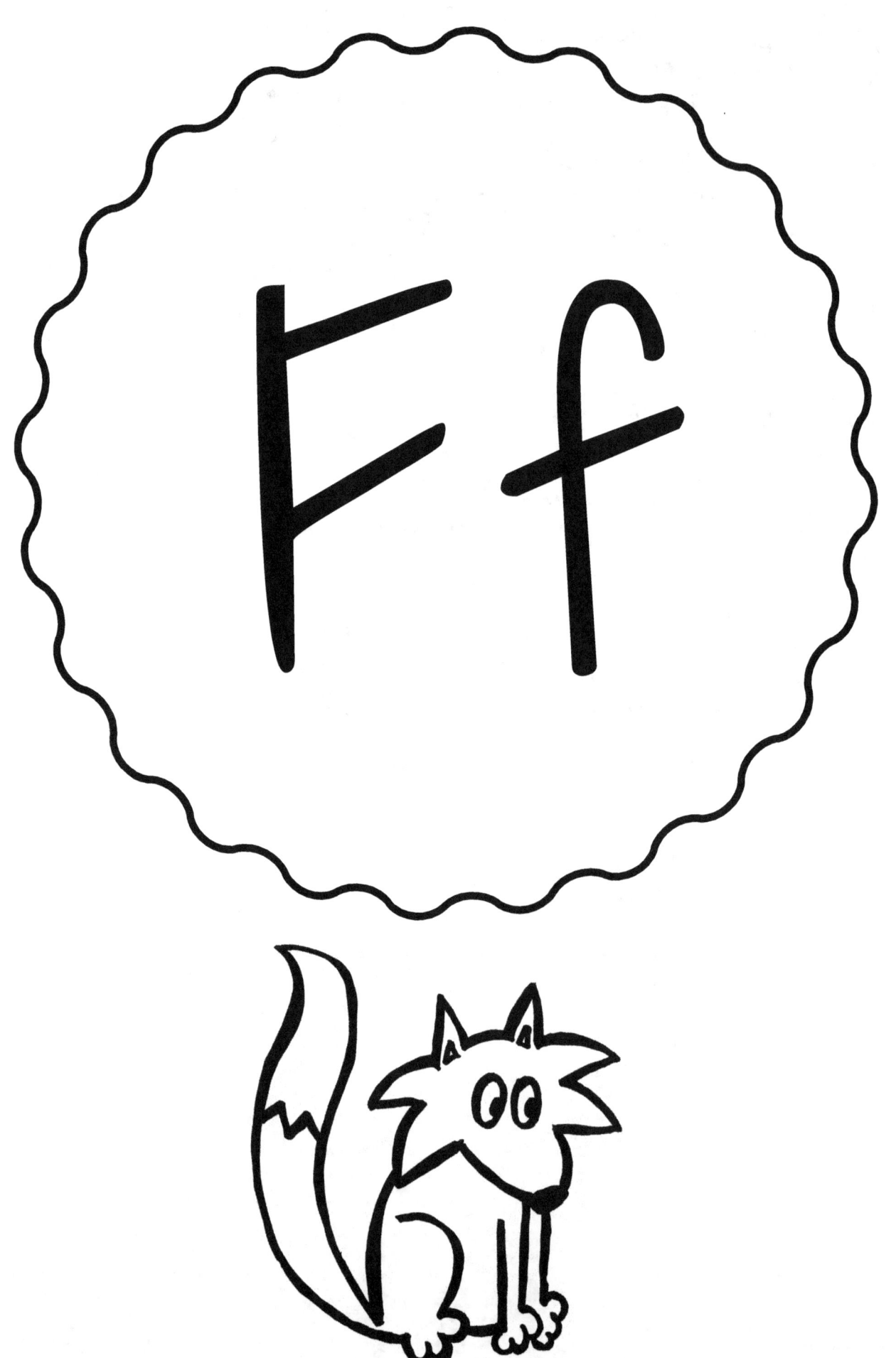

Color the picture, then trace and write the letters below.

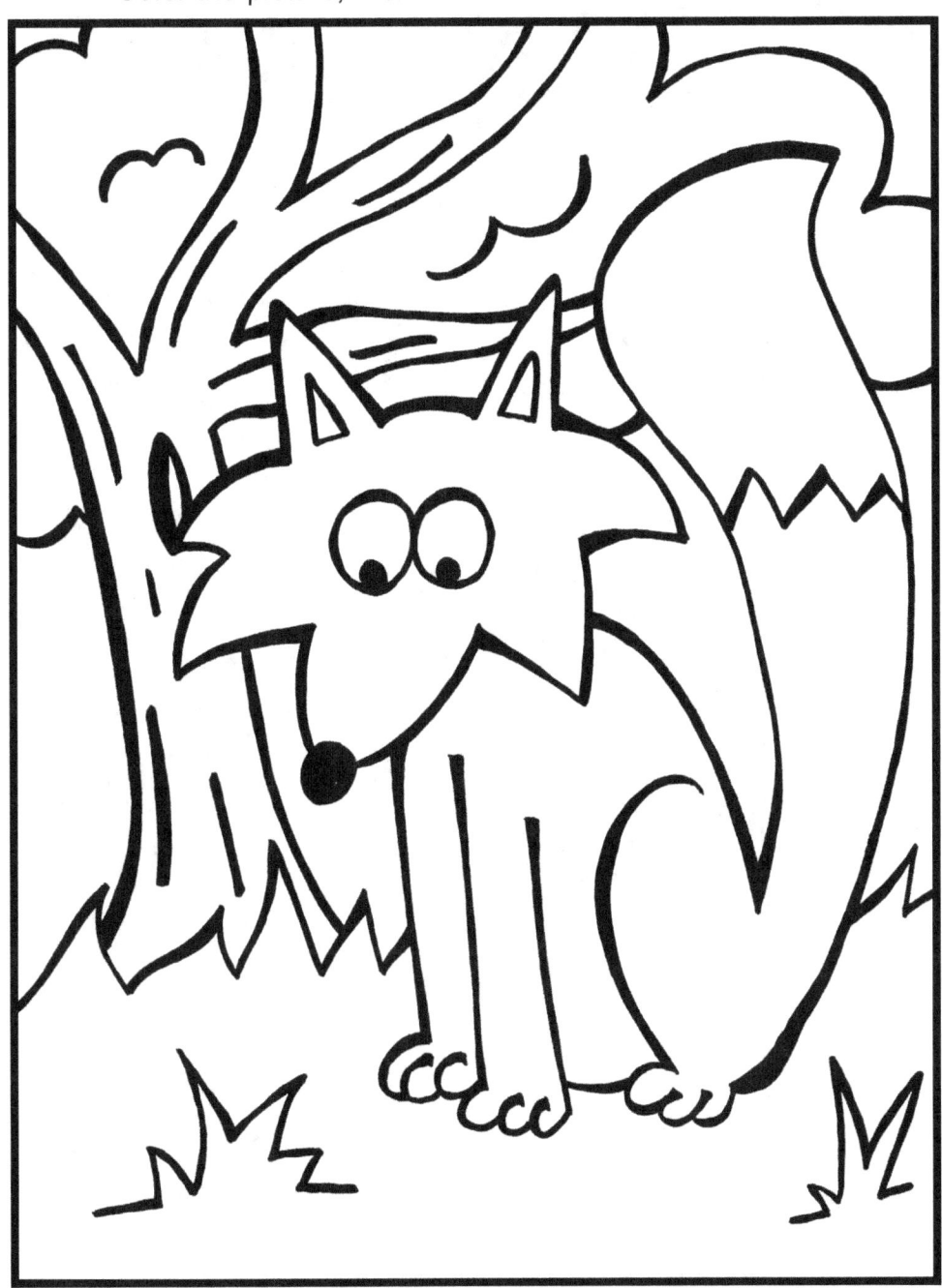

Color the picture, then trace and write the word below.

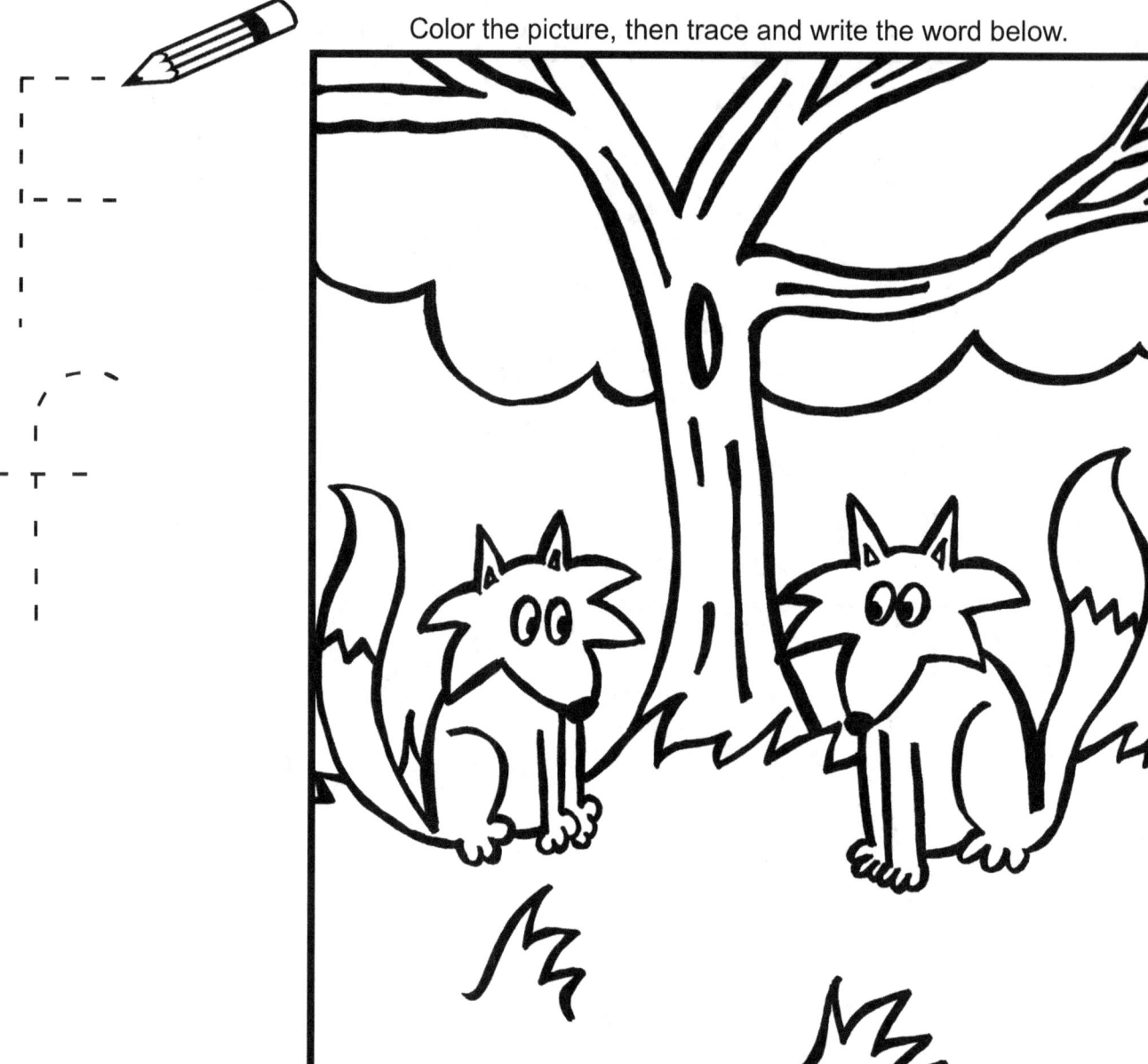

fox

fox

Color the picture, then trace and write the phrase below.

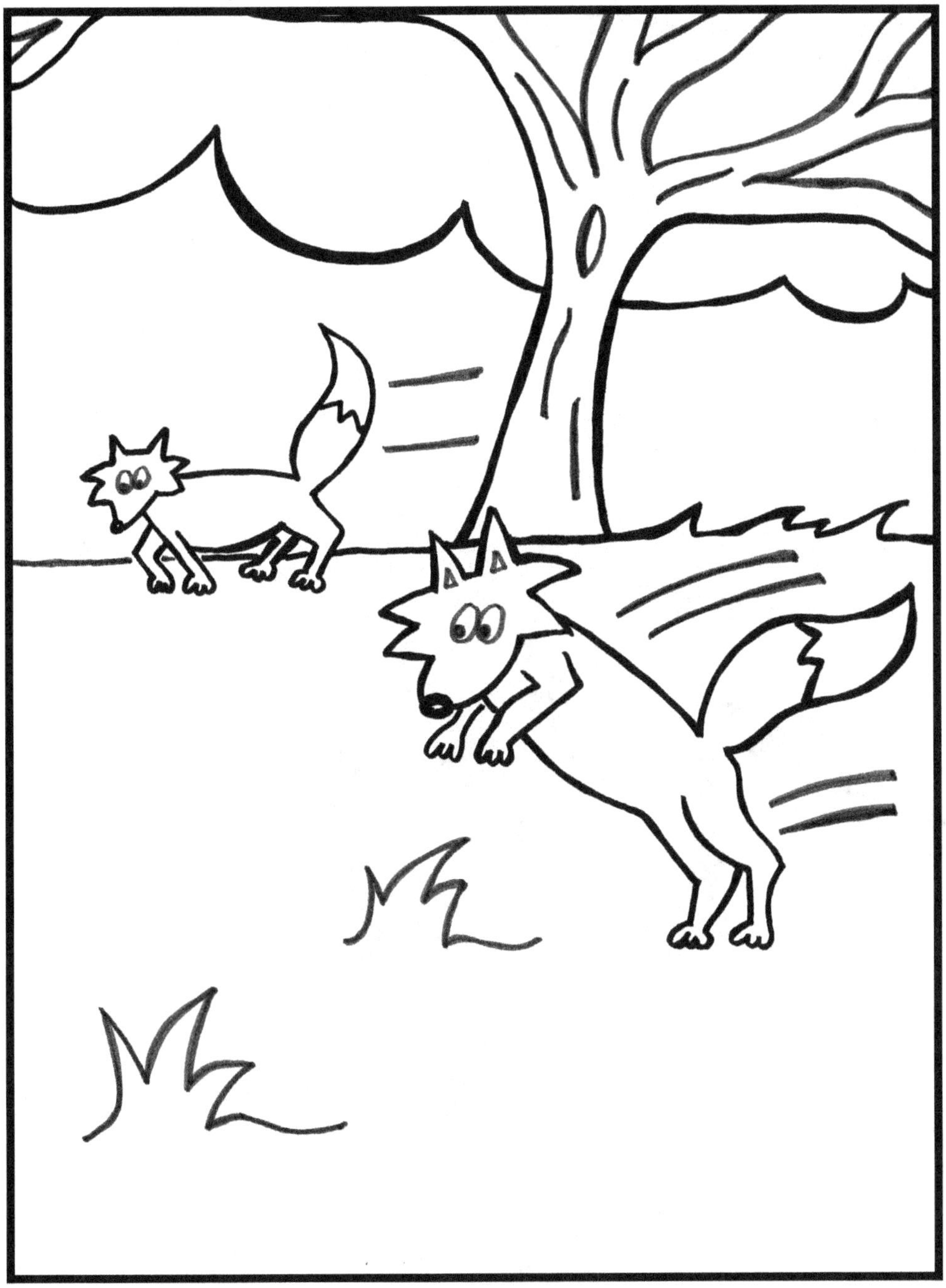

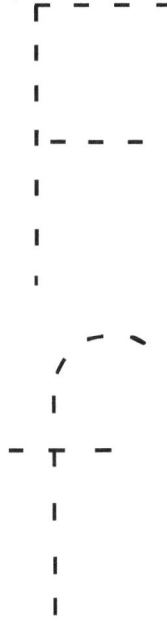

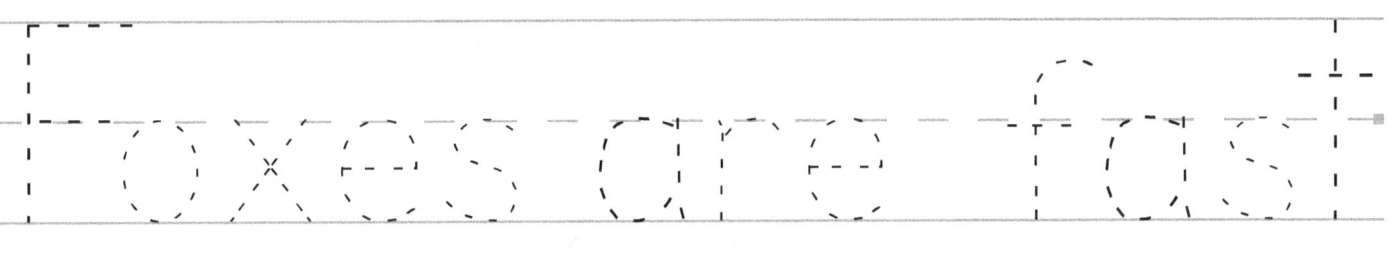

Foxes are fast

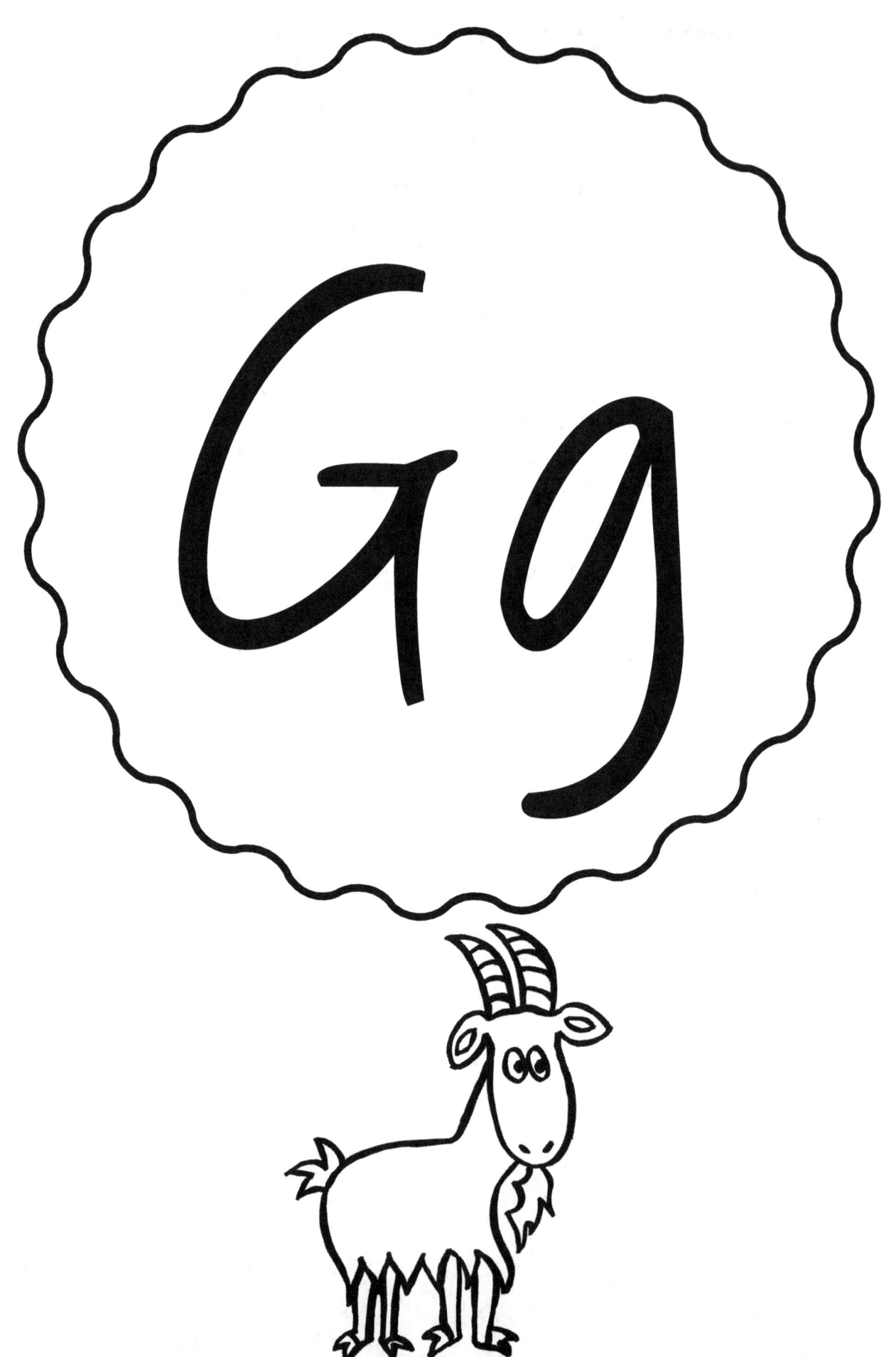

Color the picture, then trace and write the letters below.

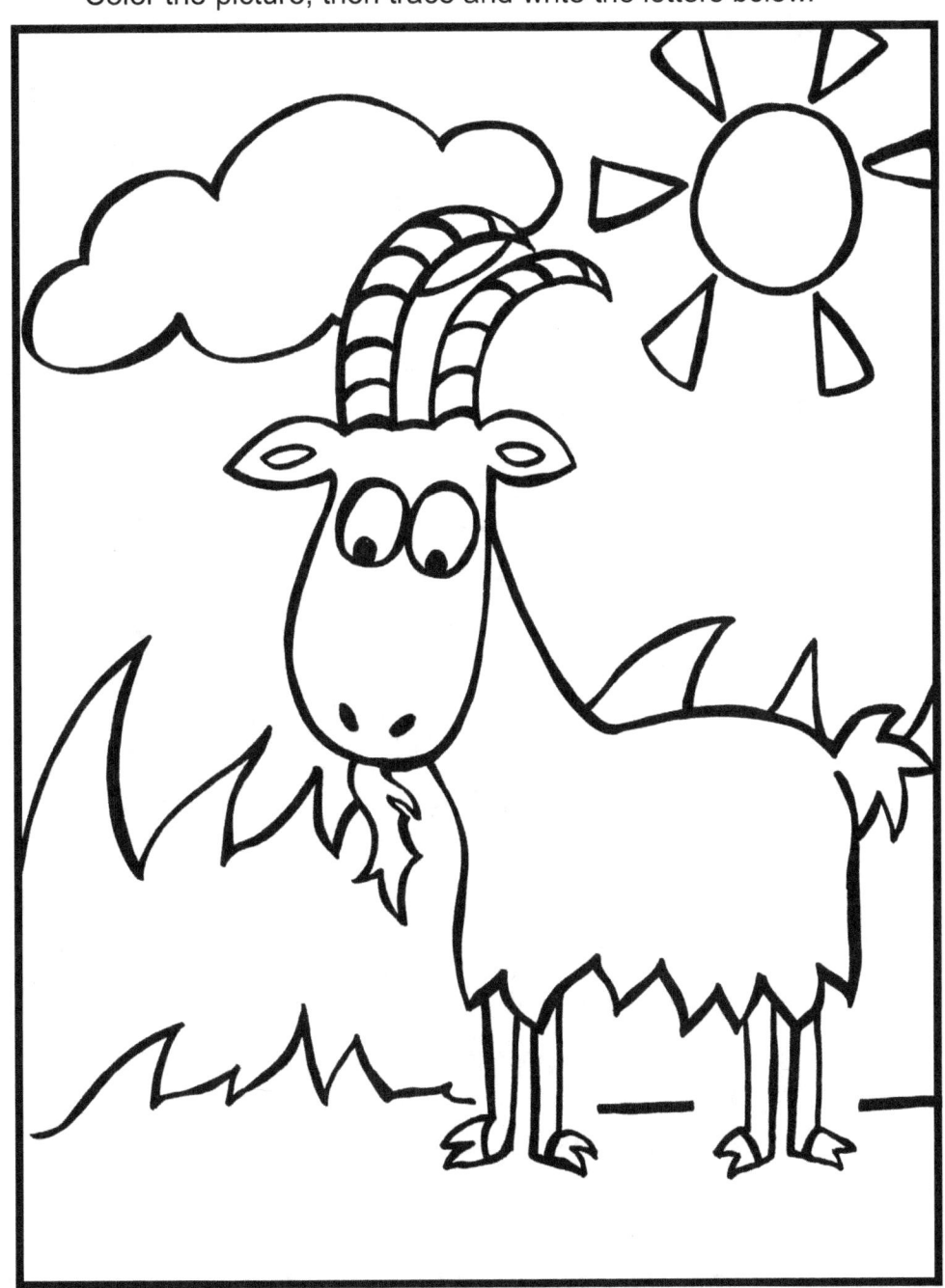

Color in the picture and trace the letters below.

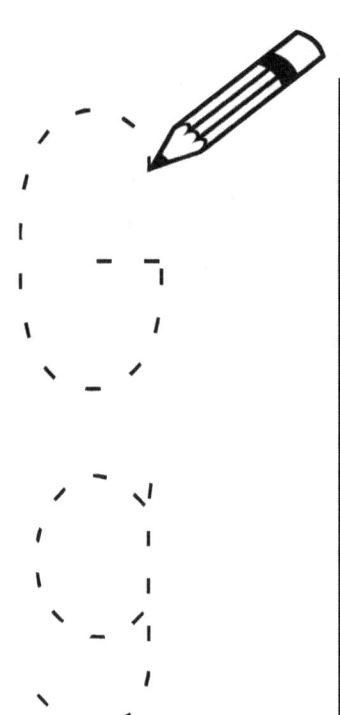

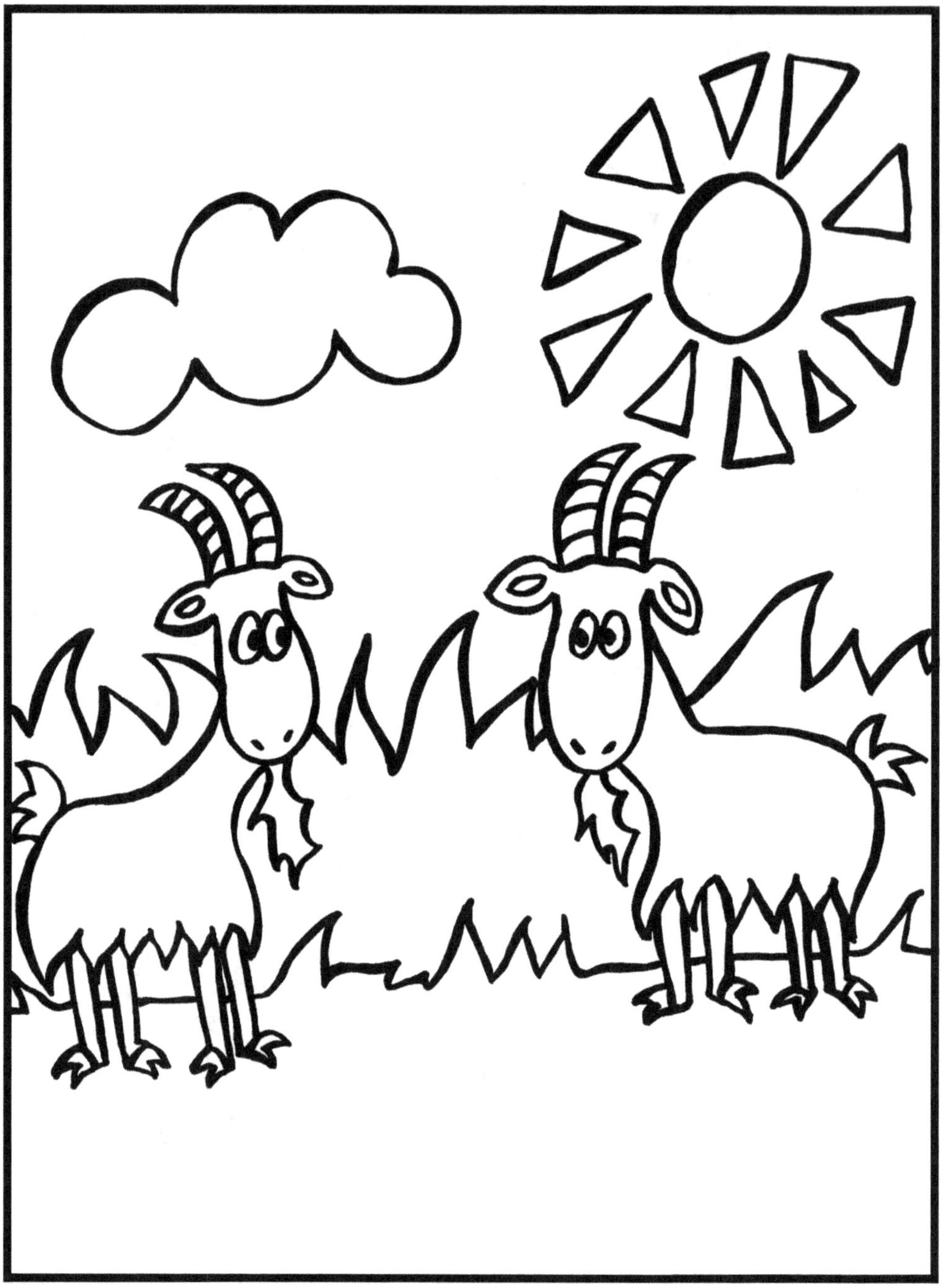

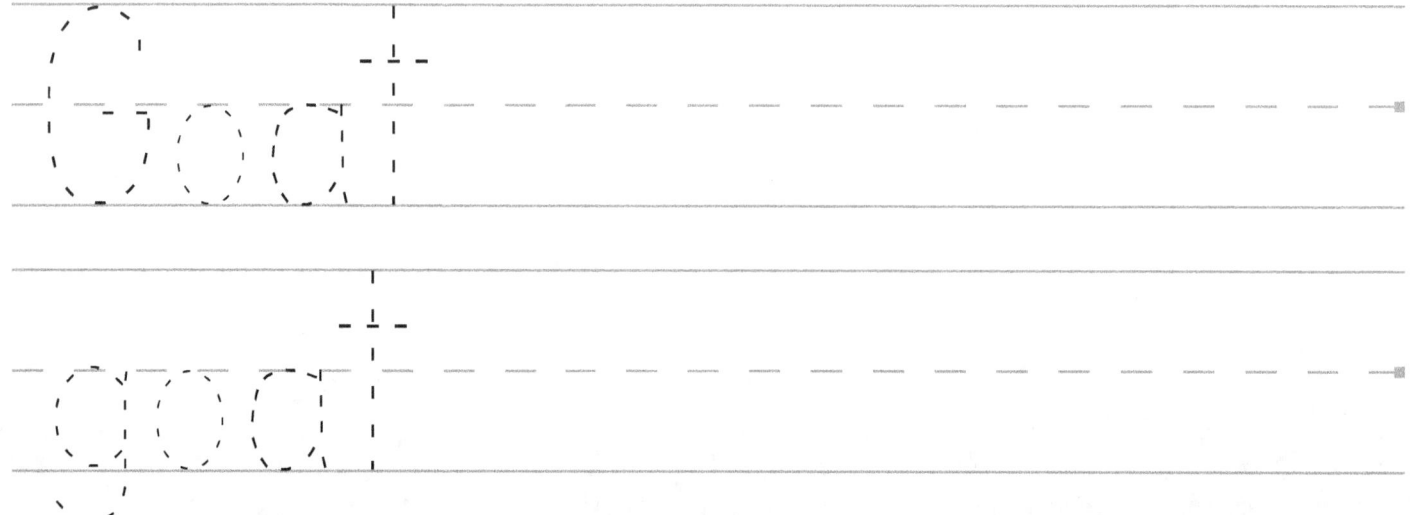

Color the picture, then trace and write the phrase below.

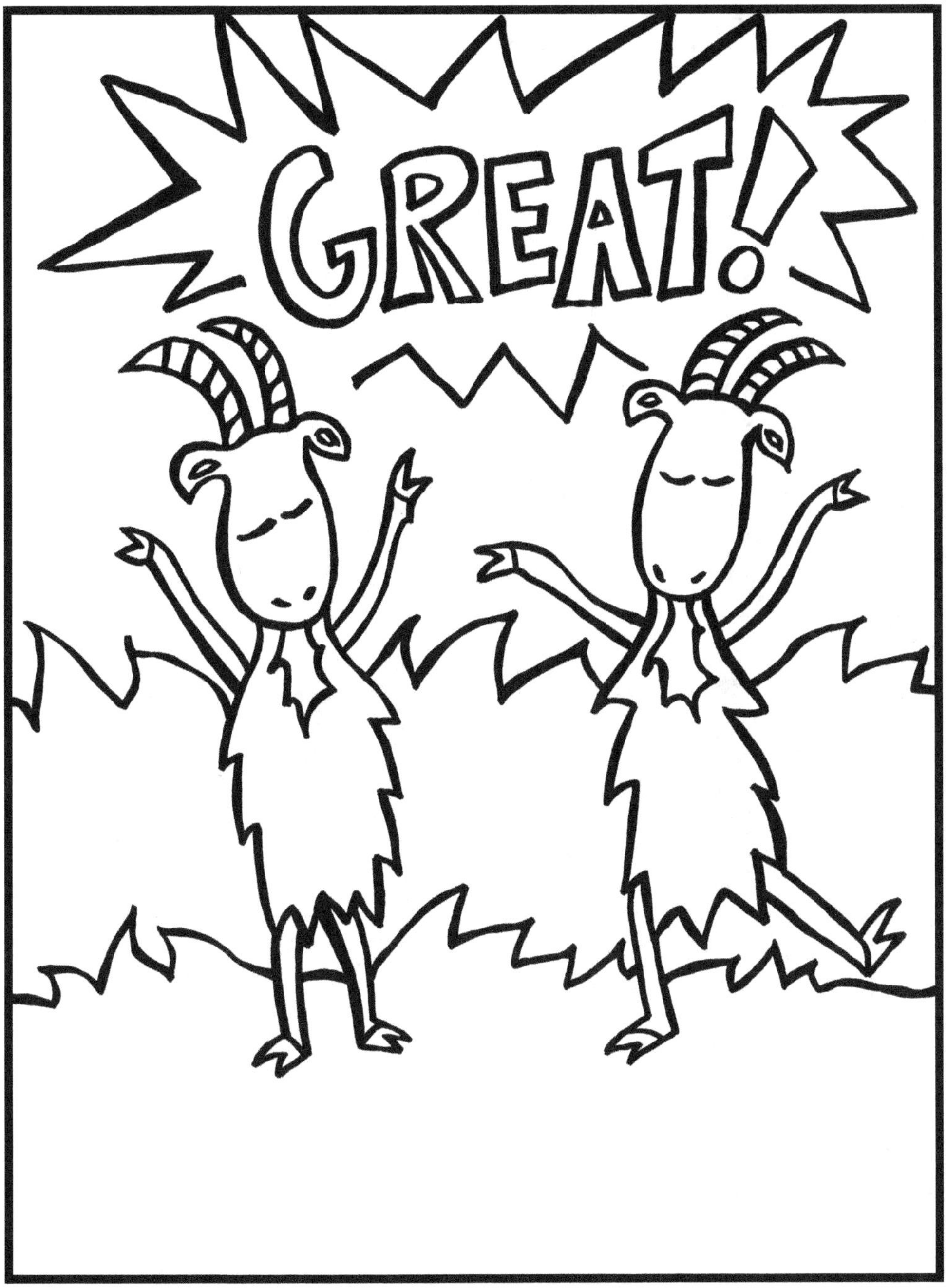

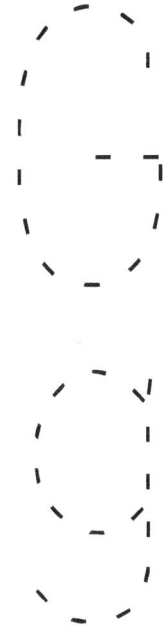

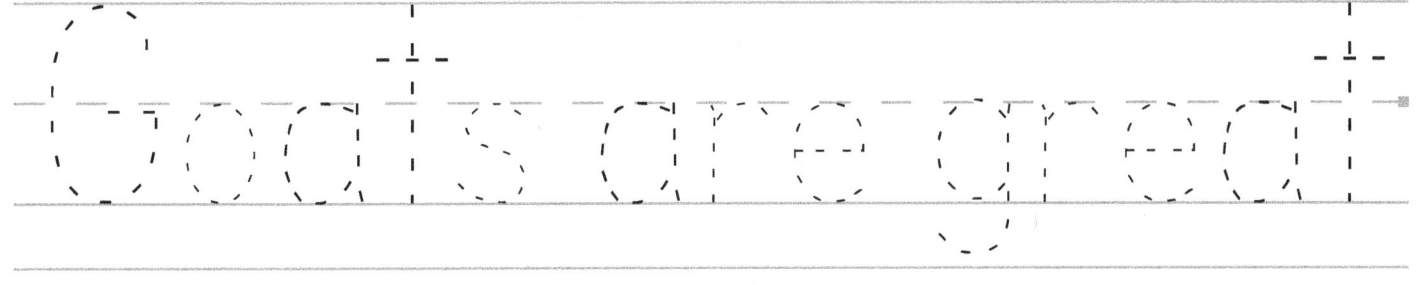

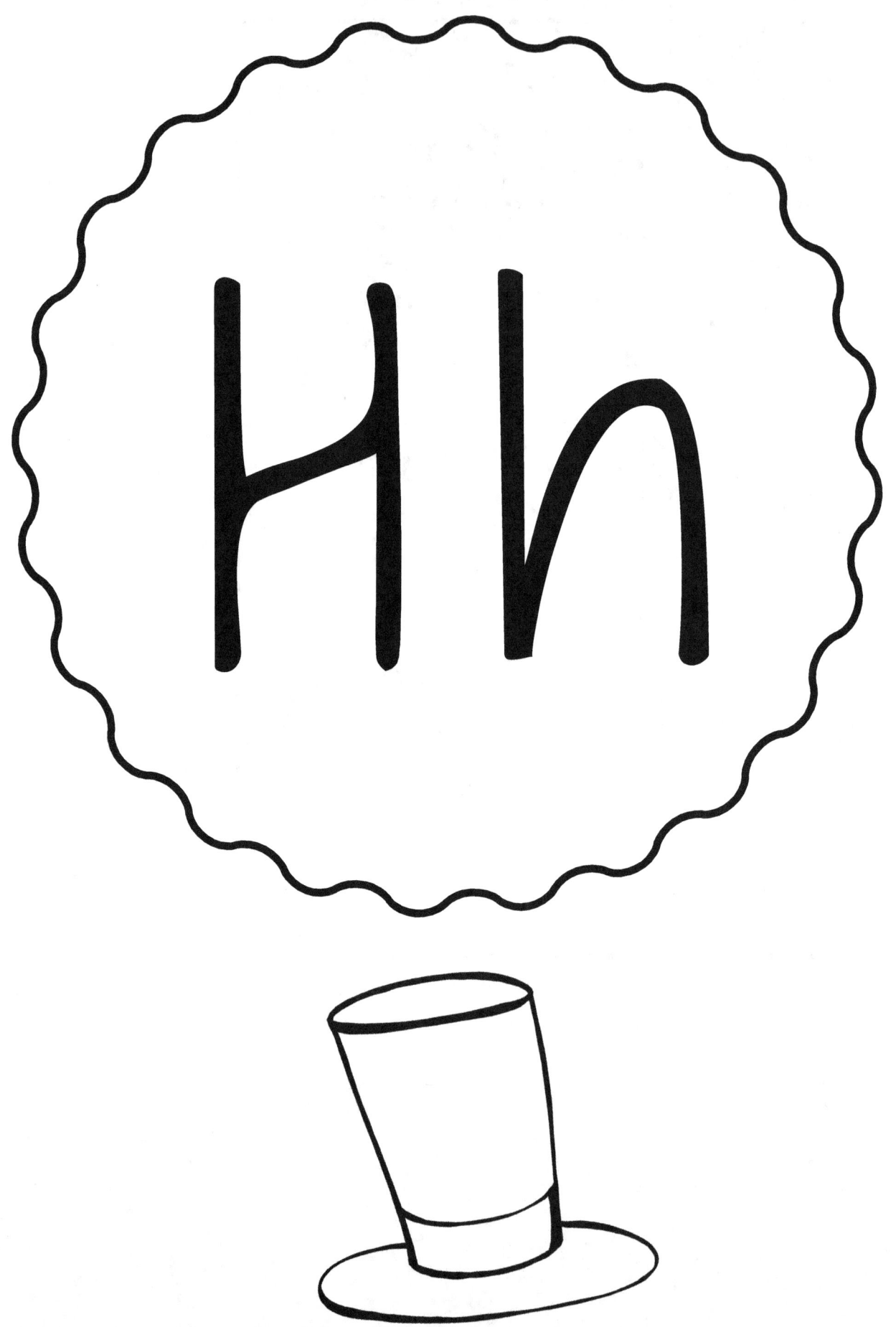

Color the picture, then trace and write the letters below.

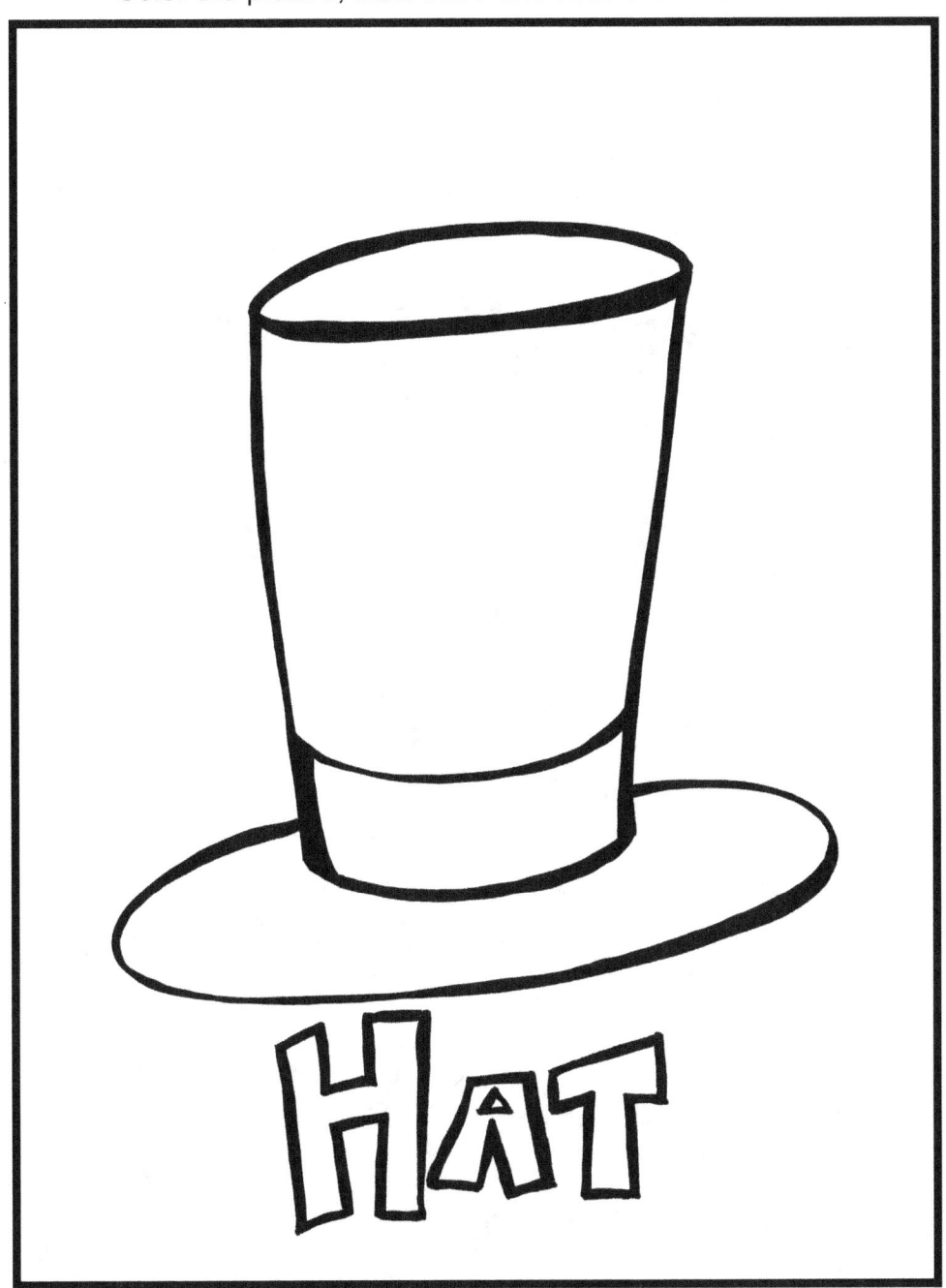

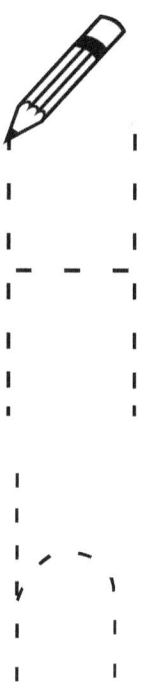

Color in the picture and trace the letters below.

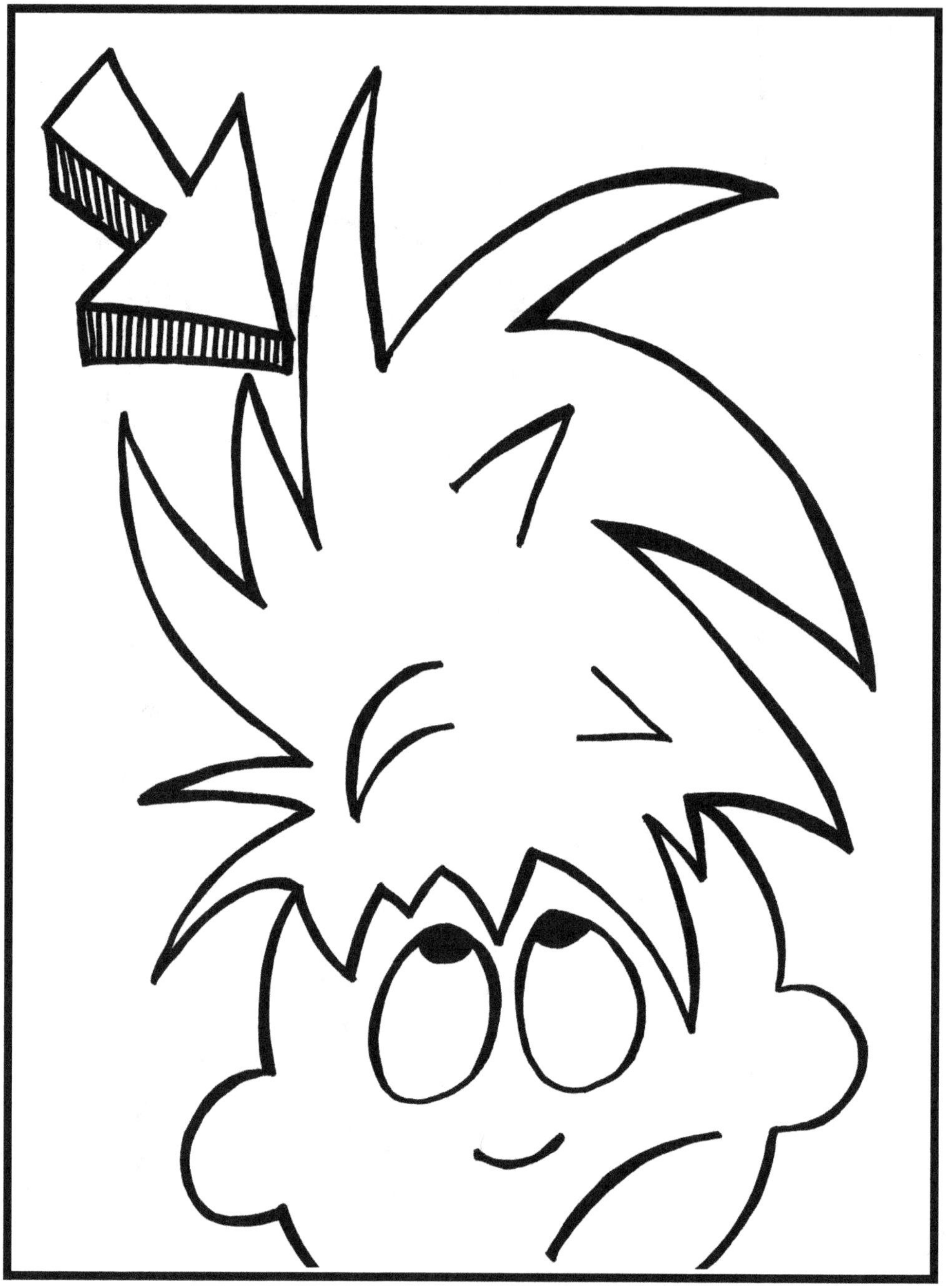

Hair

hair

Color the picture, then trace and write the phrase below.

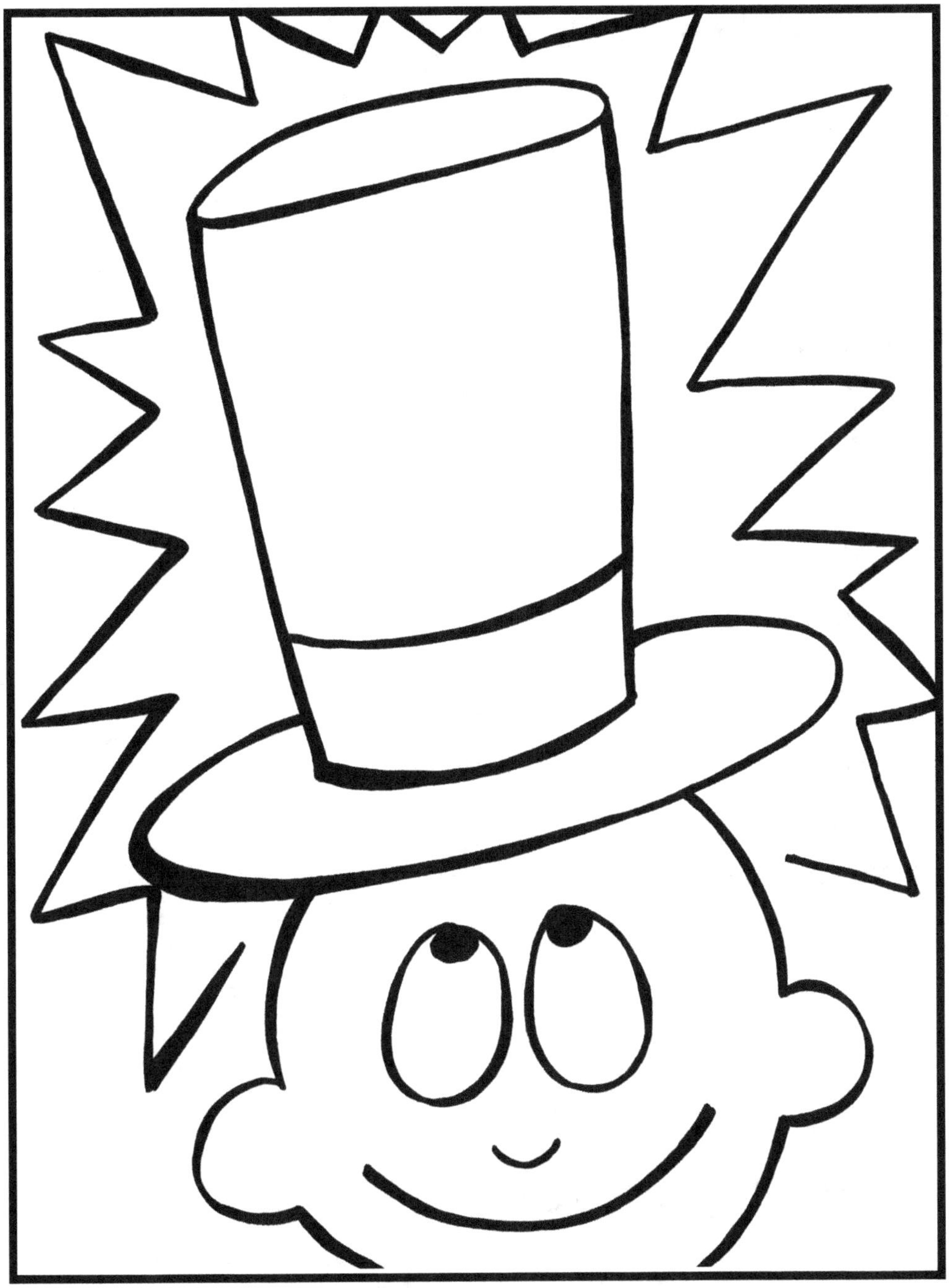

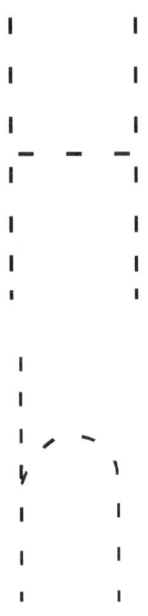

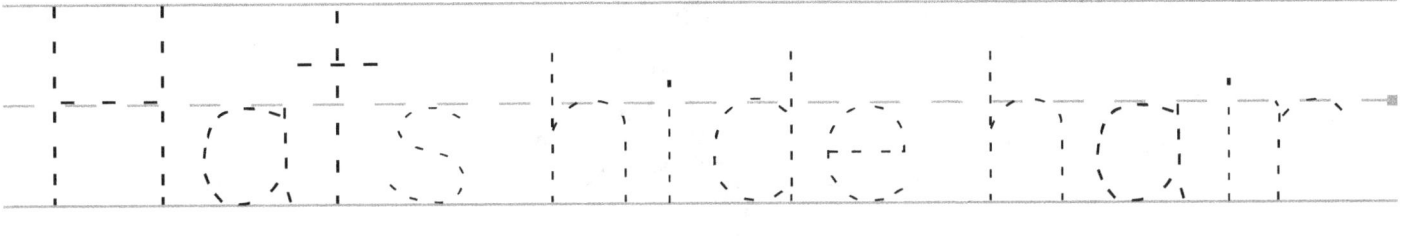

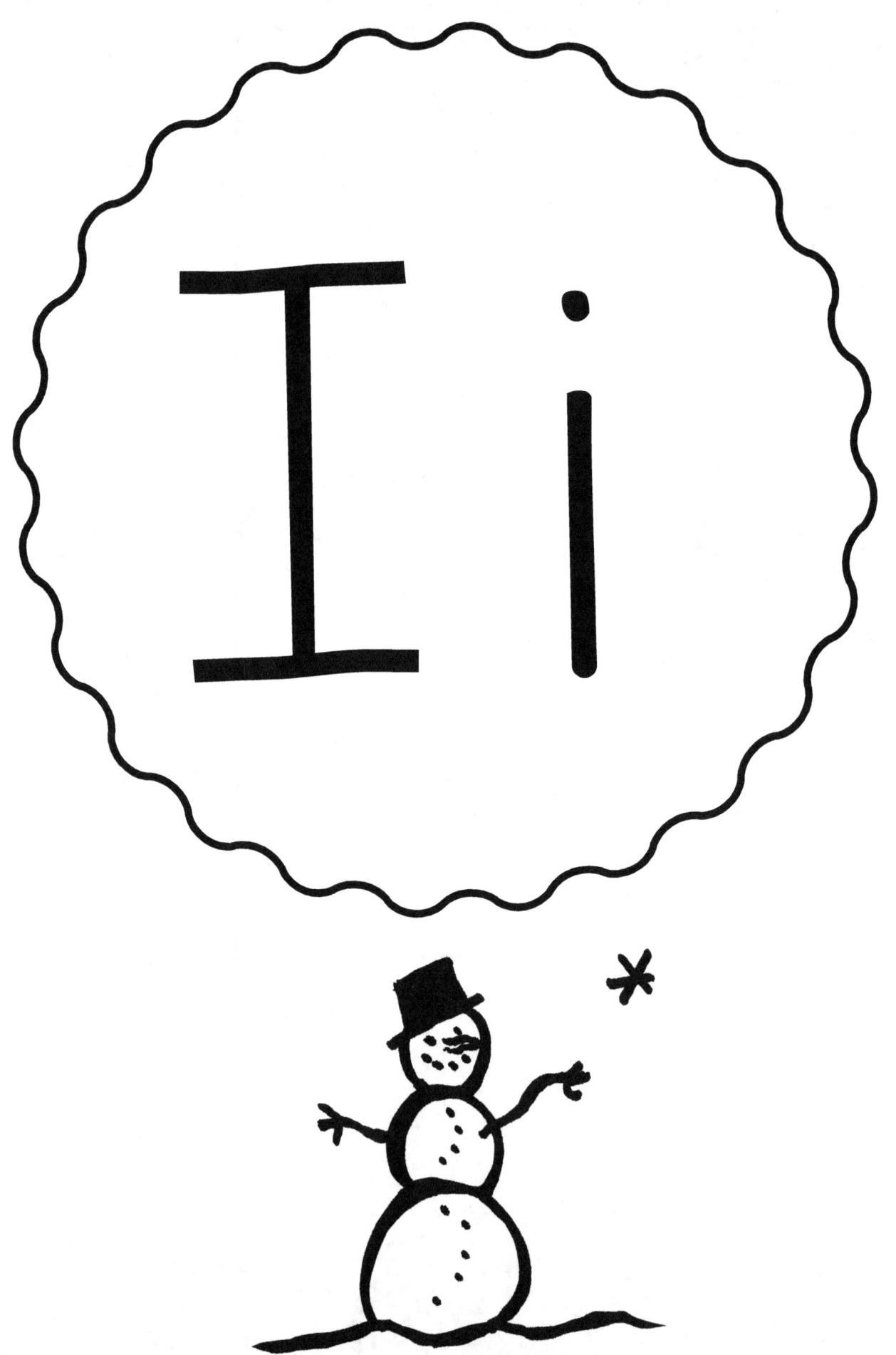

Color the picture, then trace and write the letters below.

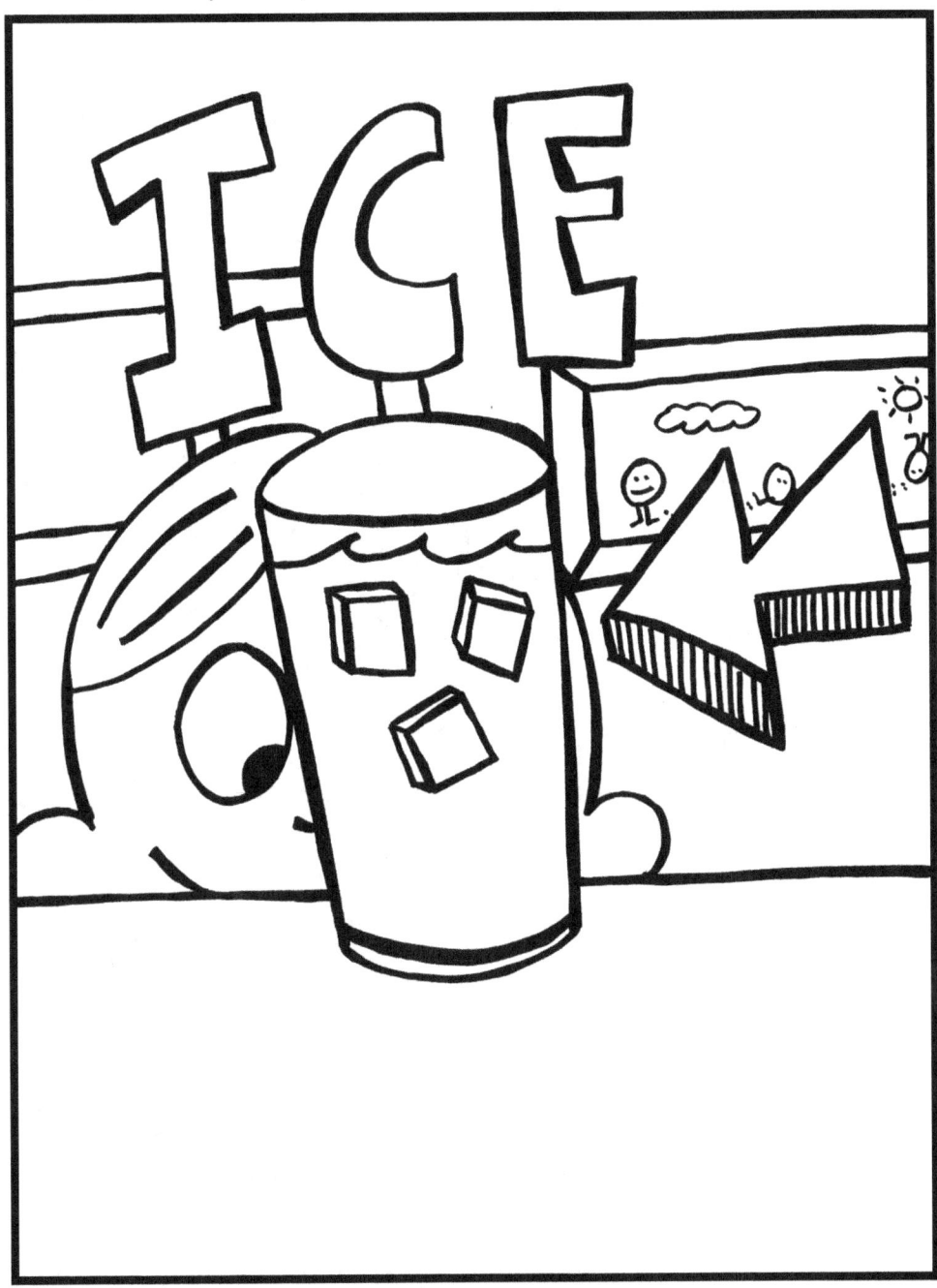

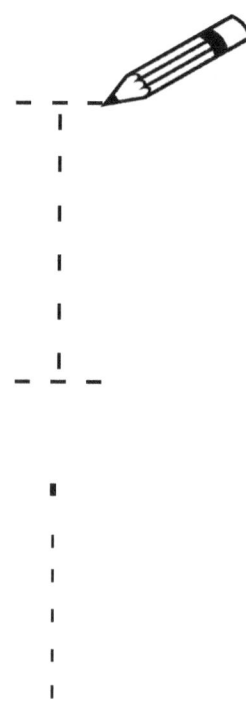

Color the picture, then trace and write the word below.

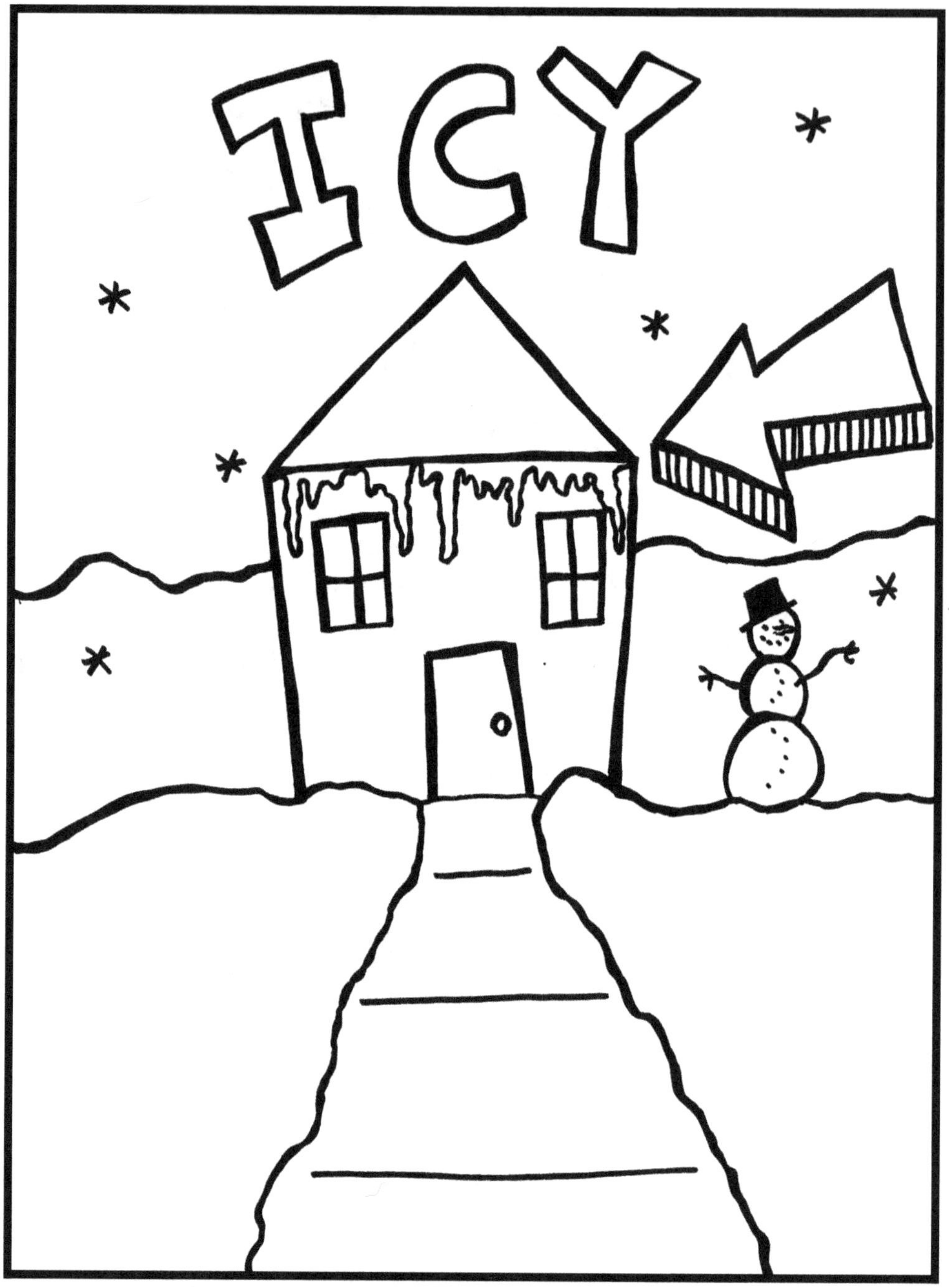

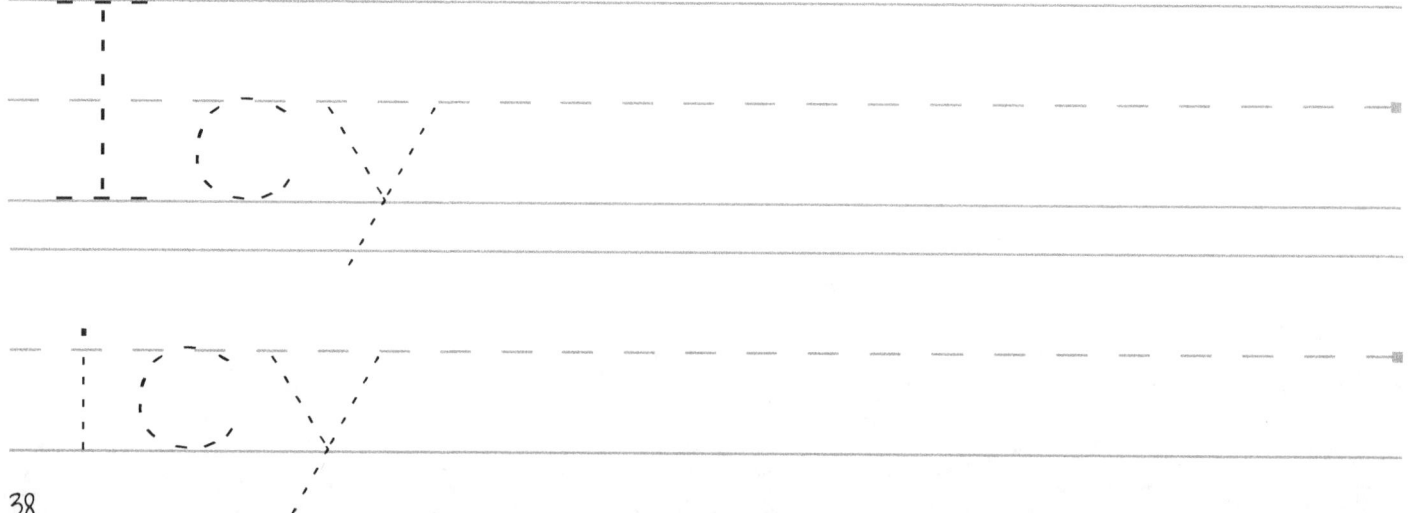

Color the picture, then trace and write the phrase below.

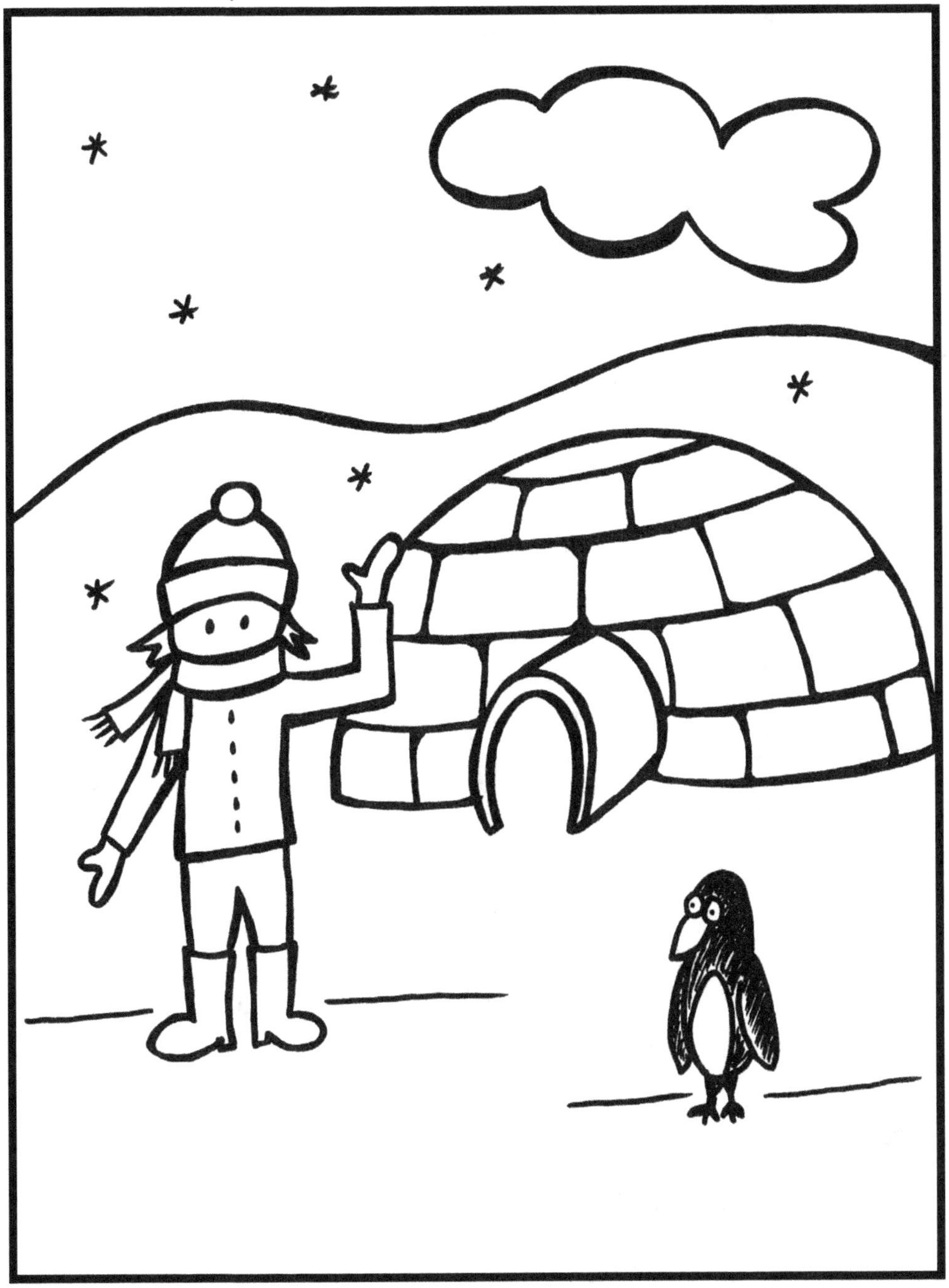

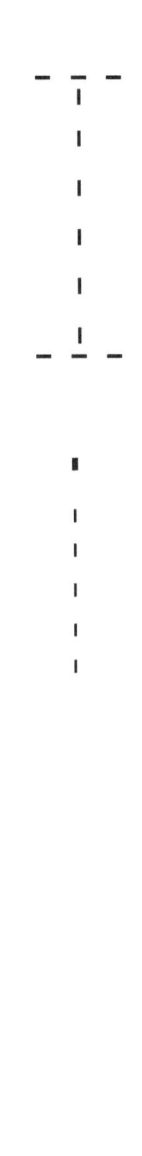

Icy igloo

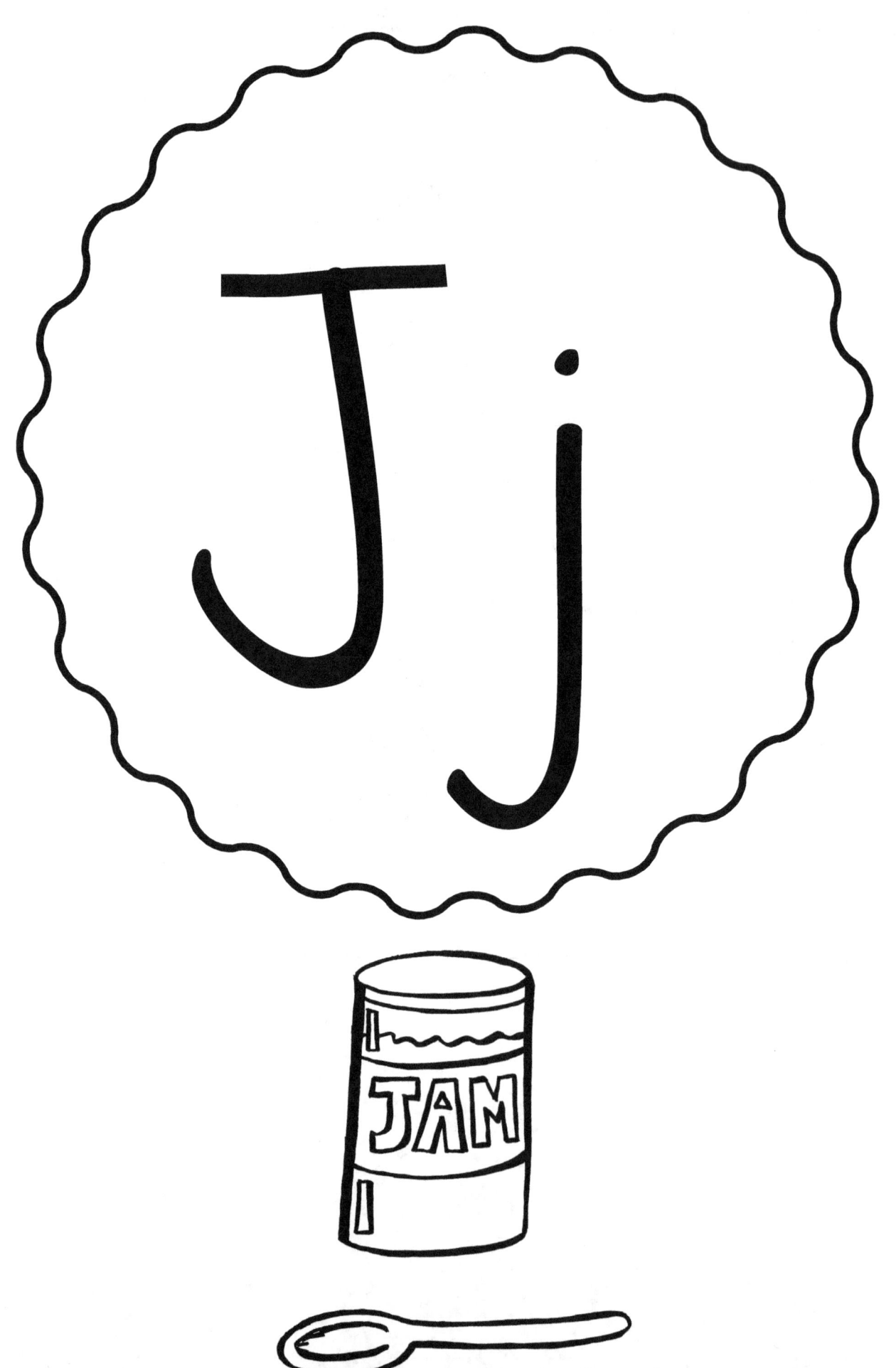

Color the picture, then trace and write the letters below.

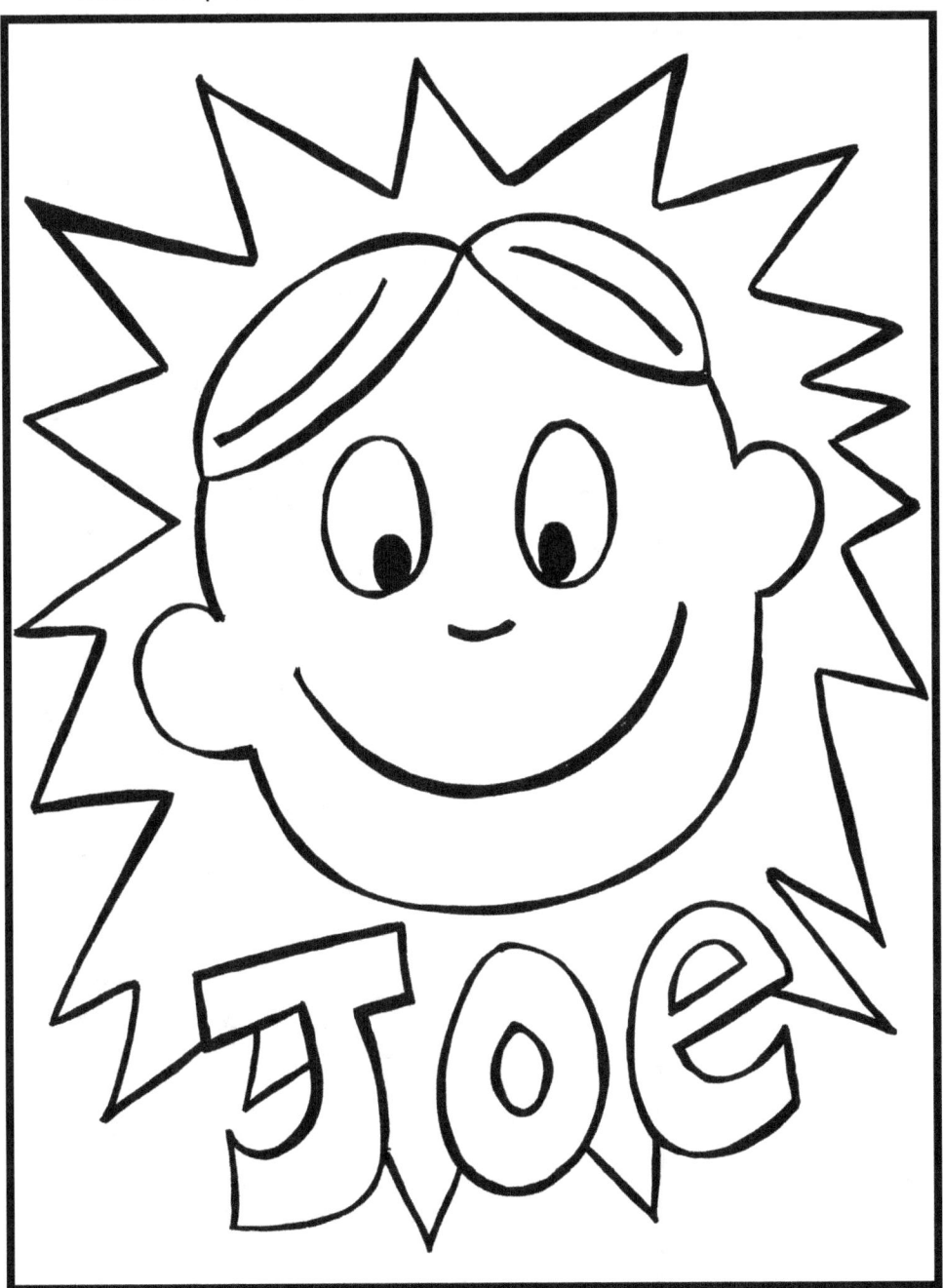

Color the picture, then trace and write the word below.

Jam

Jam

Color the picture, then trace and write the phrase below.

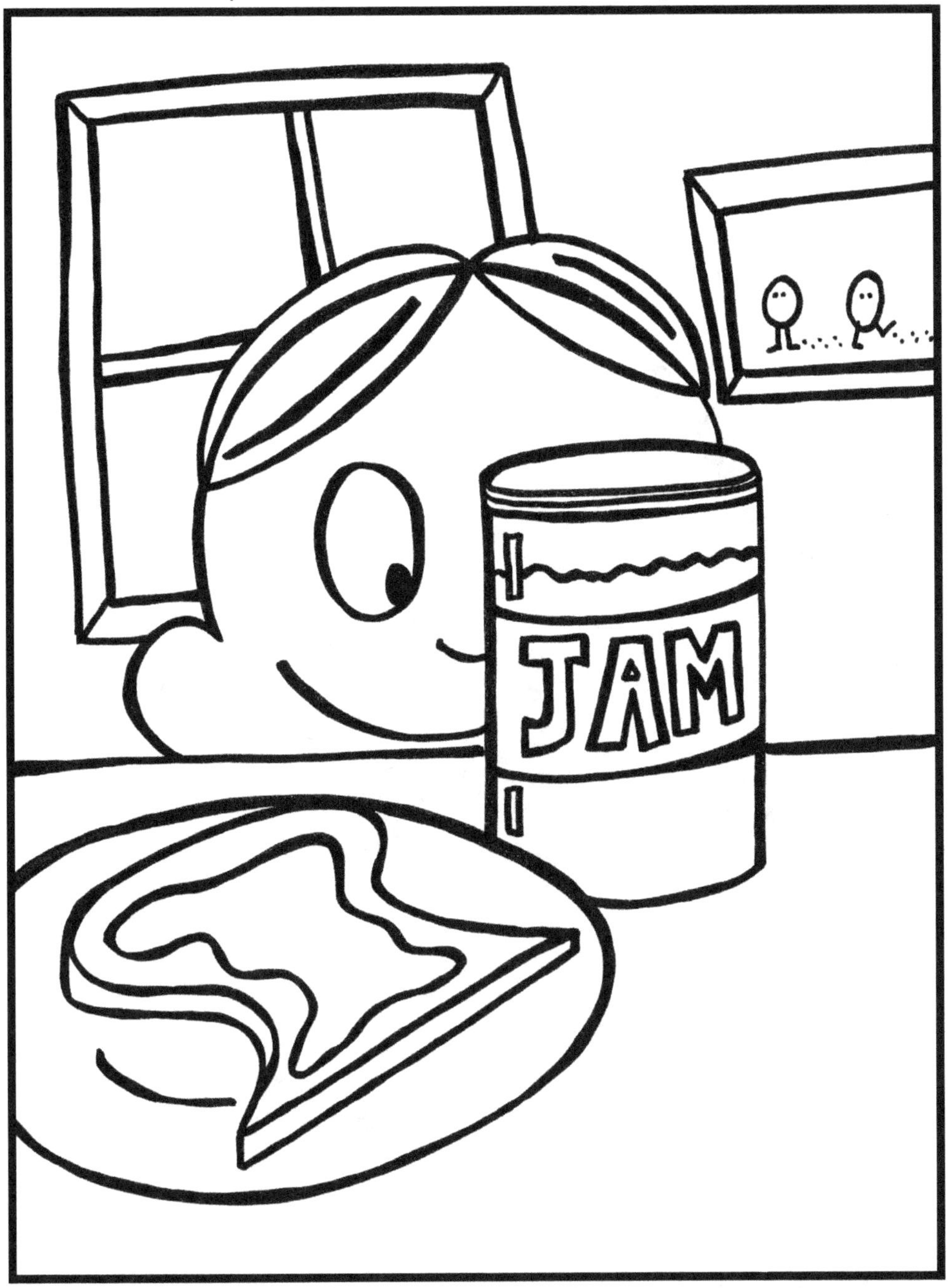

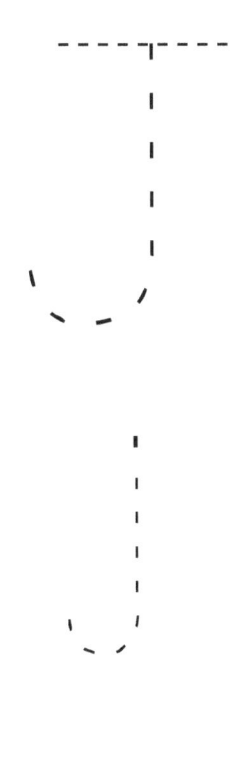

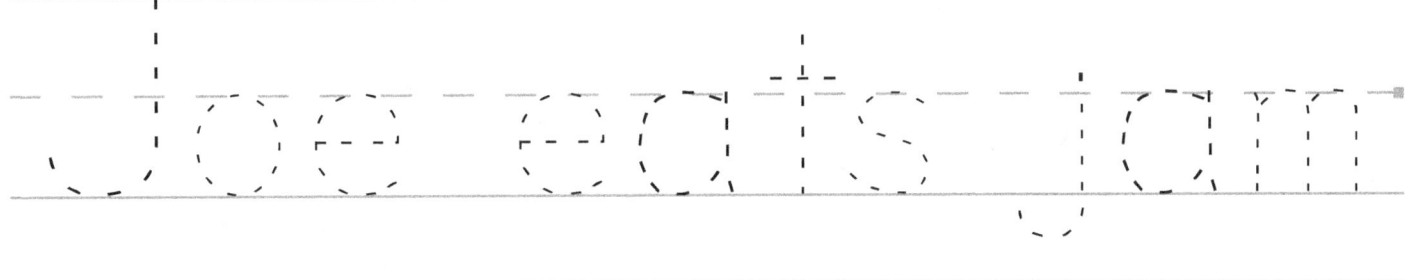

Joe eats jam

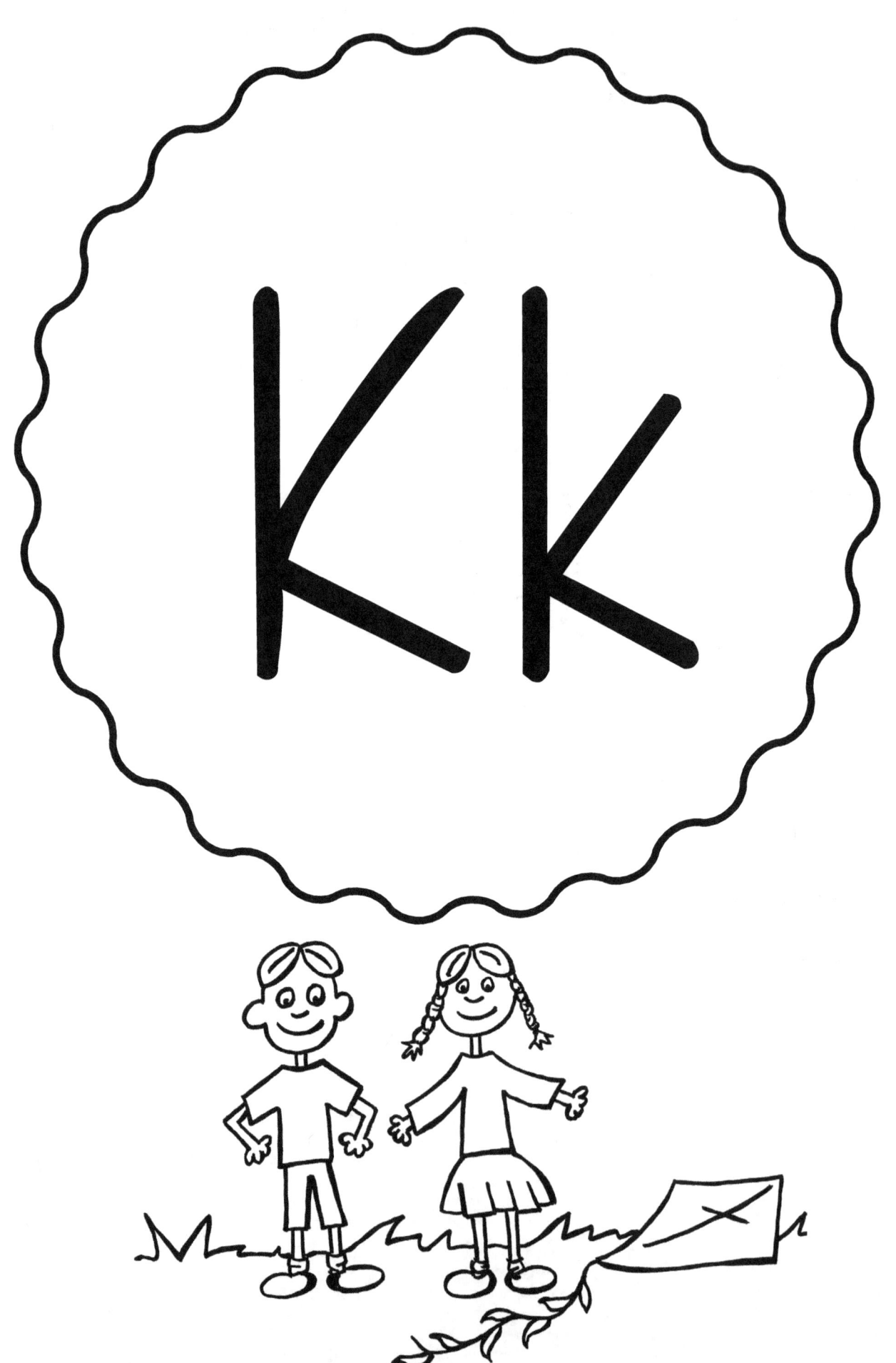

Color the picture, then trace and write the letters below.

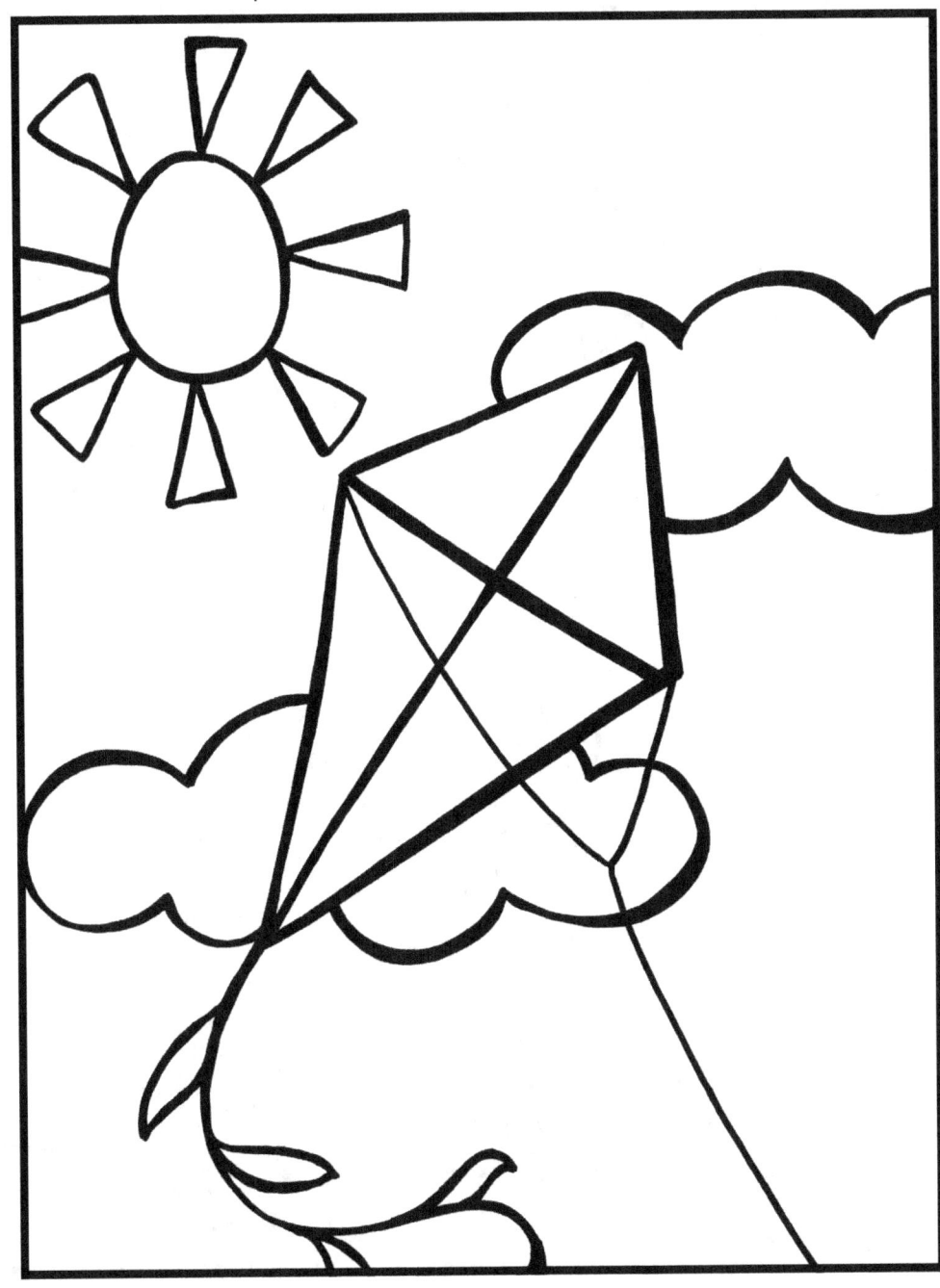

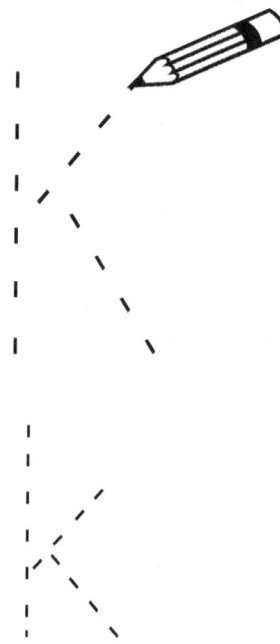

Color the picture, then trace and write the word below.

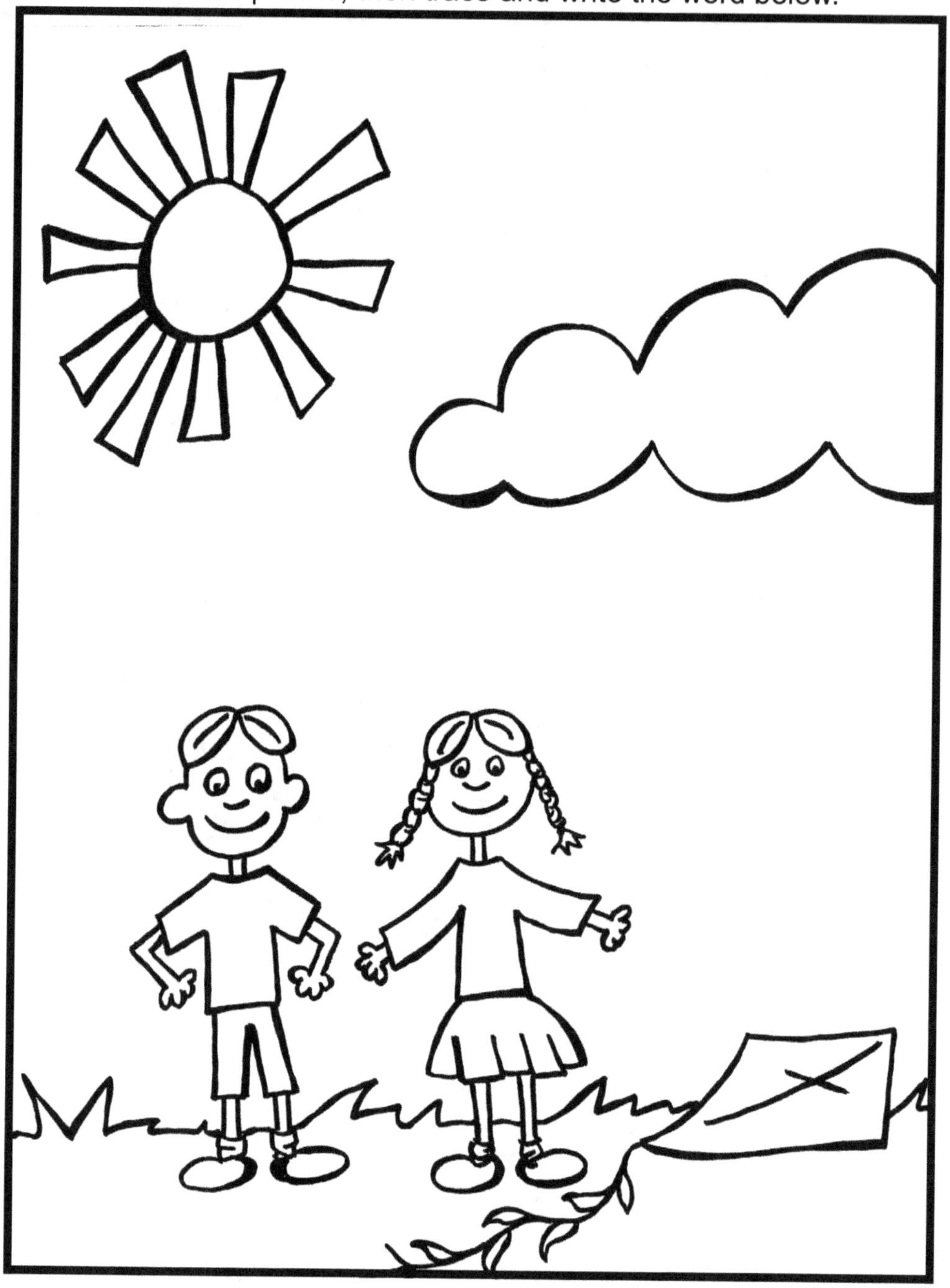

Kid

kid

Color the picture, then trace and write the phrase below.

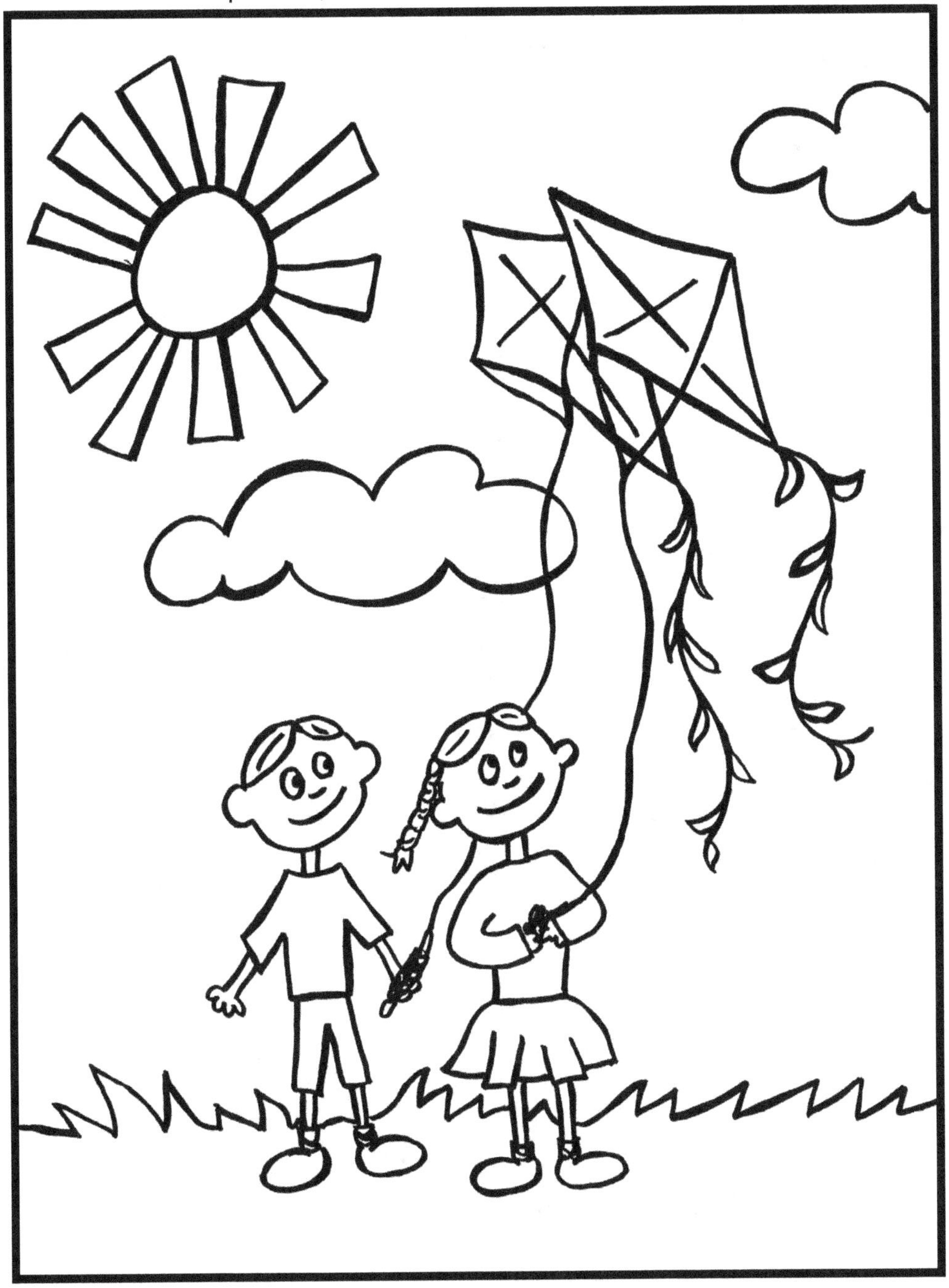

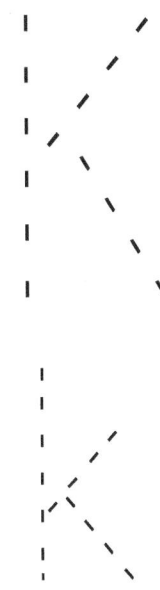

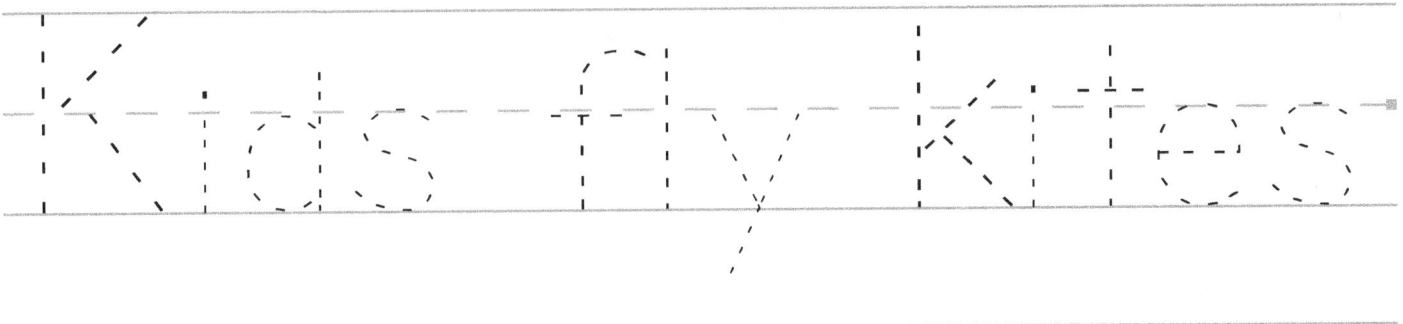

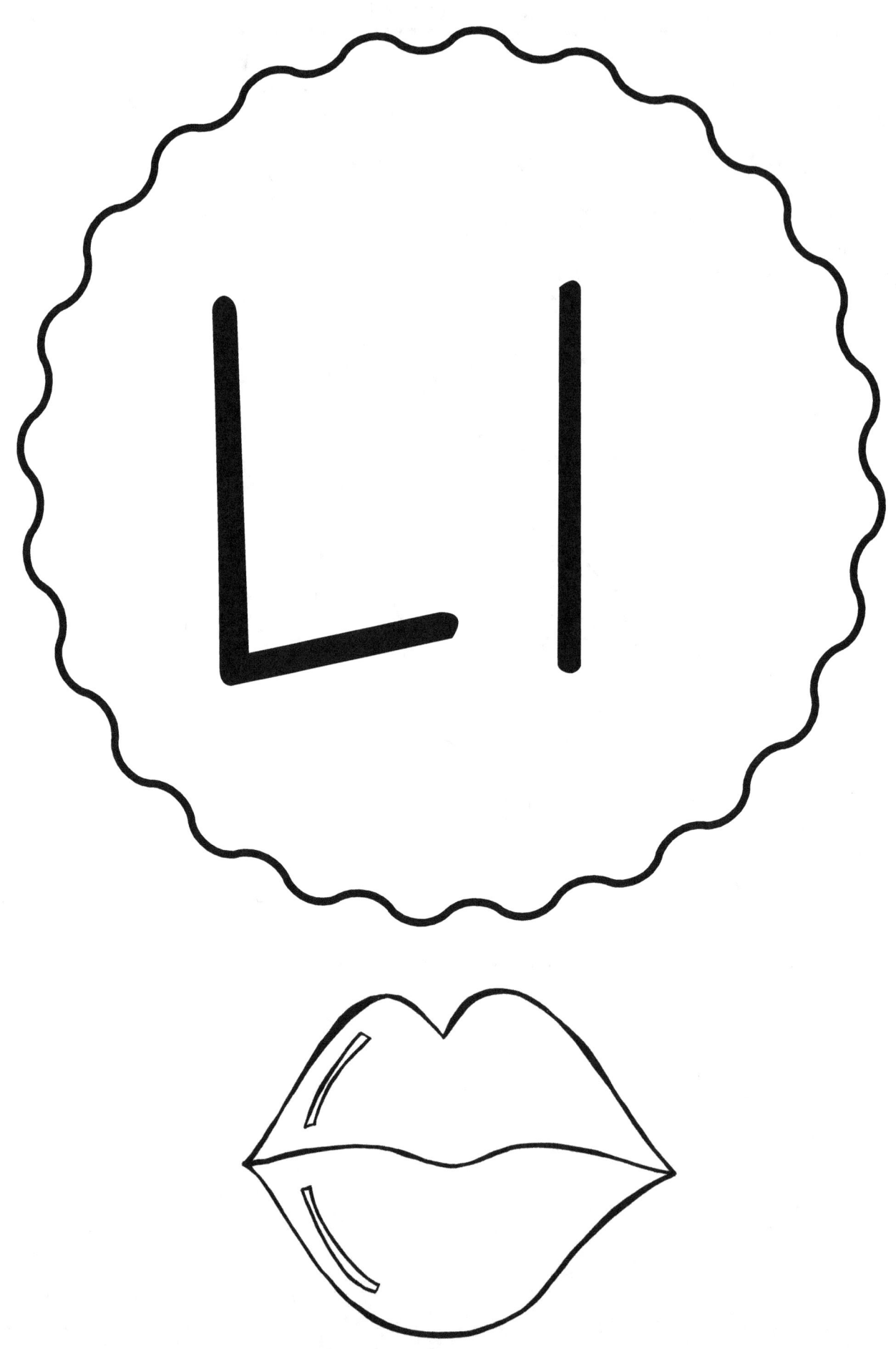

Color in the picture and trace the letters below.

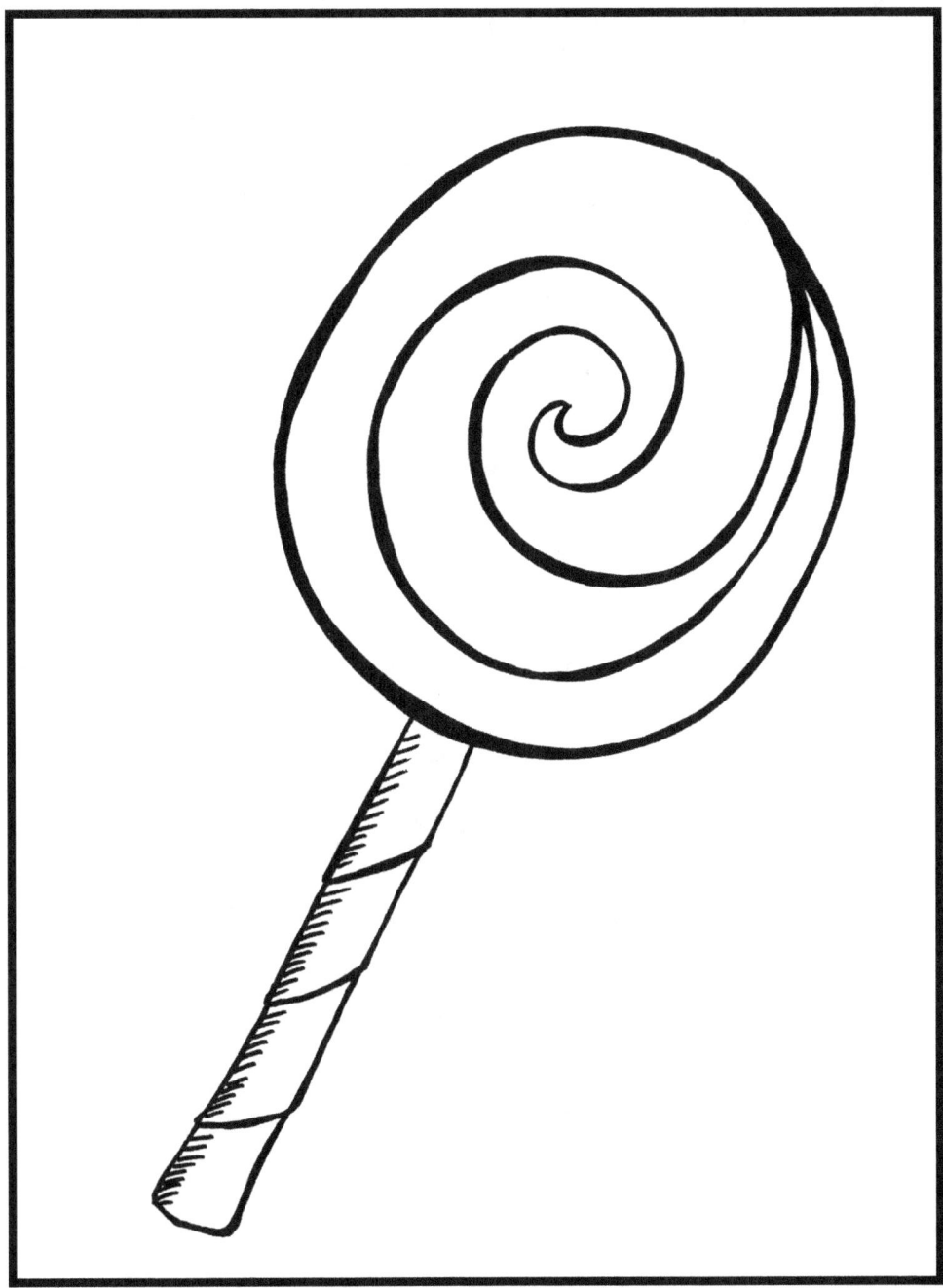

Color in the picture and trace the letters below.

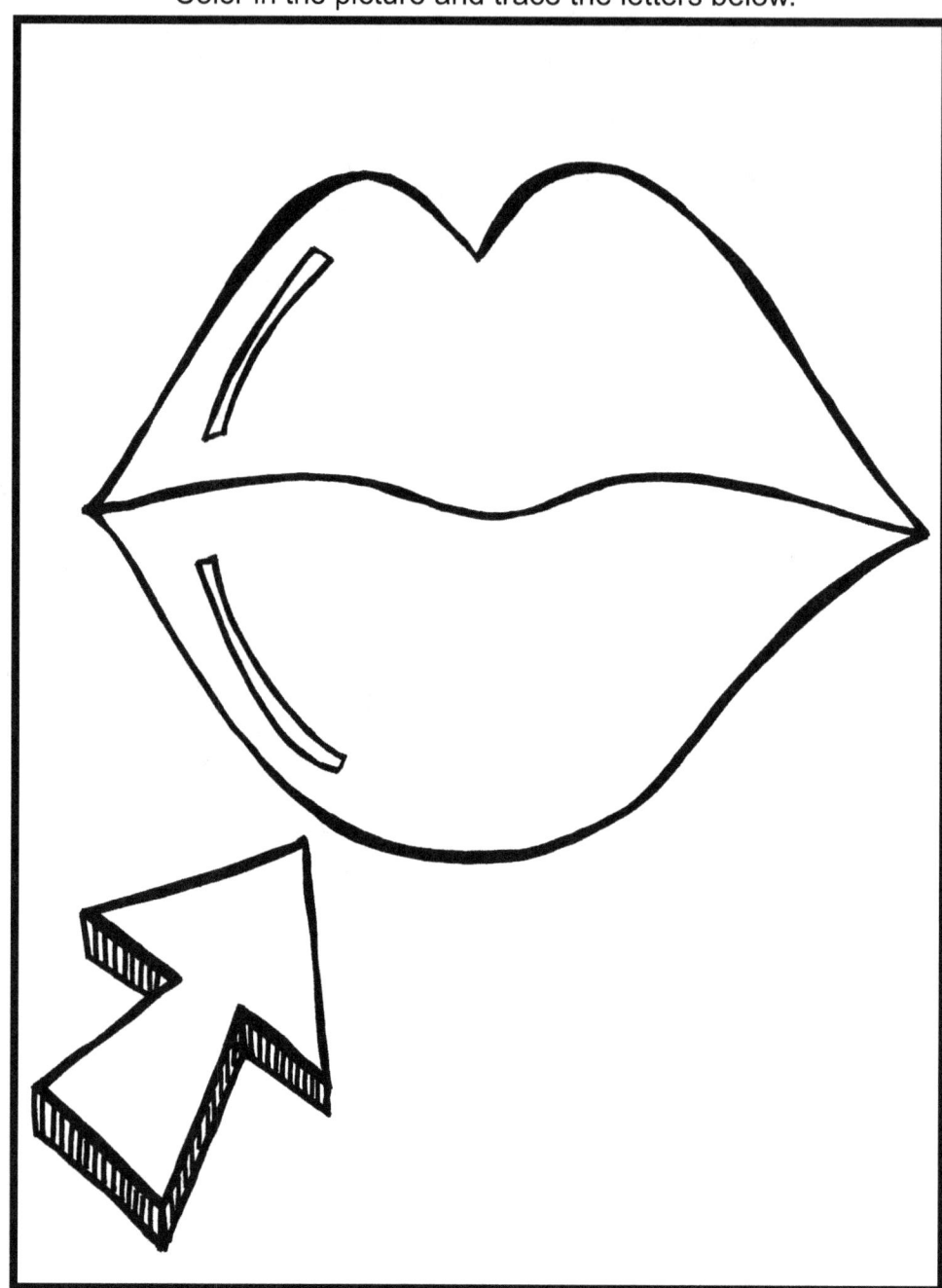

Lip
lip

Color the picture, then trace and write the phrase below.

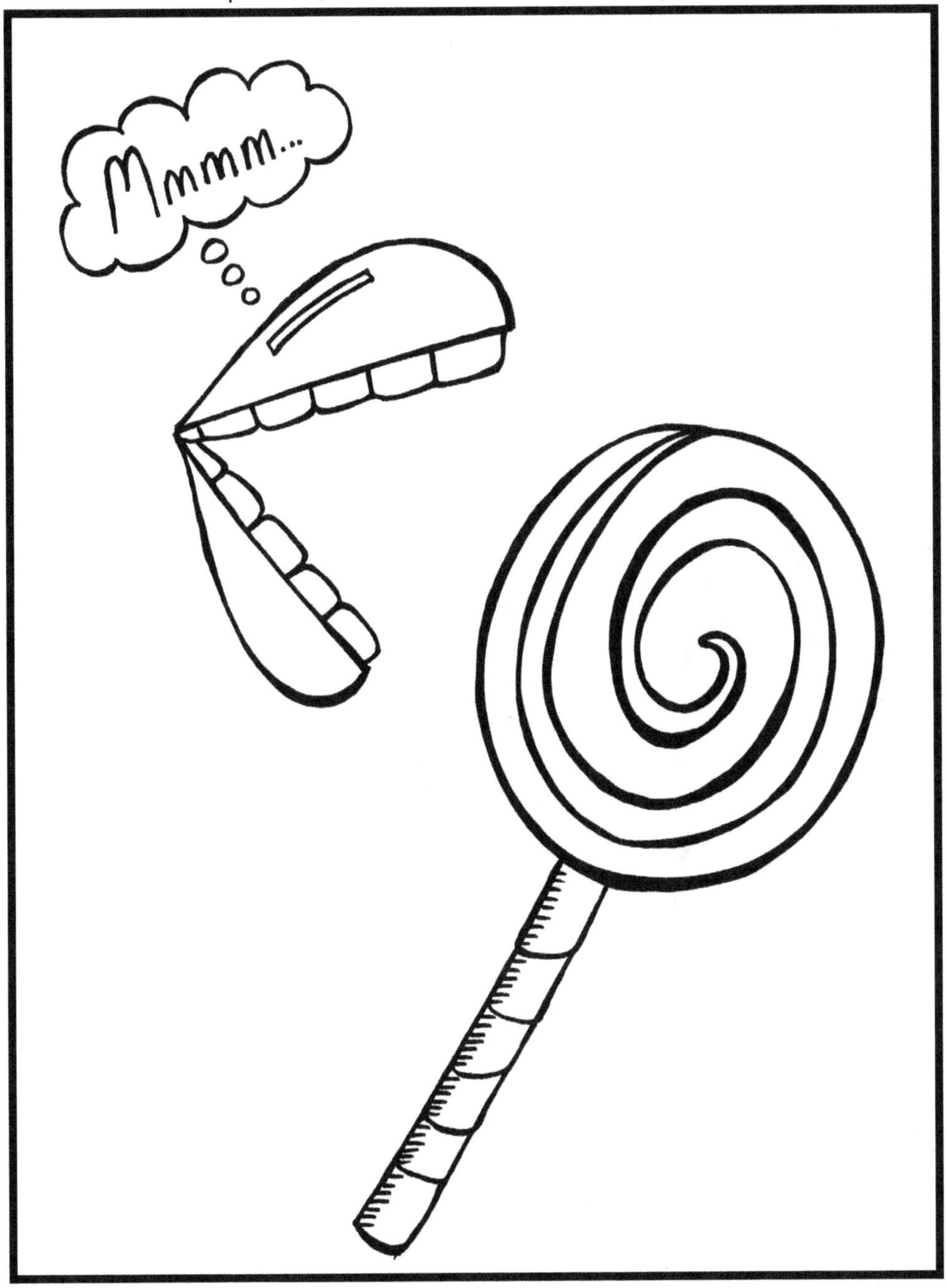

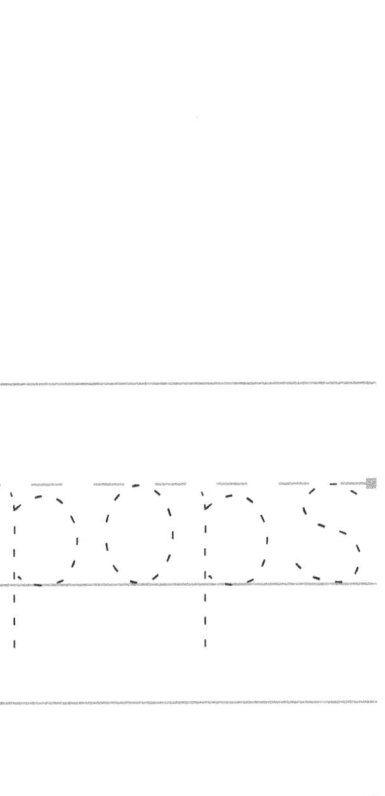

Lips like lollipops

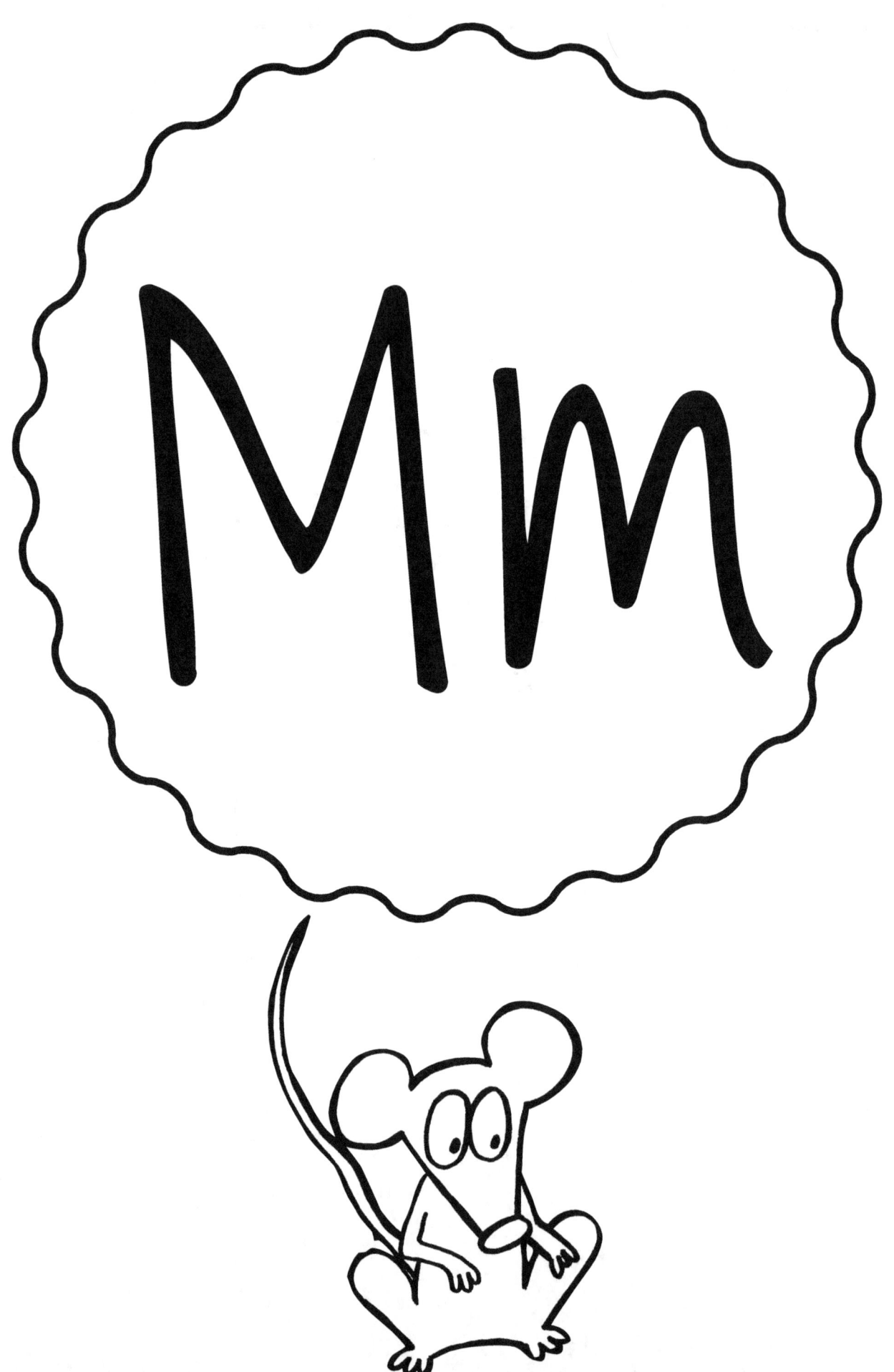

Color the picture, then trace and write the letters below.

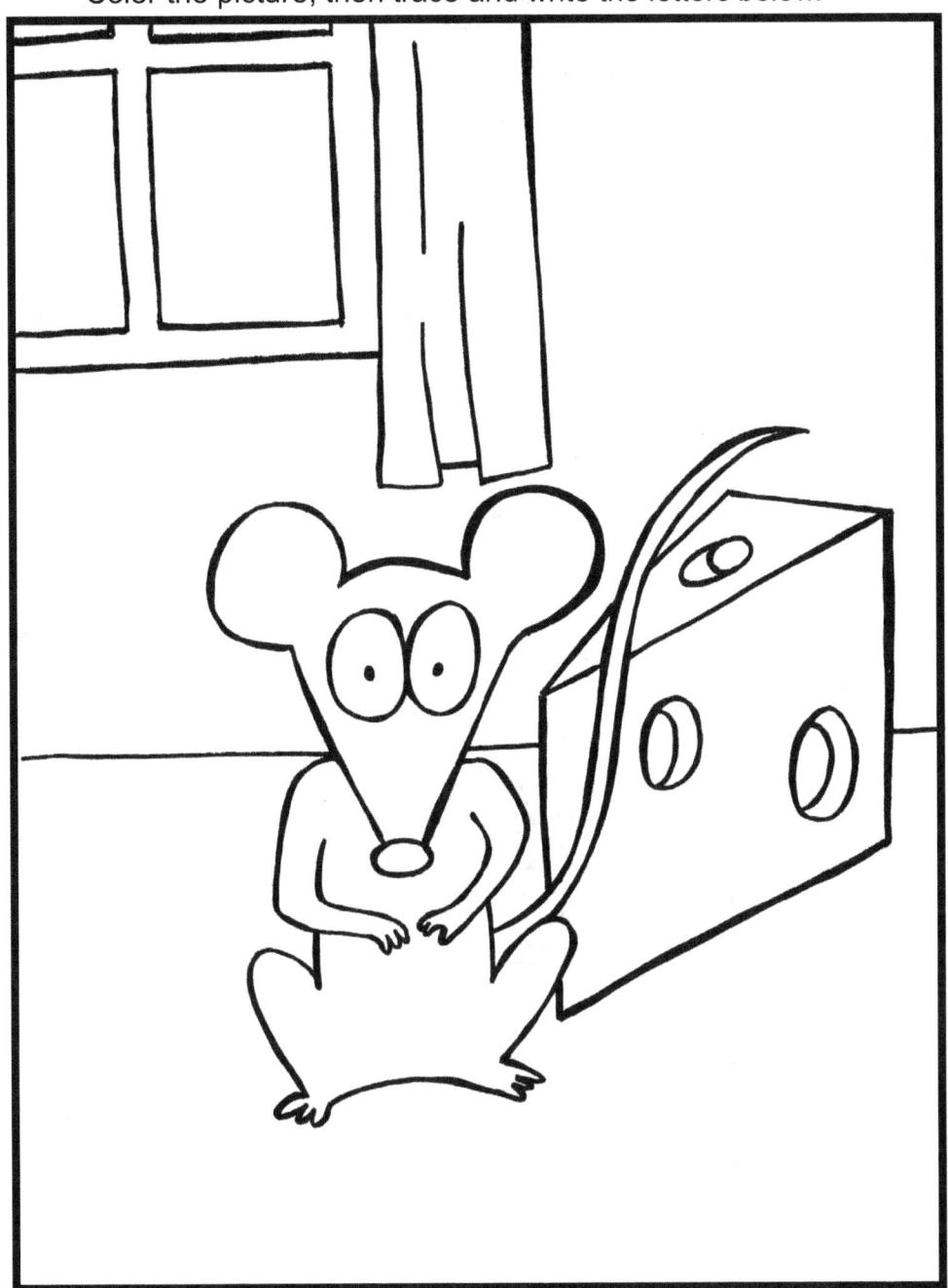

Color in the picture and trace the letters below.

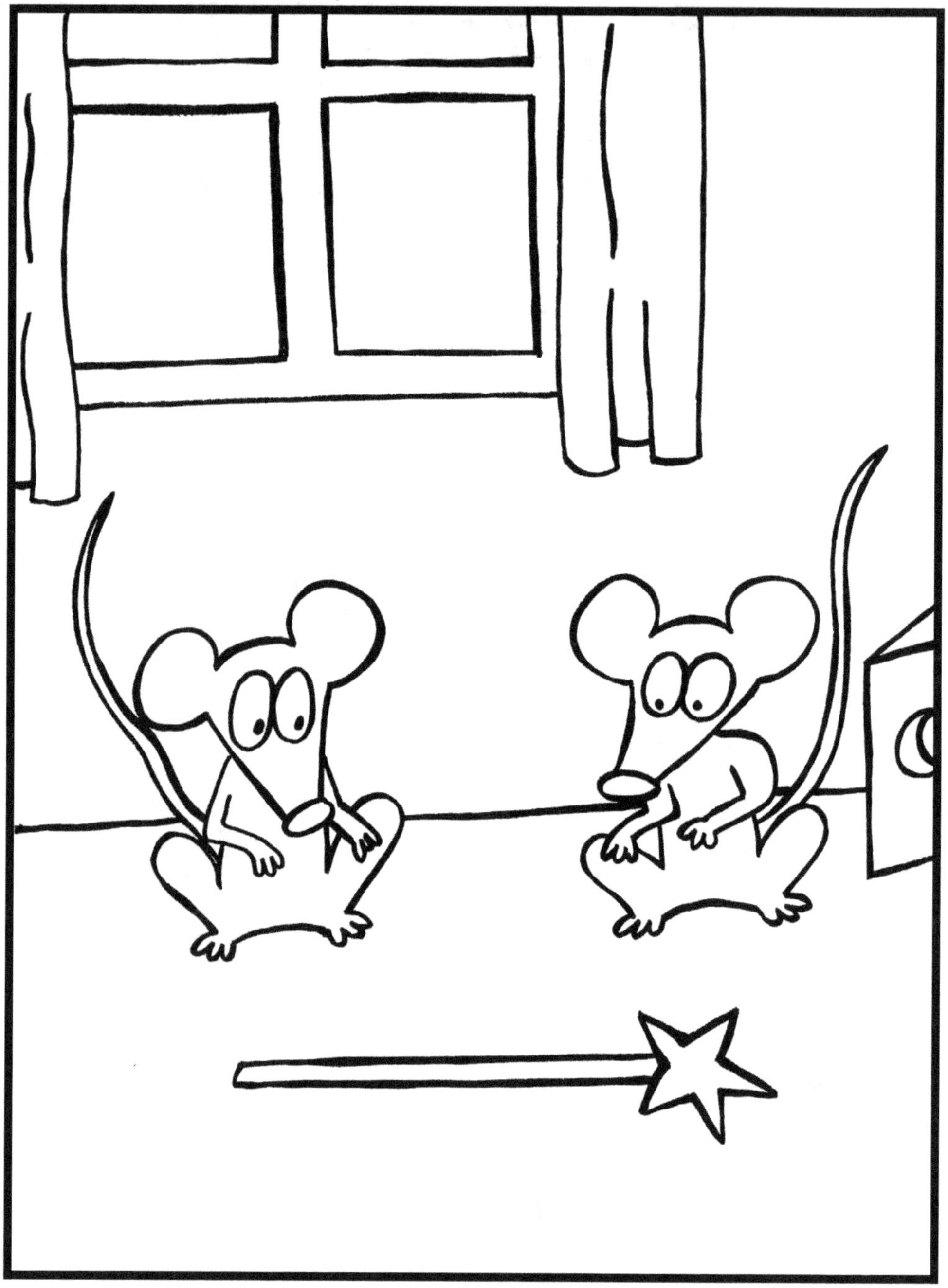

M m

Mice

mice

Color the picture, then trace and write the phrase below.

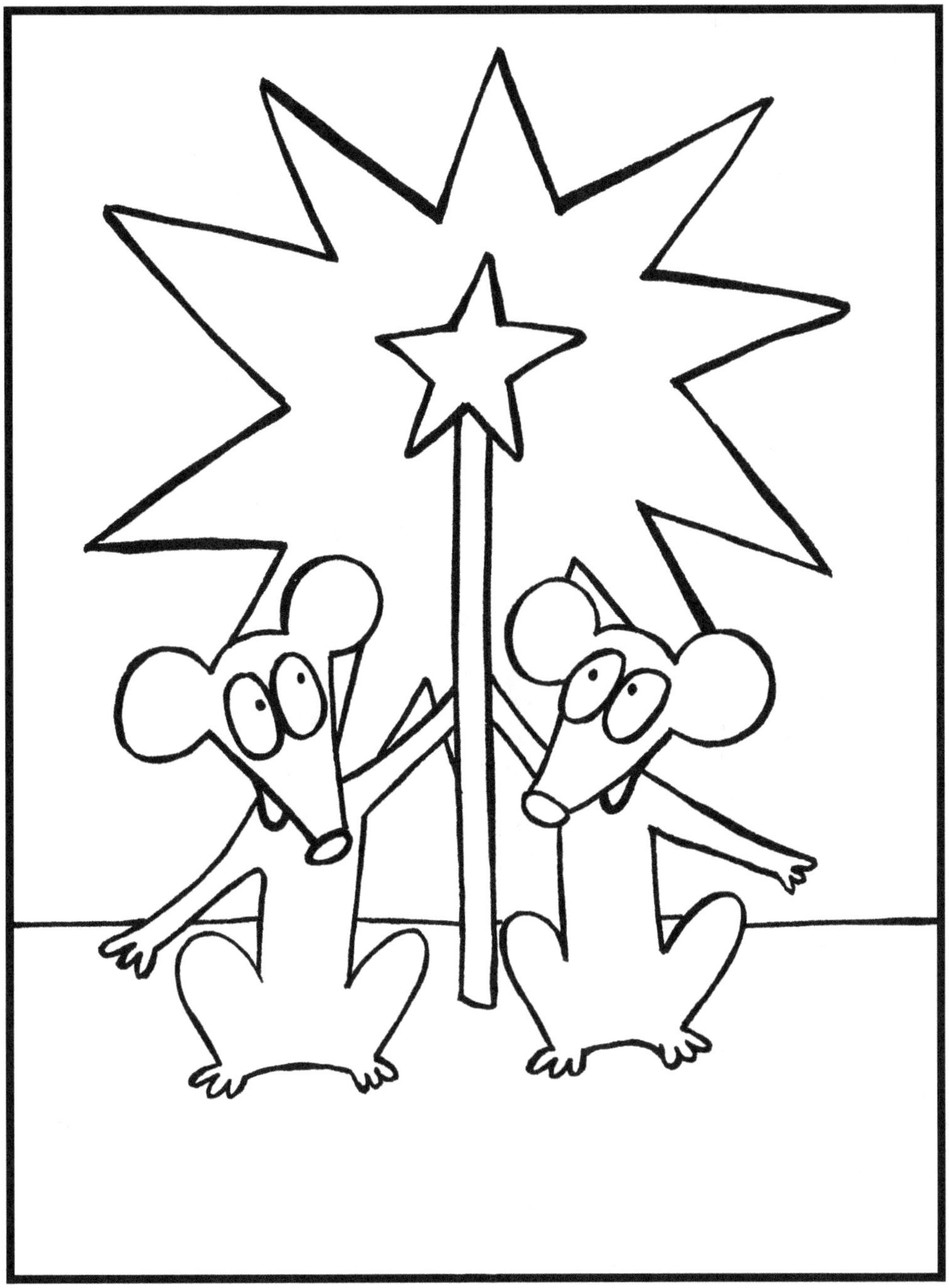

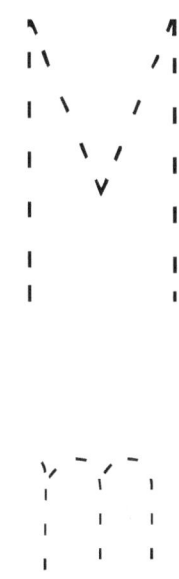

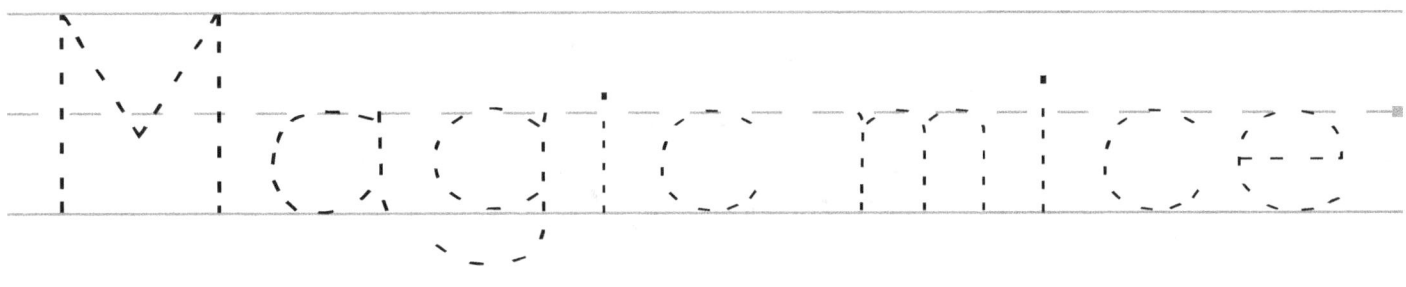

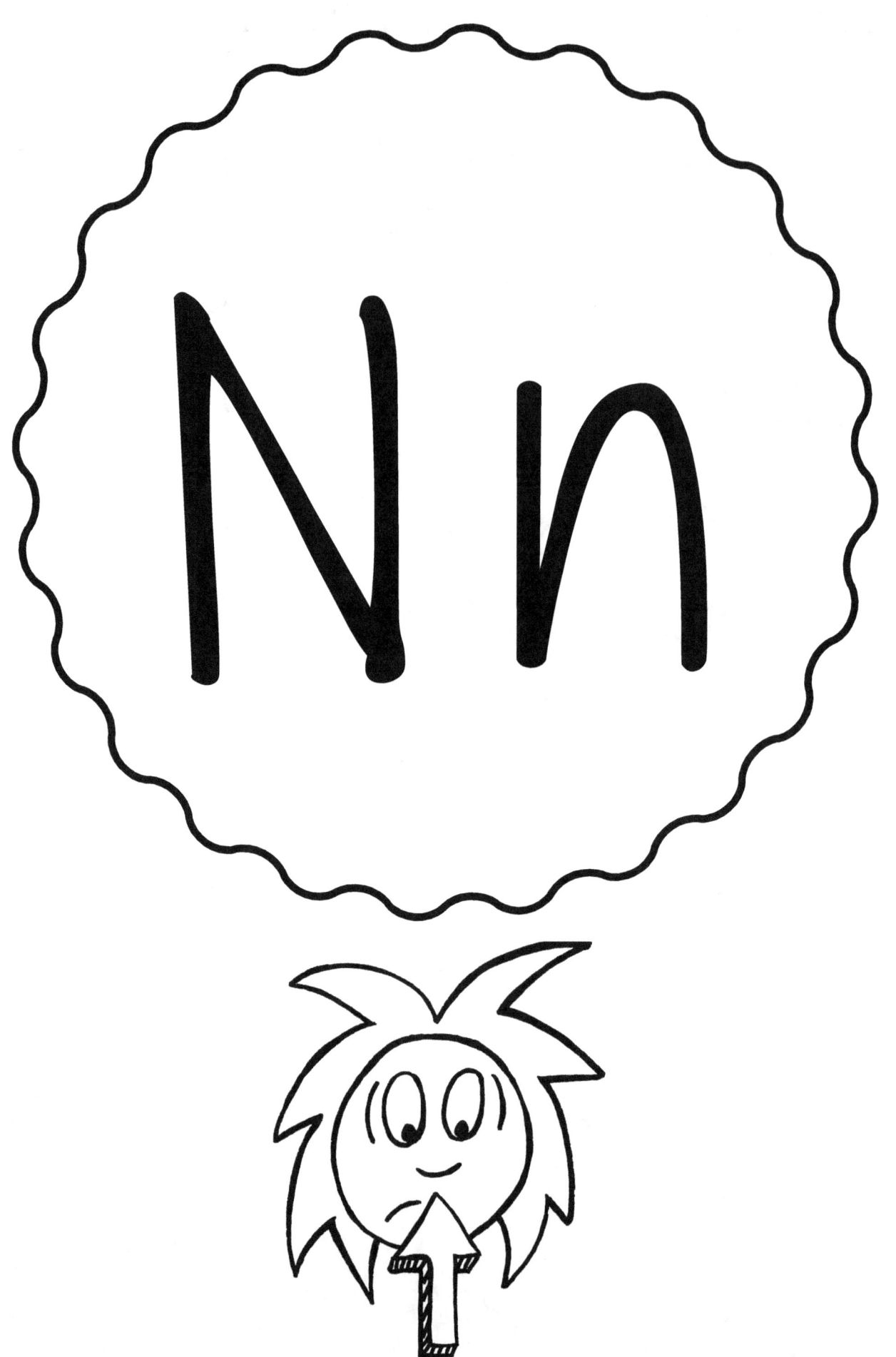

Color the picture, then trace and write the letters below.

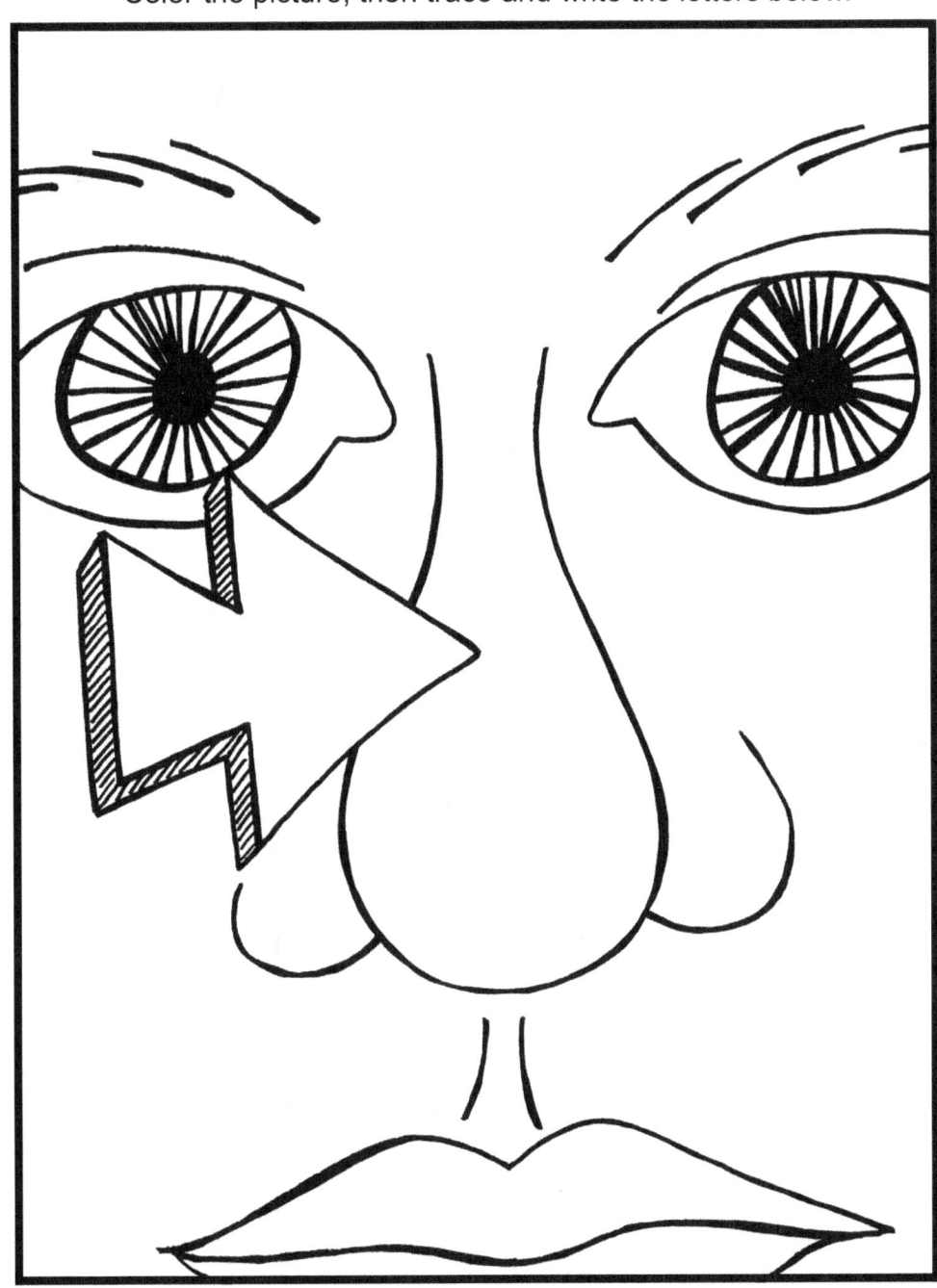

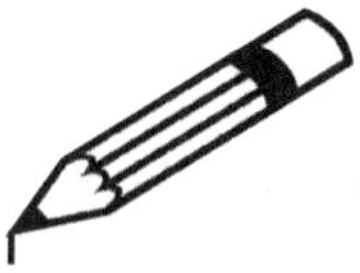

Color the picture, then trace and write the word below.

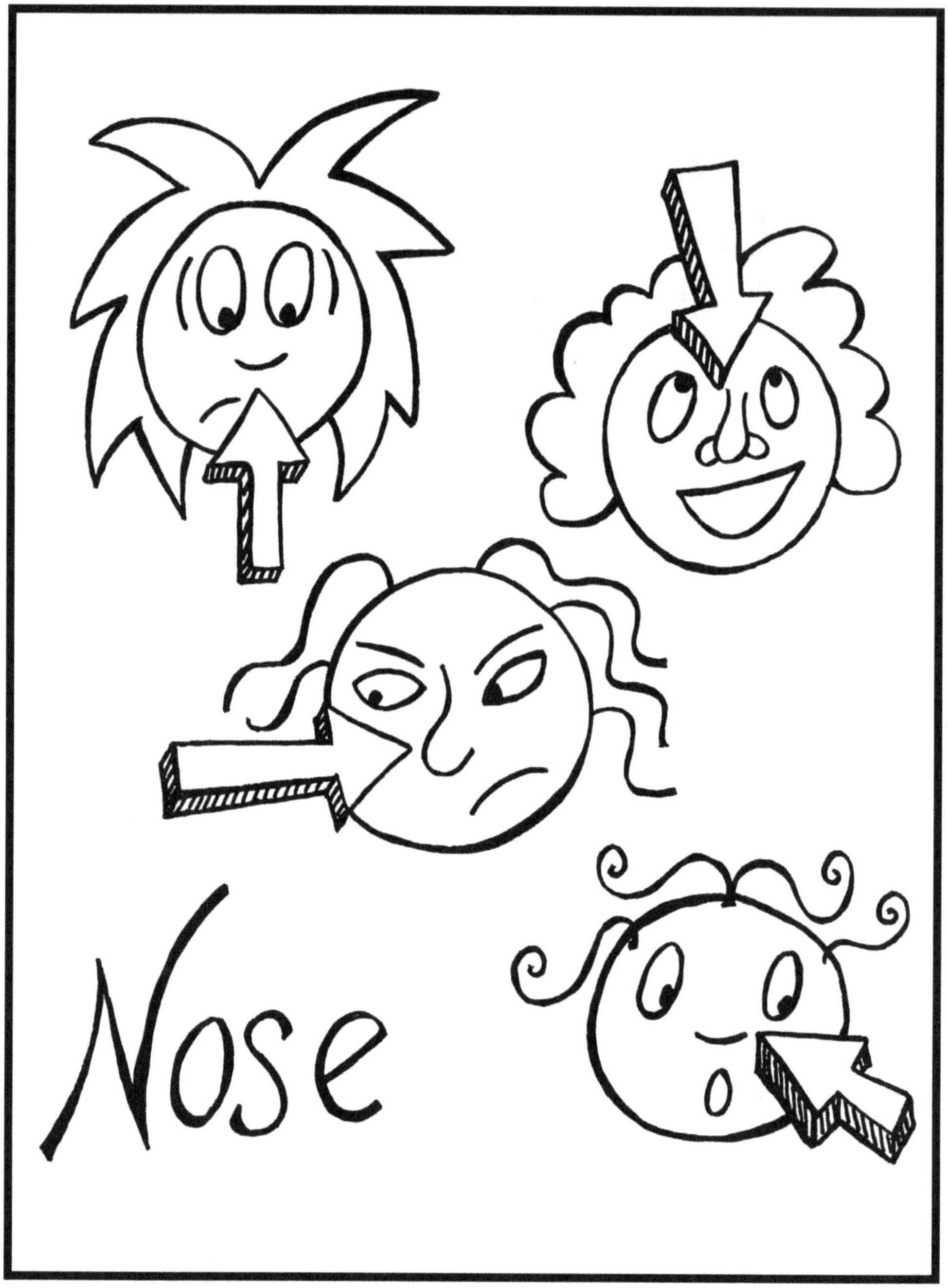

N n

Nose

Nose

nose

Color the picture, then trace and write the phrase below.

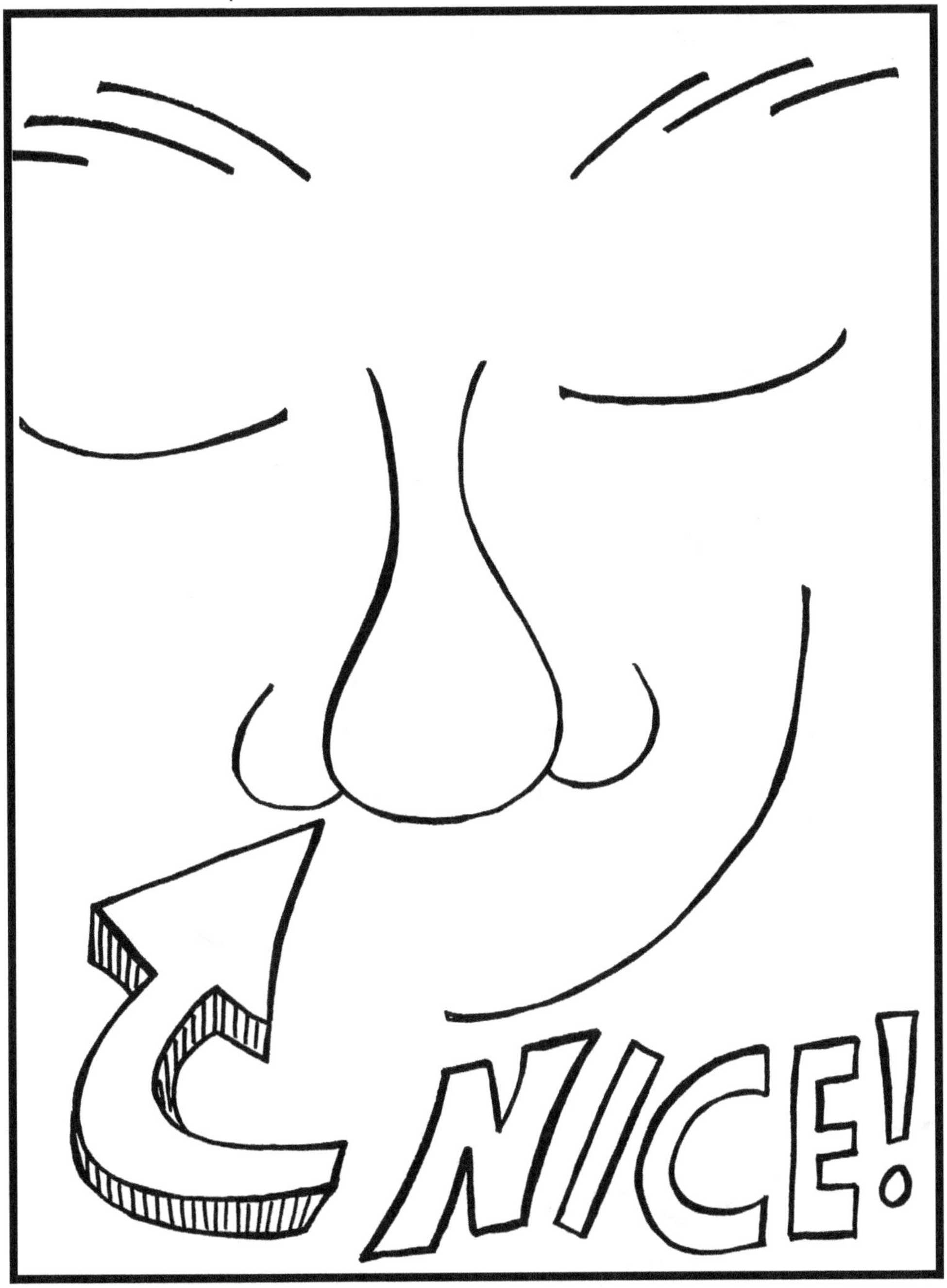

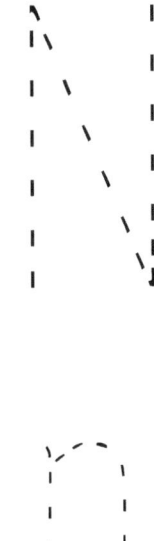

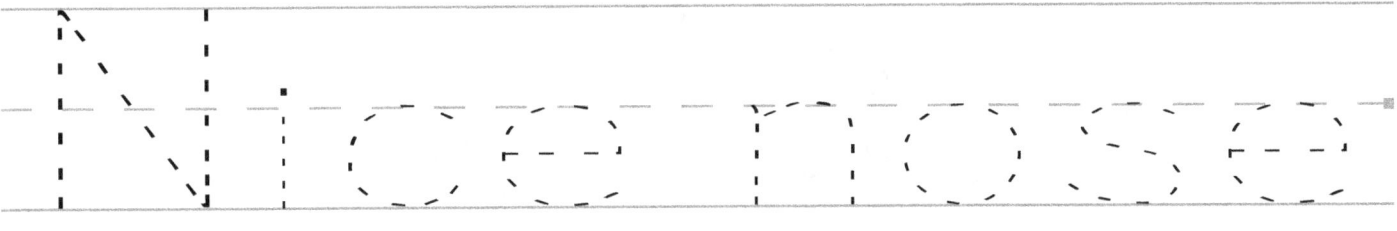

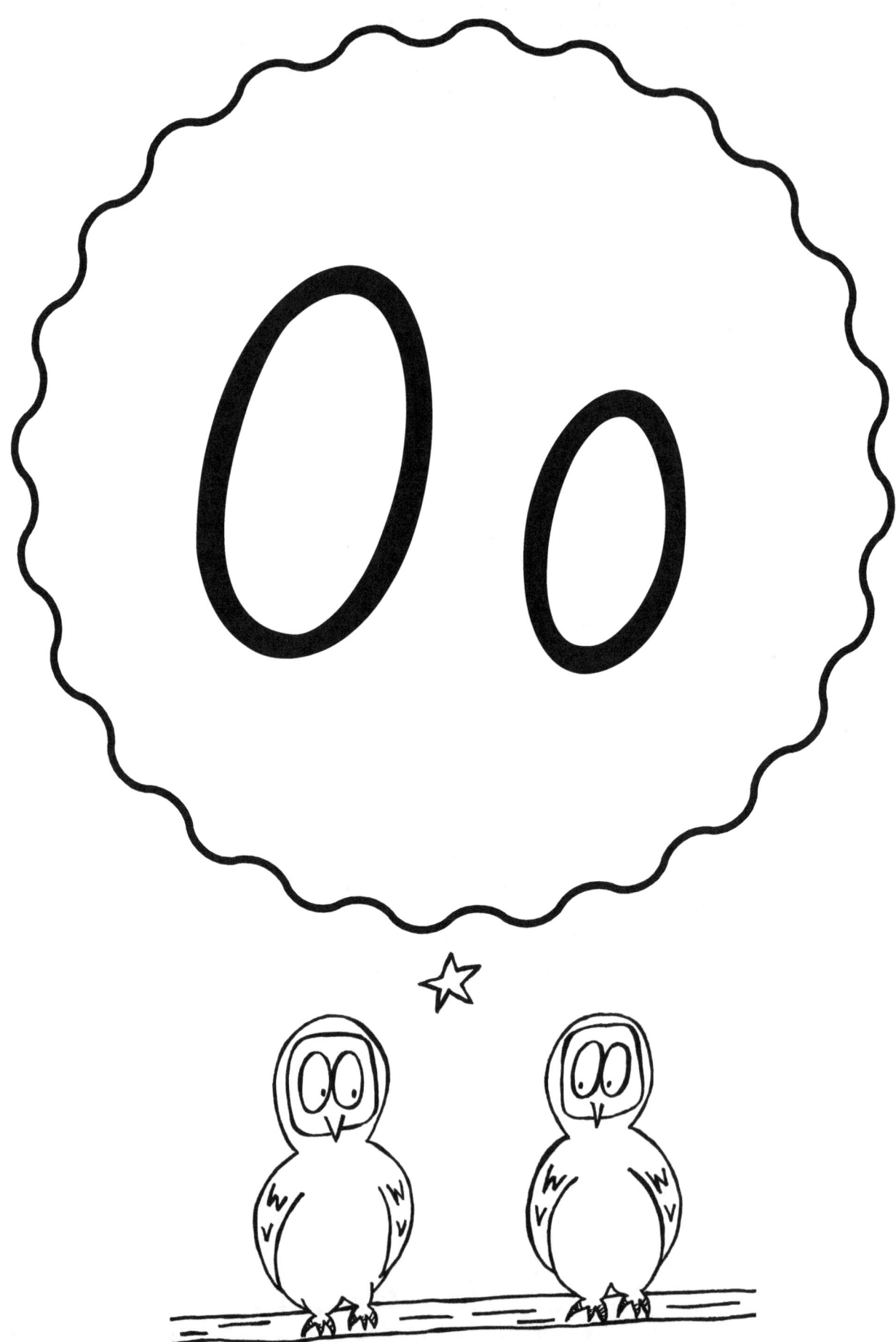

Color the picture, then trace and write the letters below.

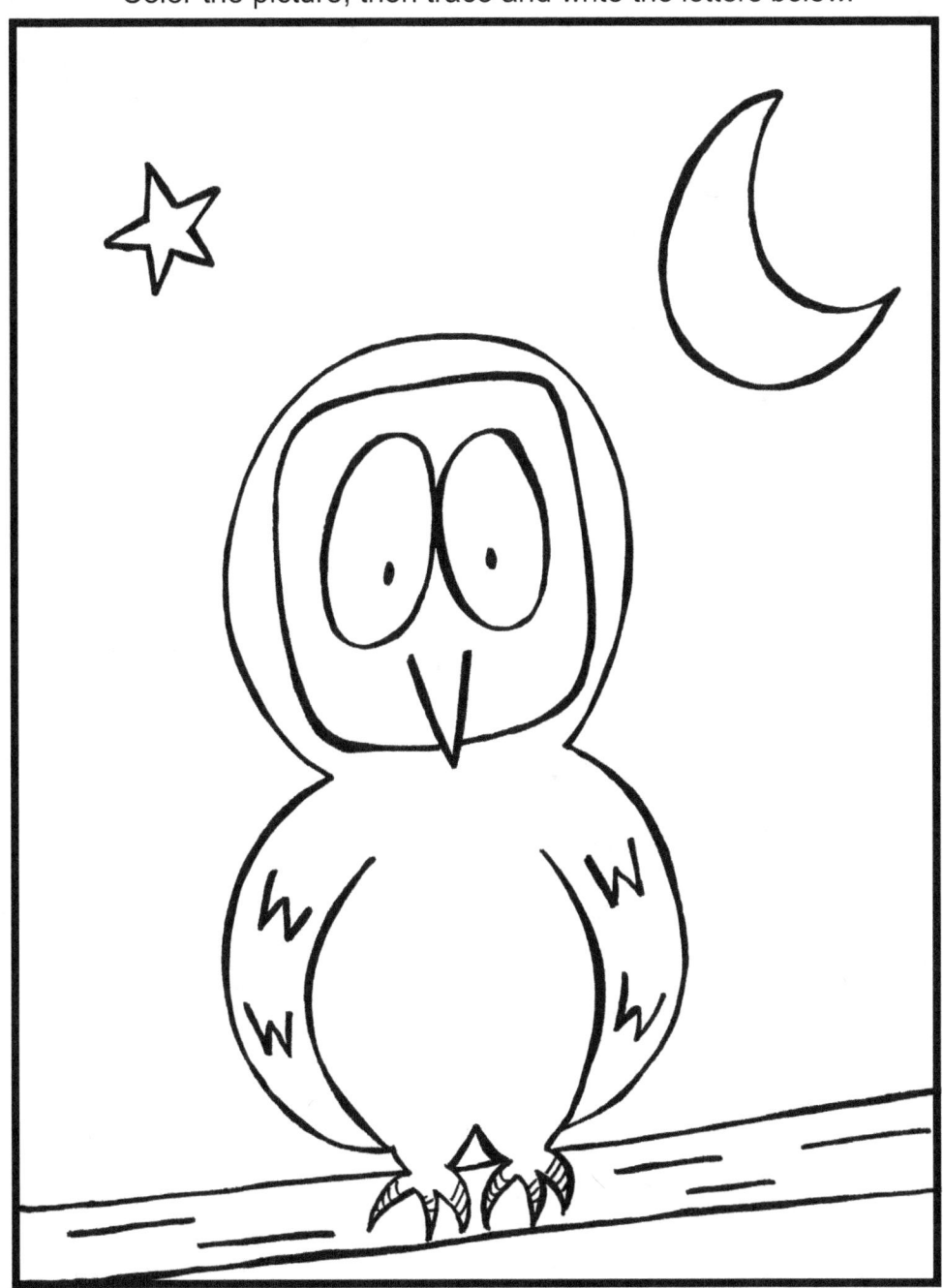

Color the picture, then trace and write the word below.

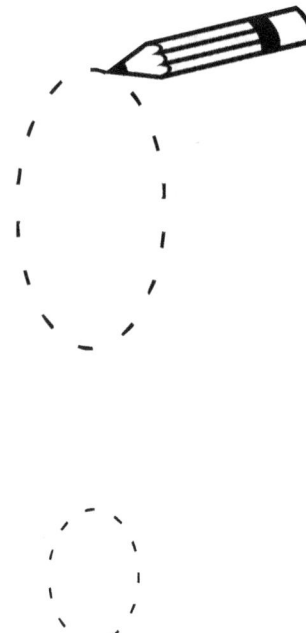

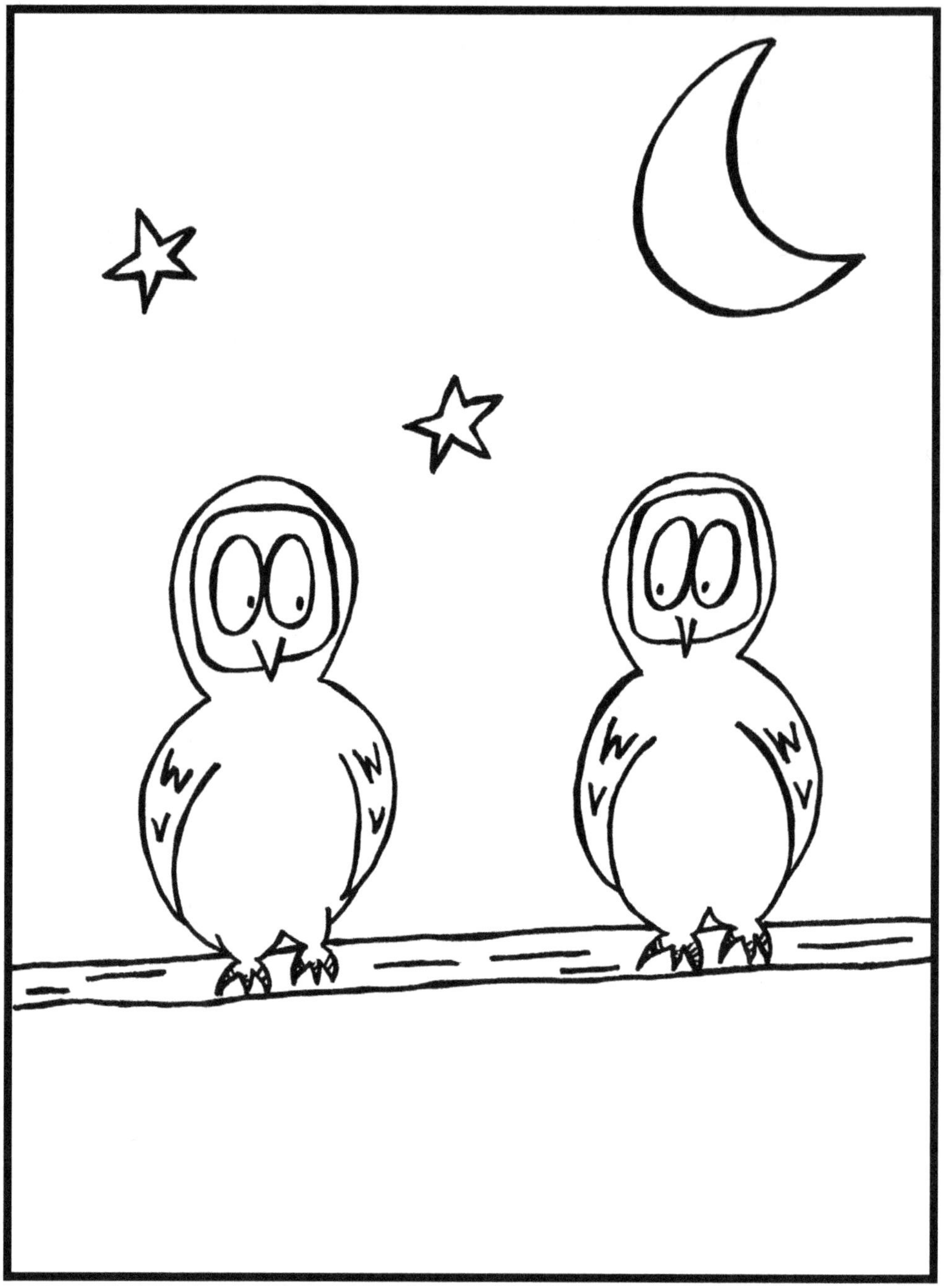

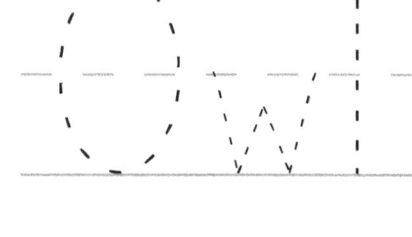

Color the picture, then trace and write the phrase below.

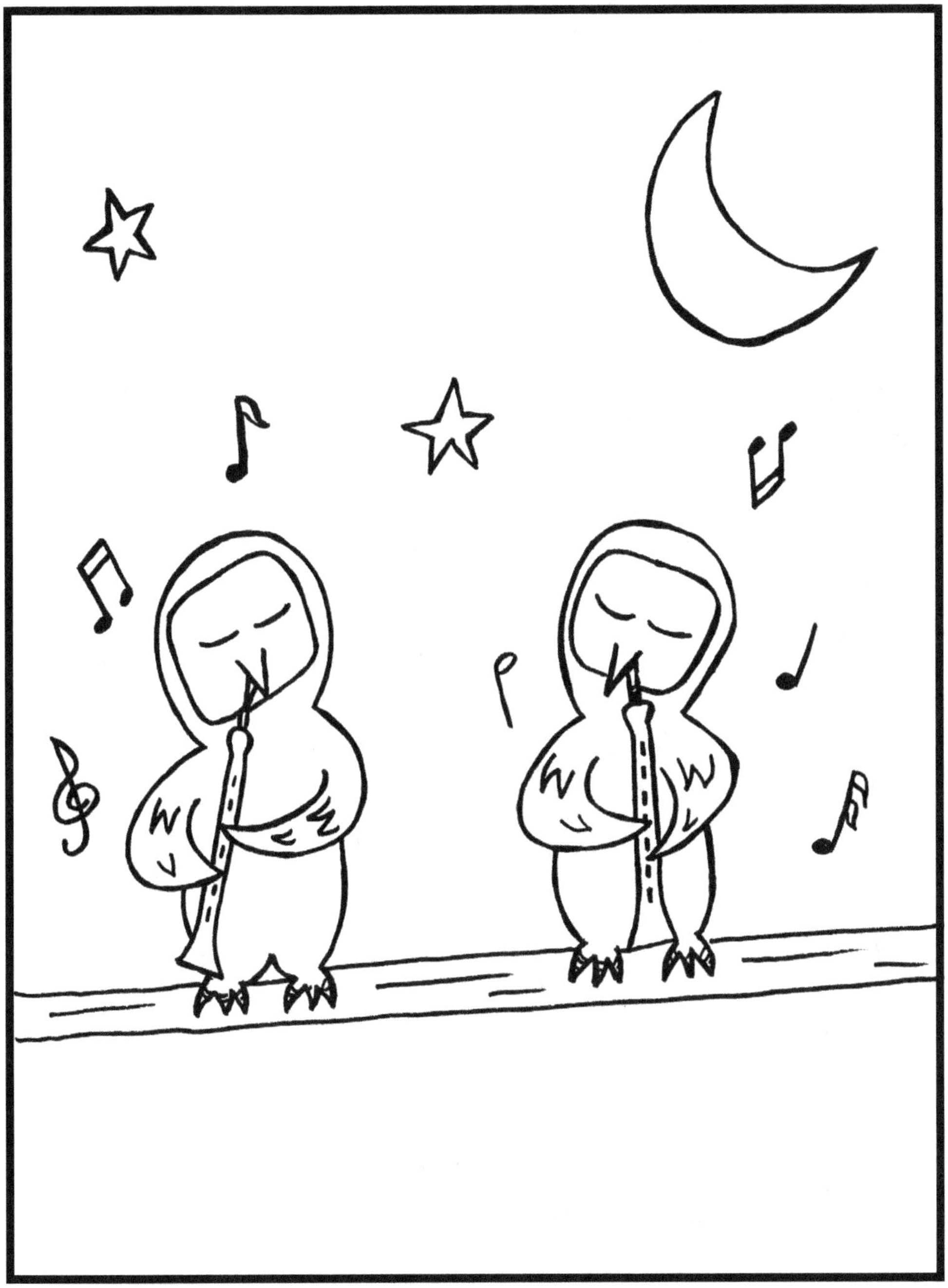

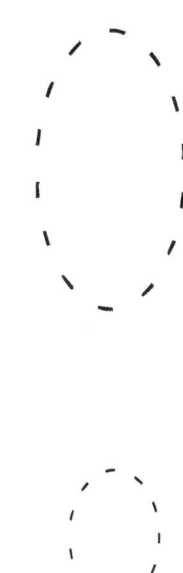

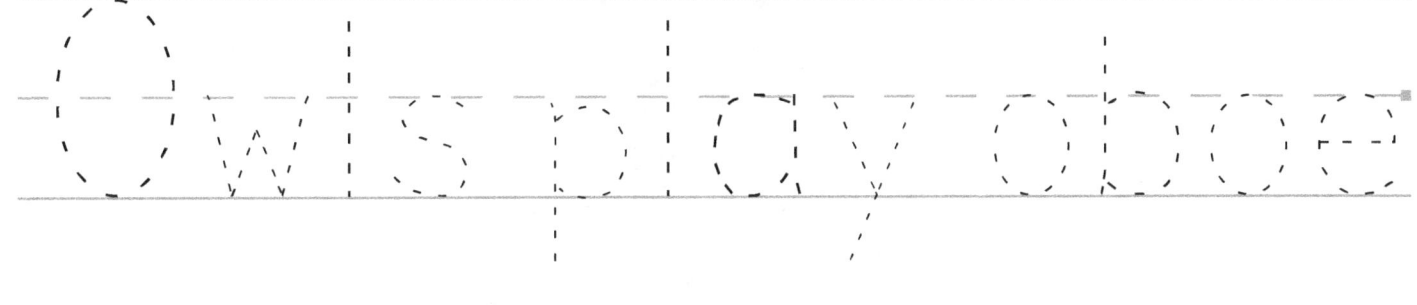

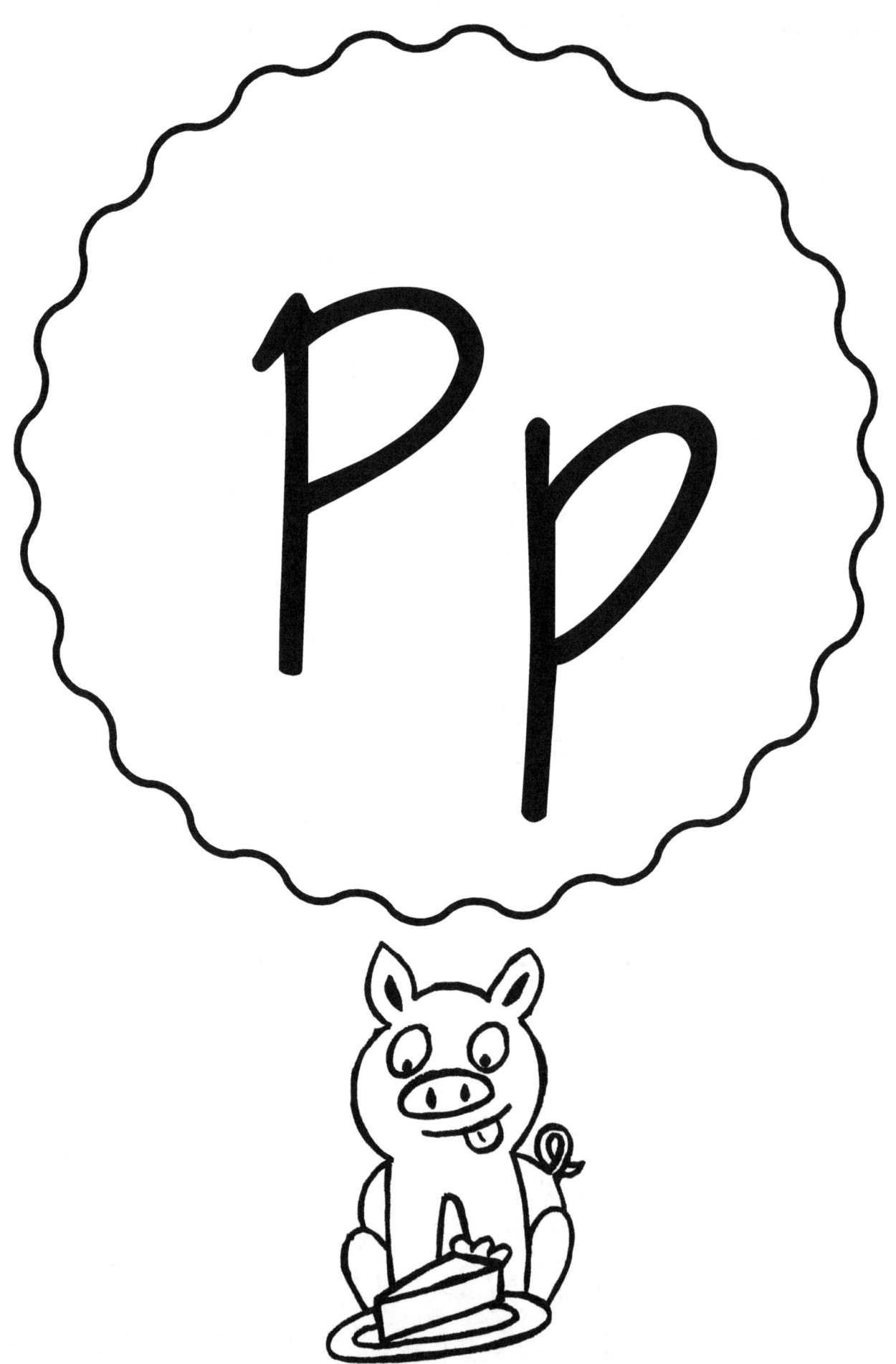

Color the picture, then trace and write the letters below.

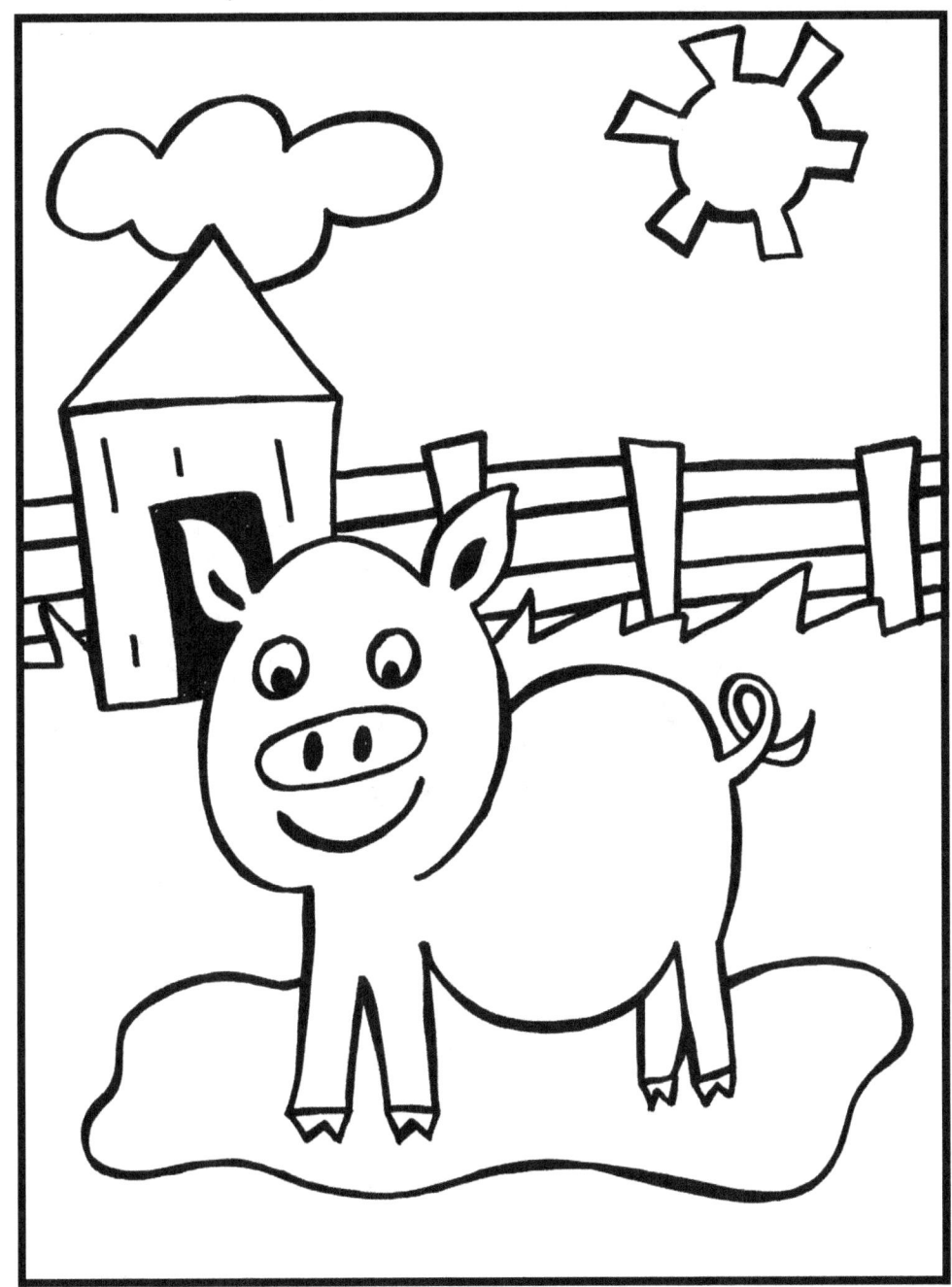

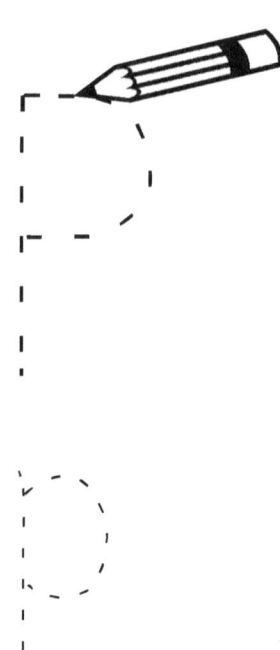

Color the picture, then trace and write the word below.

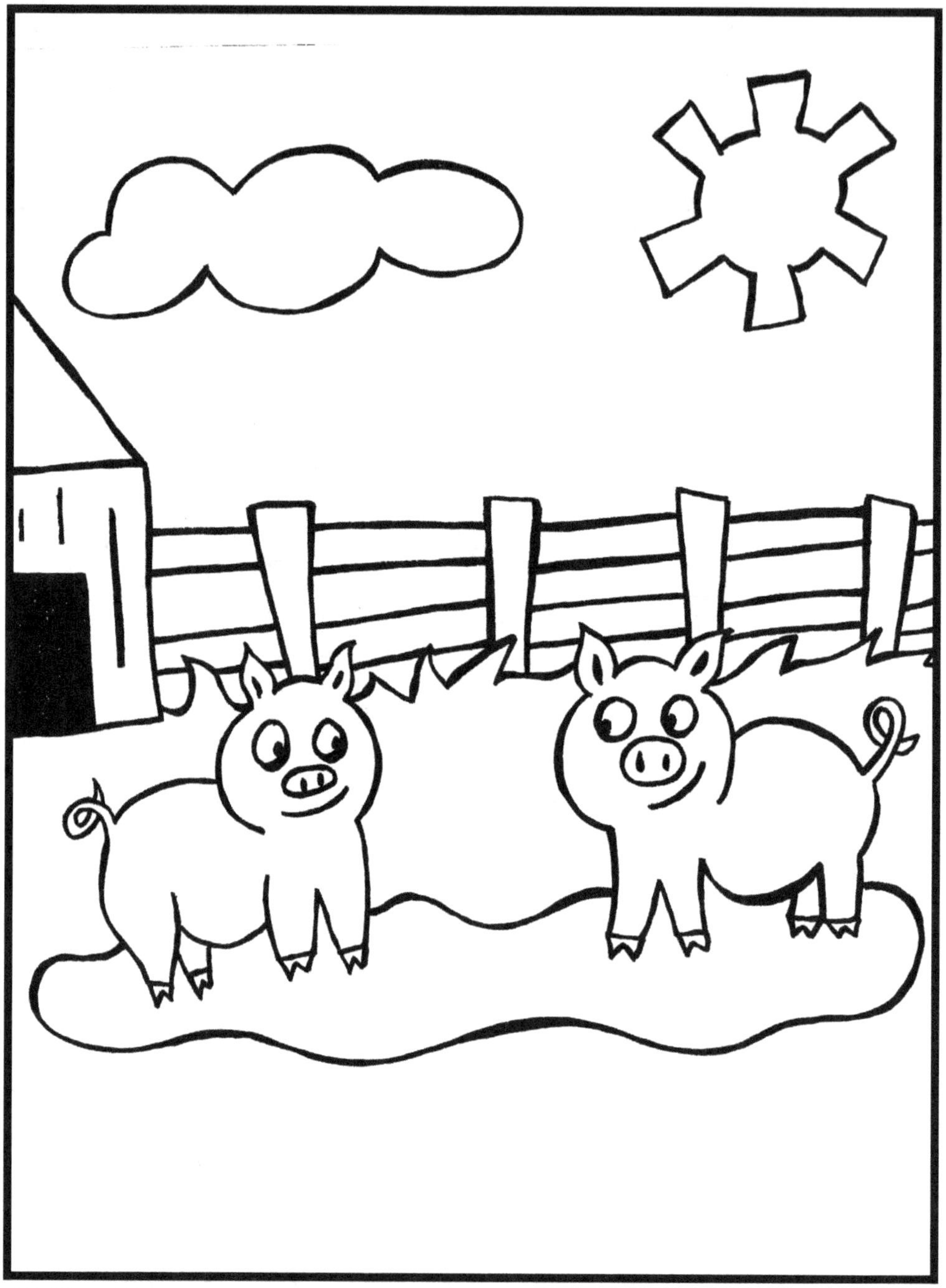

Pig

pig

Color the picture, then trace and write the phrase below.

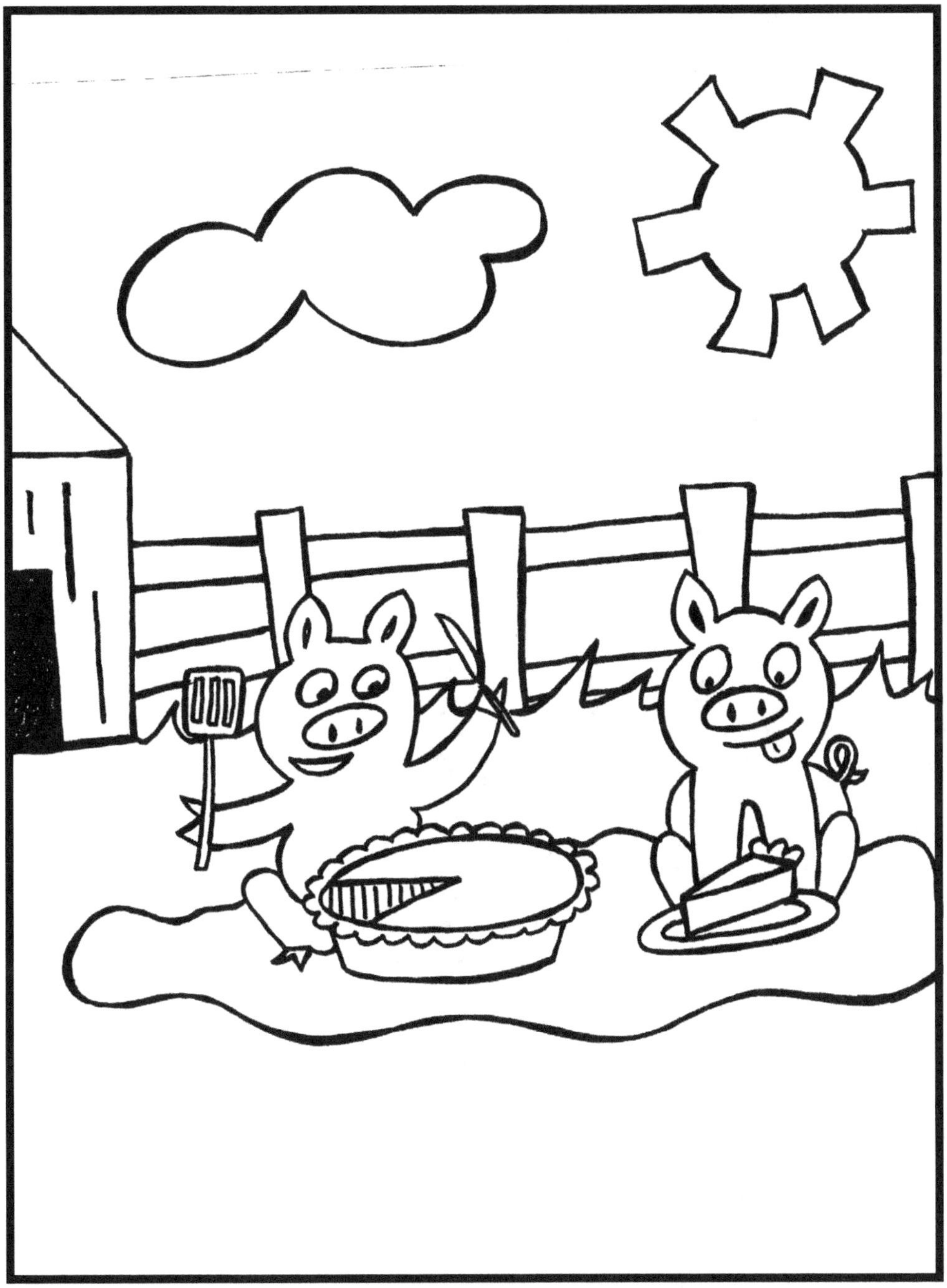

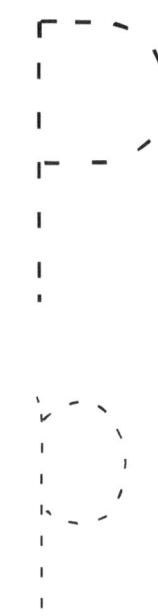

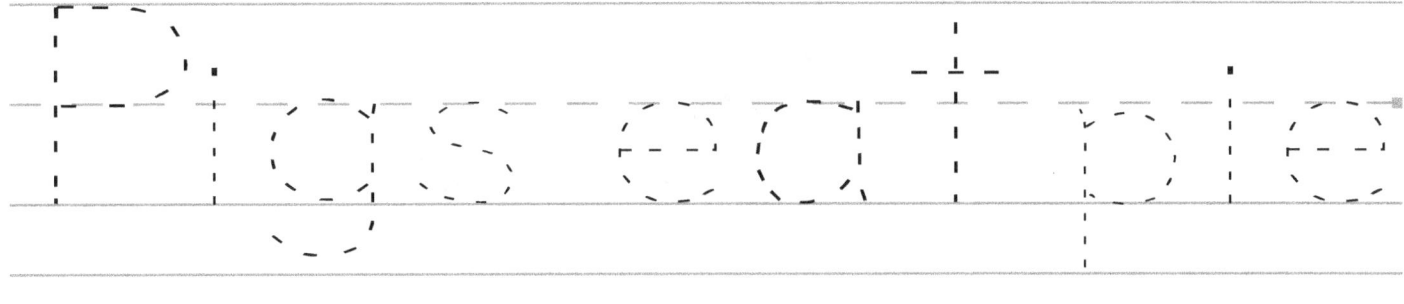

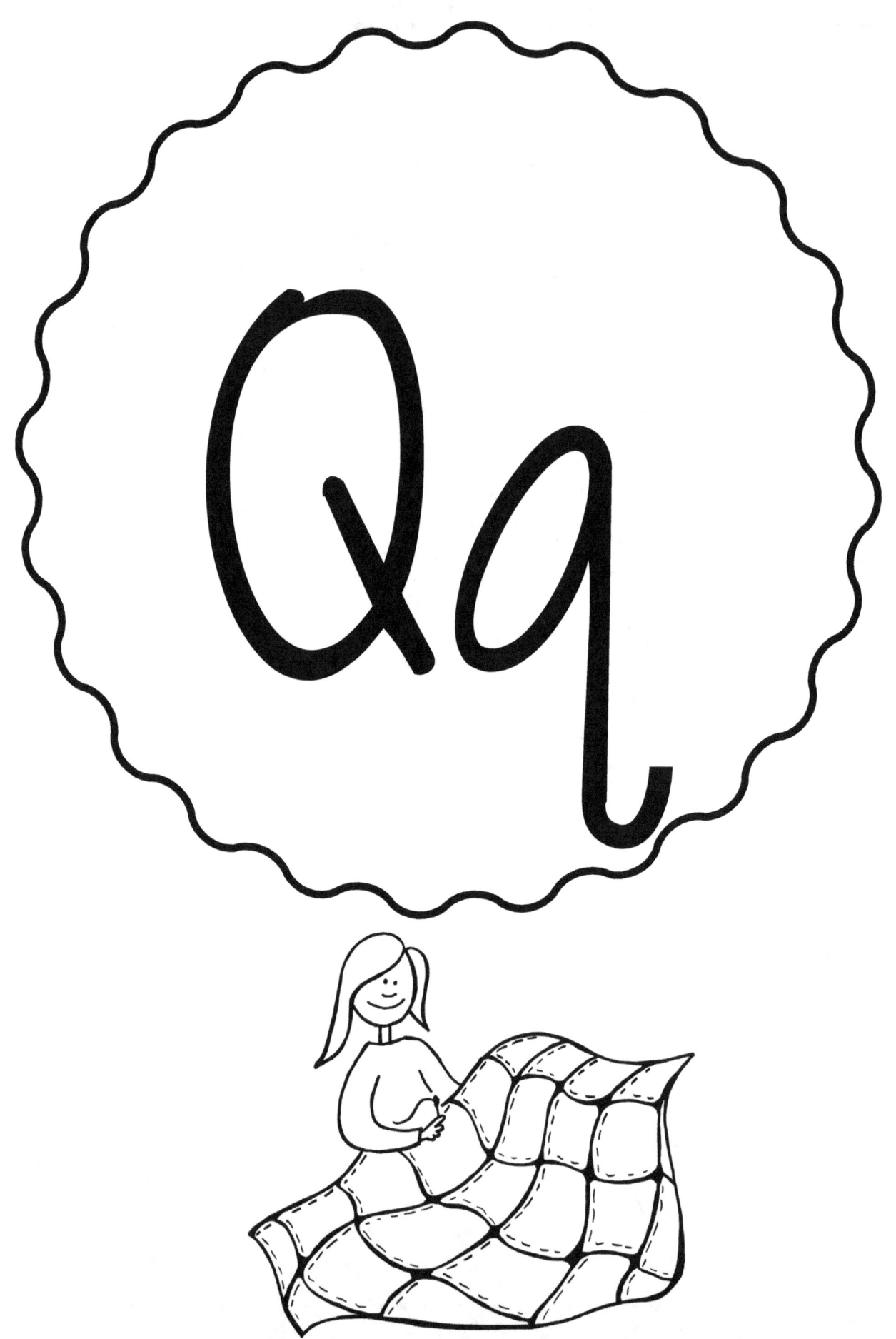

Color in the picture and trace the letters below.

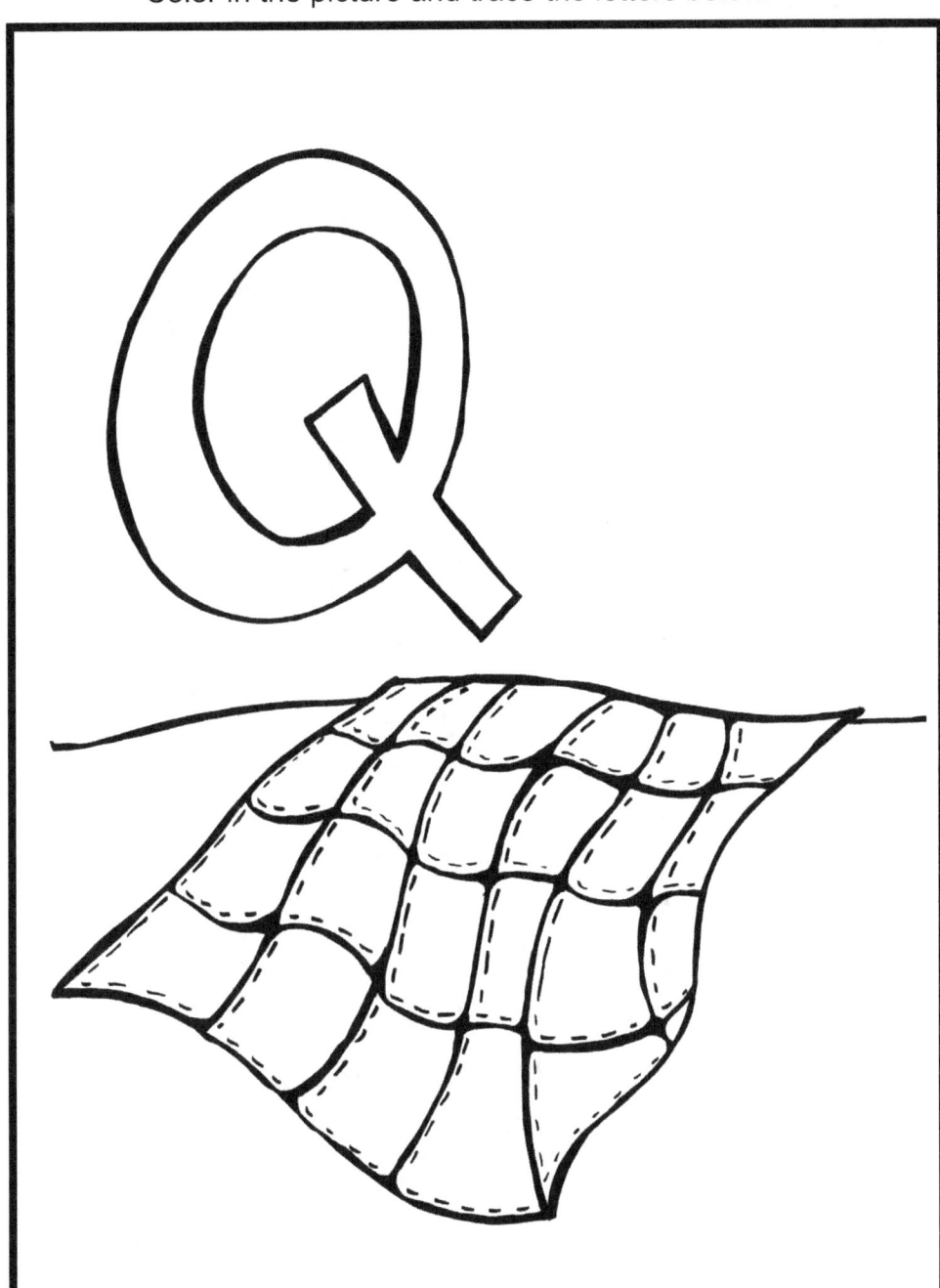

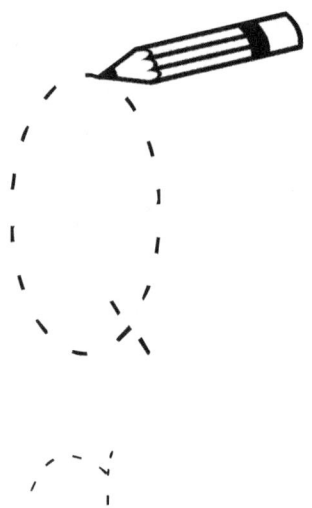

Color in the picture and trace the letters below.

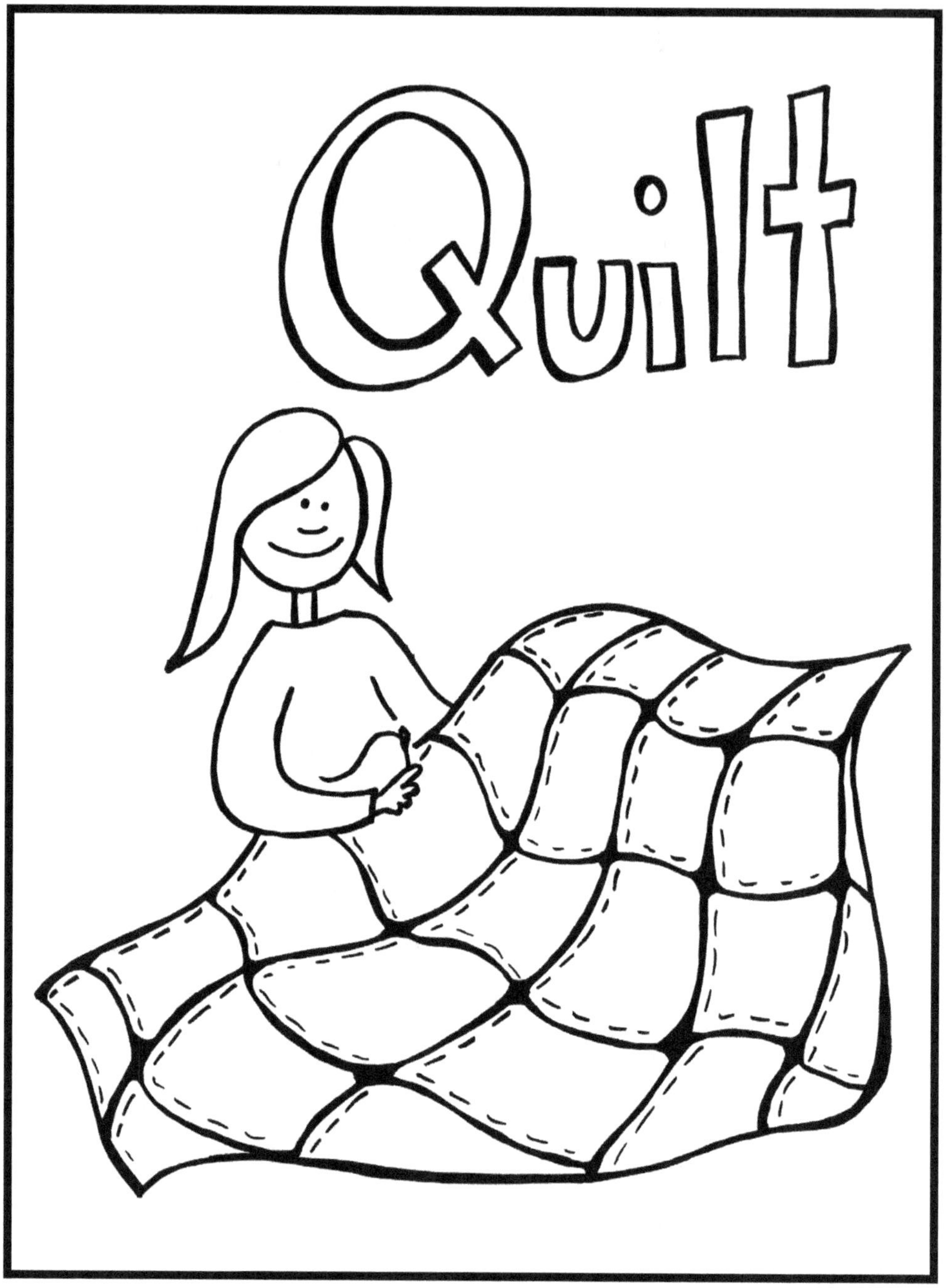

Quilt

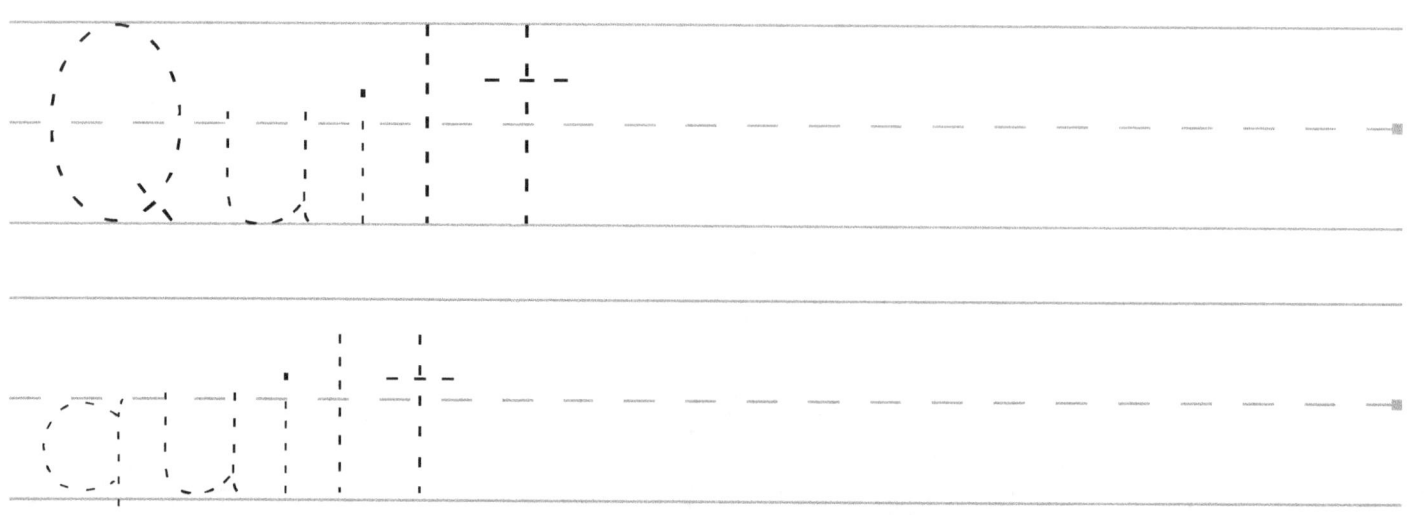

Color the picture, then trace and write the phrase below.

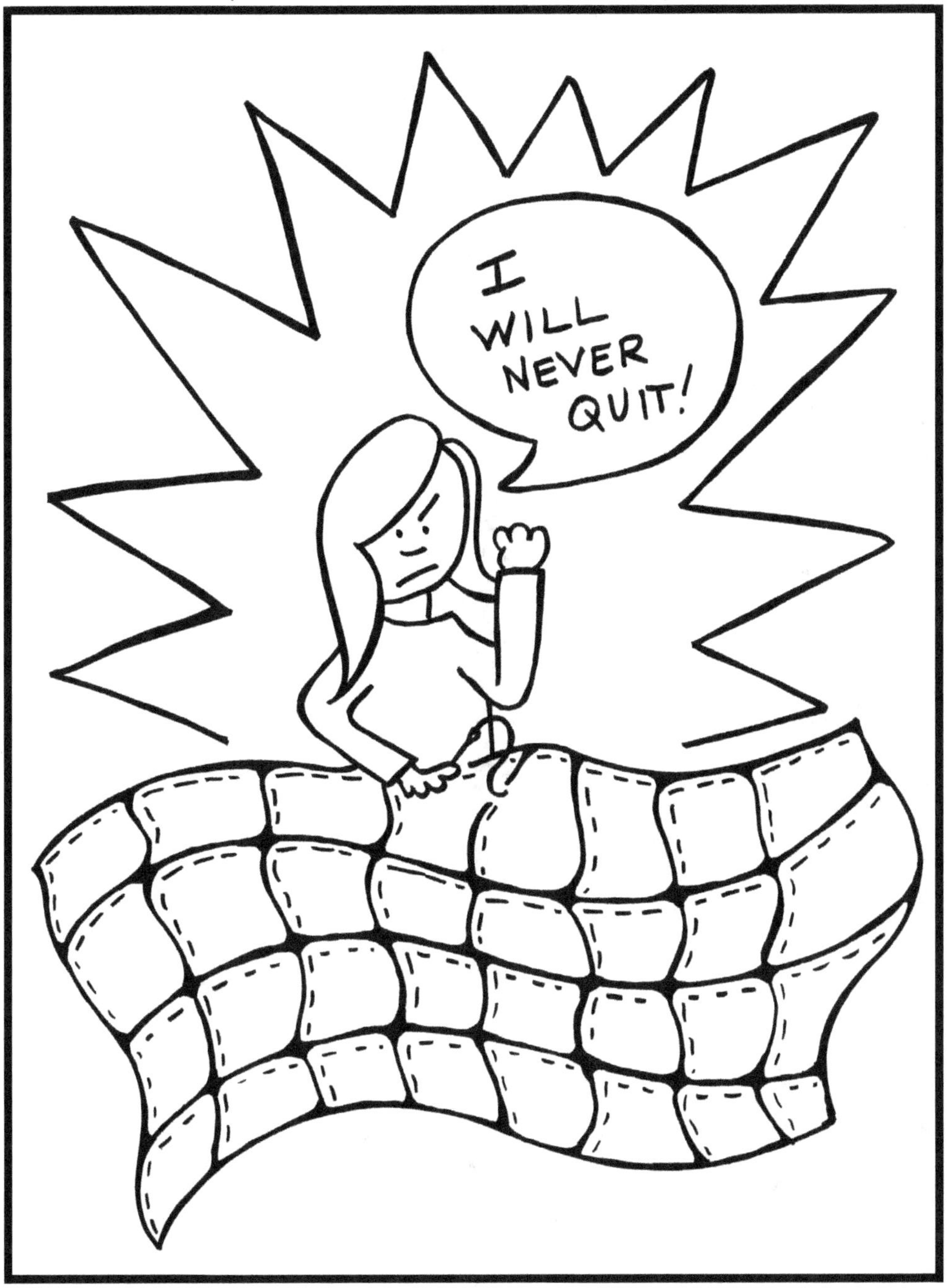

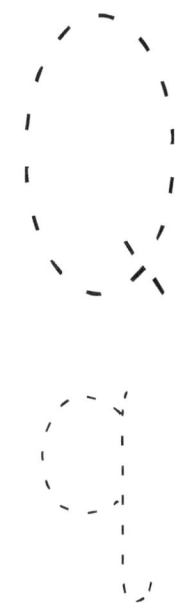

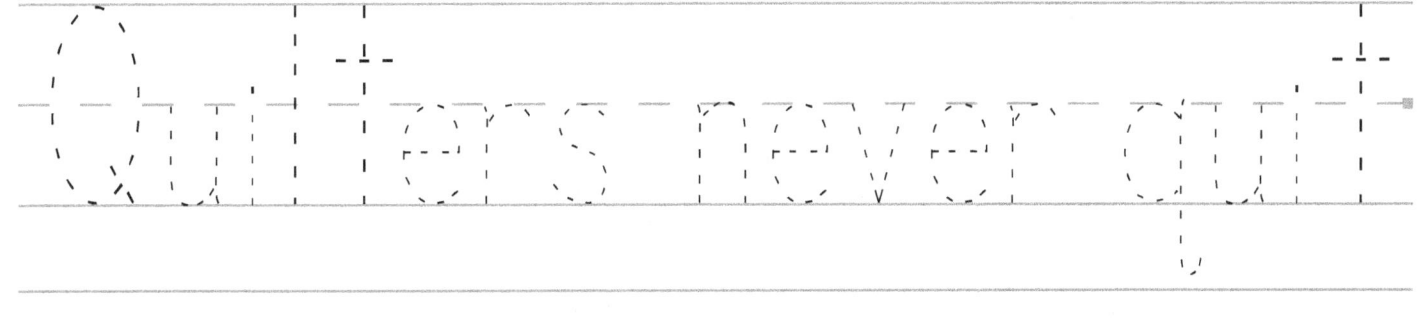

Quilters never quit

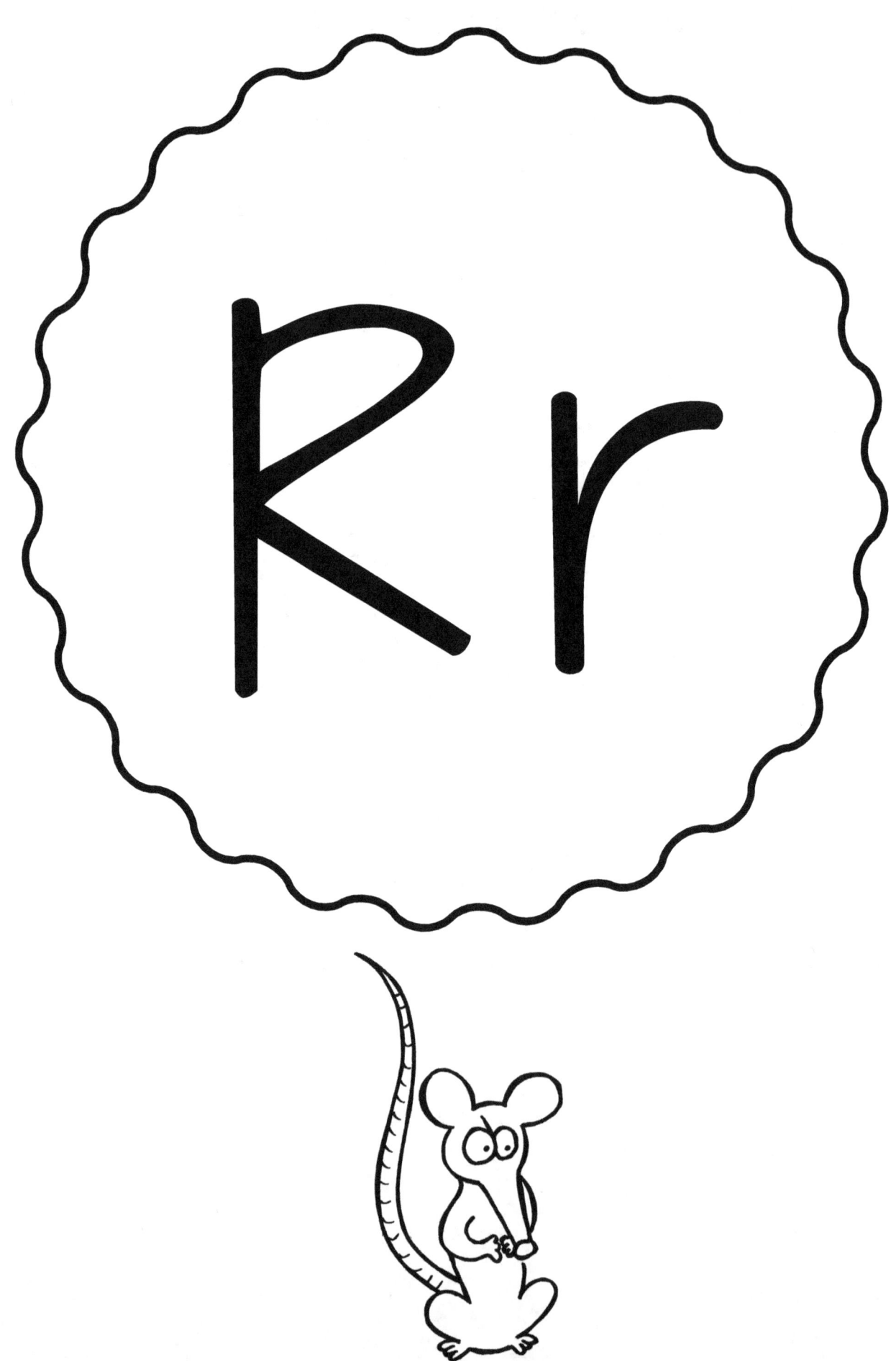

Color the picture, then trace and write the letters below.

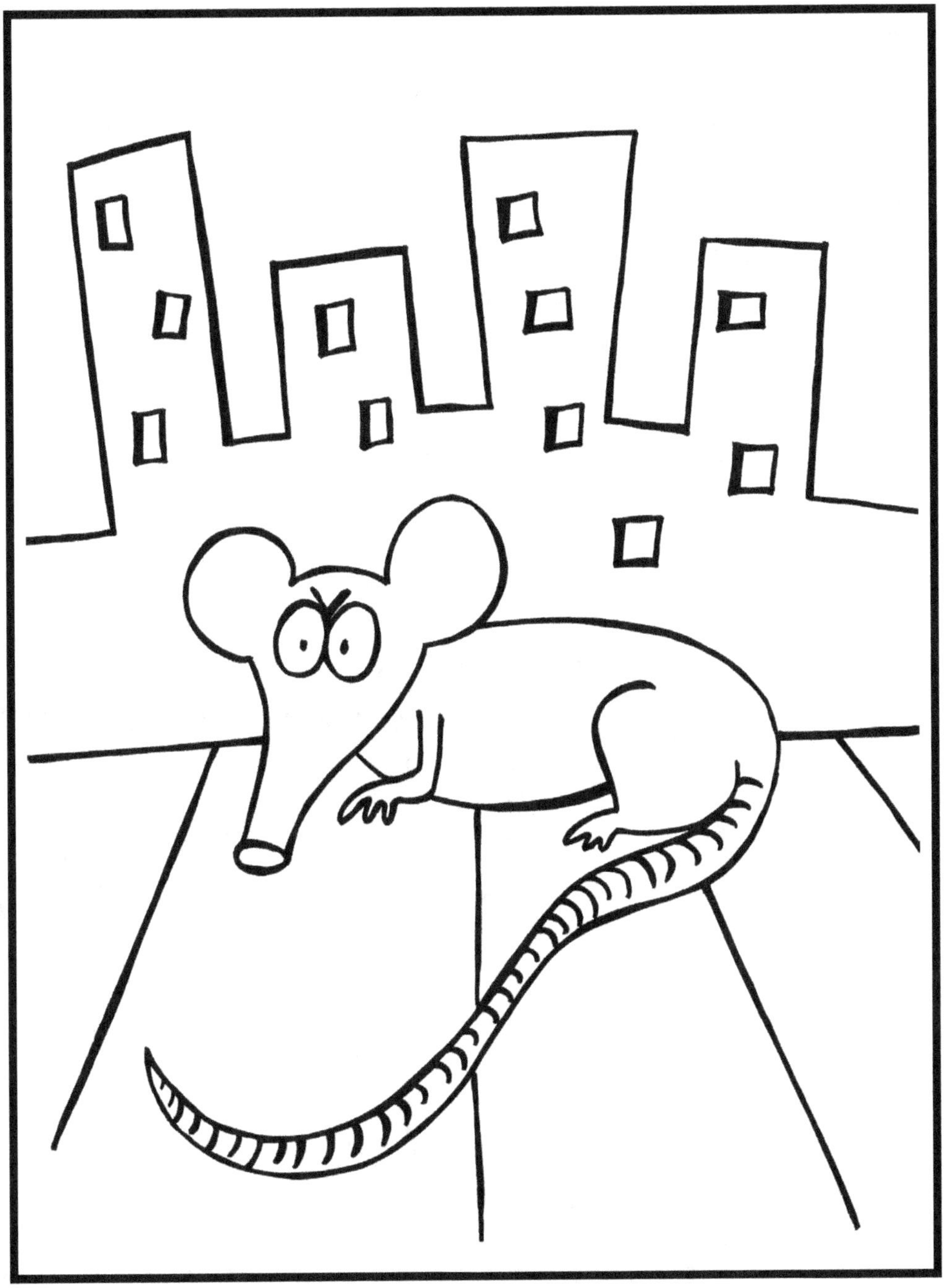

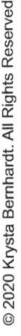

Color in the picture and trace the letters below.

Rat

rat

Color the picture, then trace and write the phrase below.

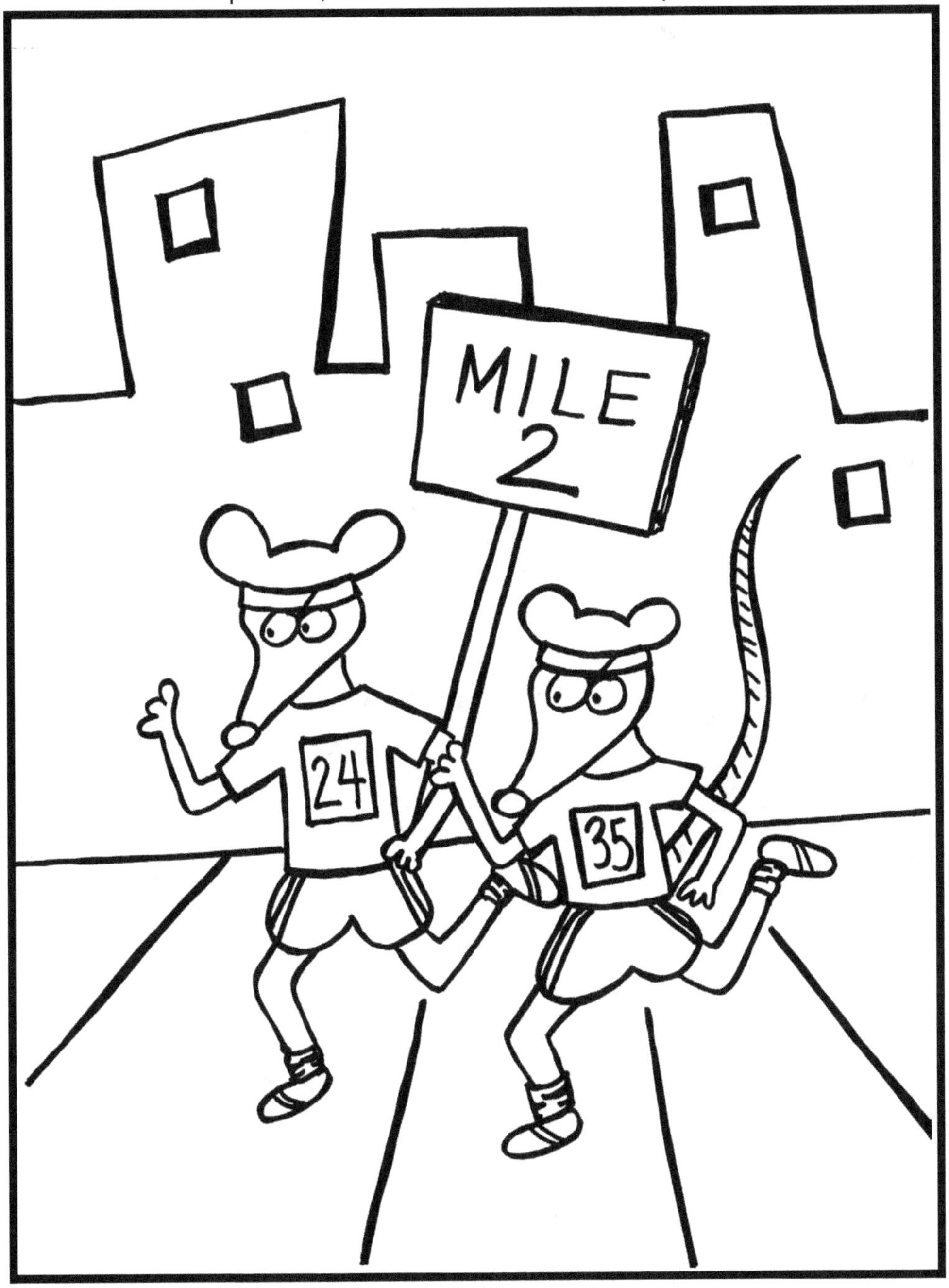

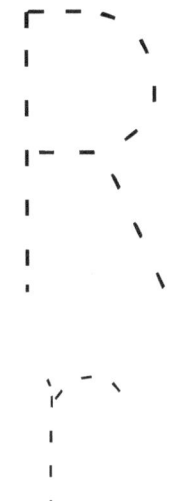

Rats run races

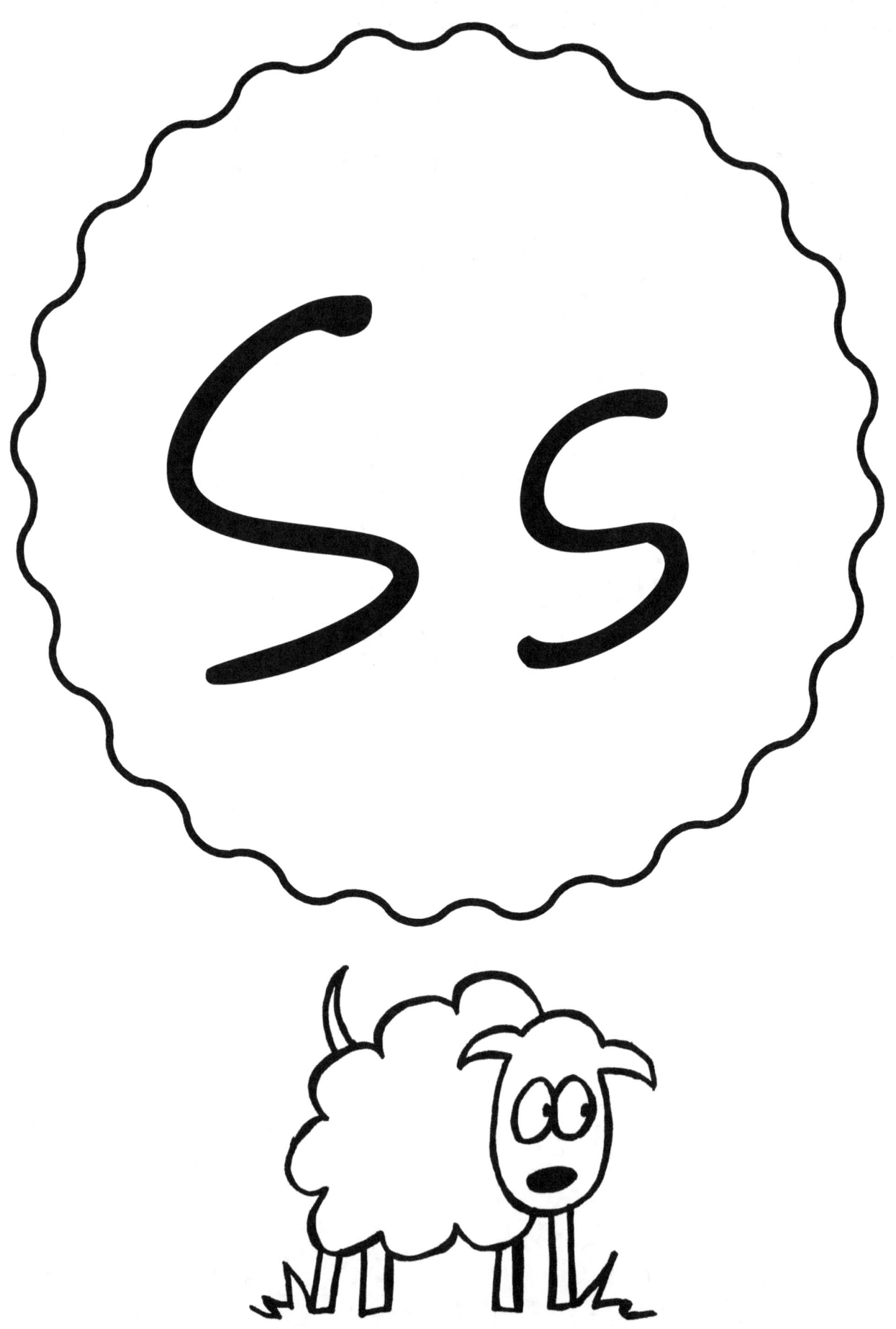

Color the picture, then trace and write the letters below.

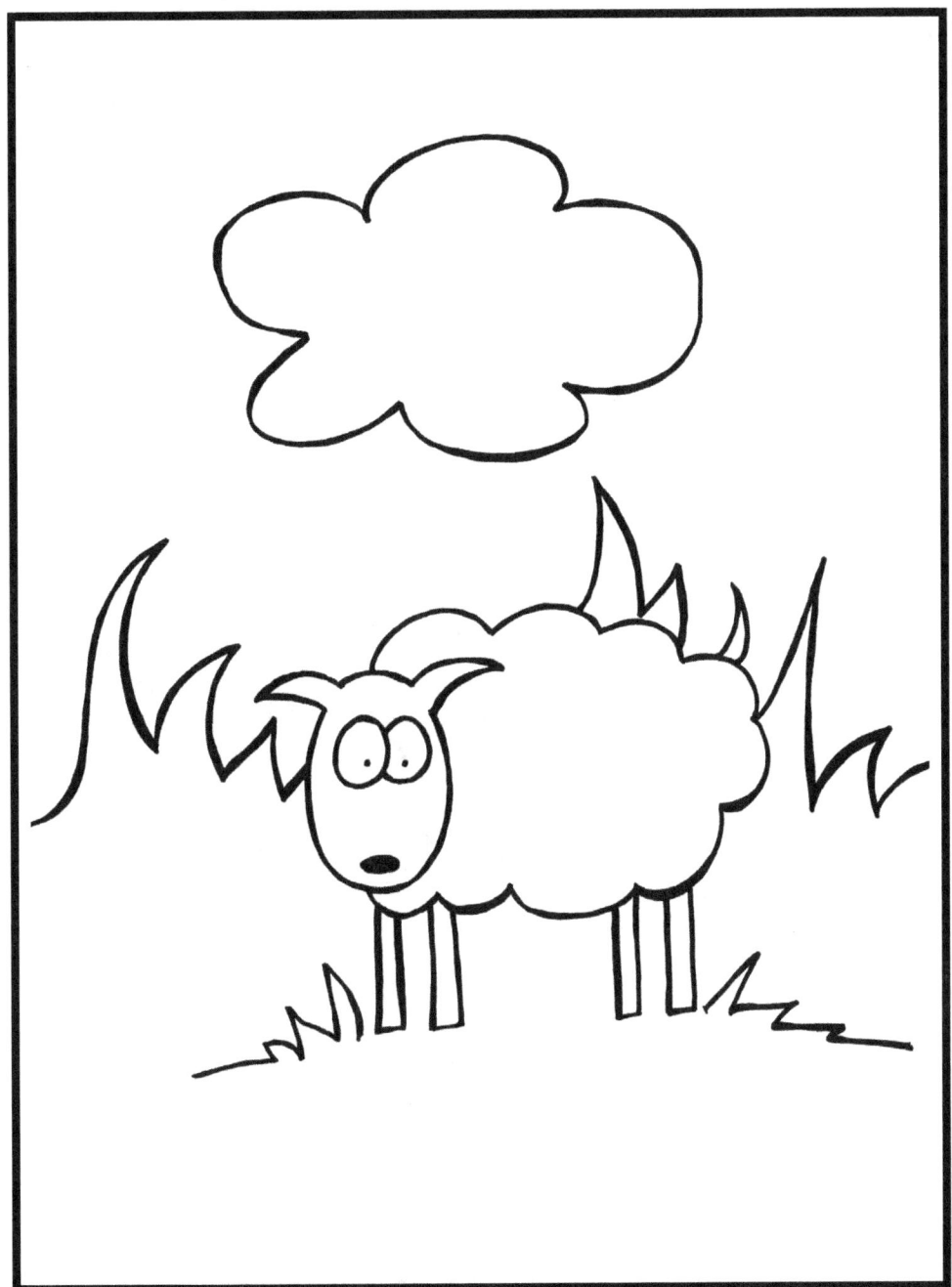

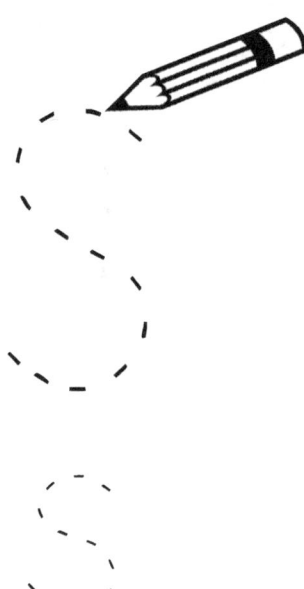

Color the picture, then trace and write the word below.

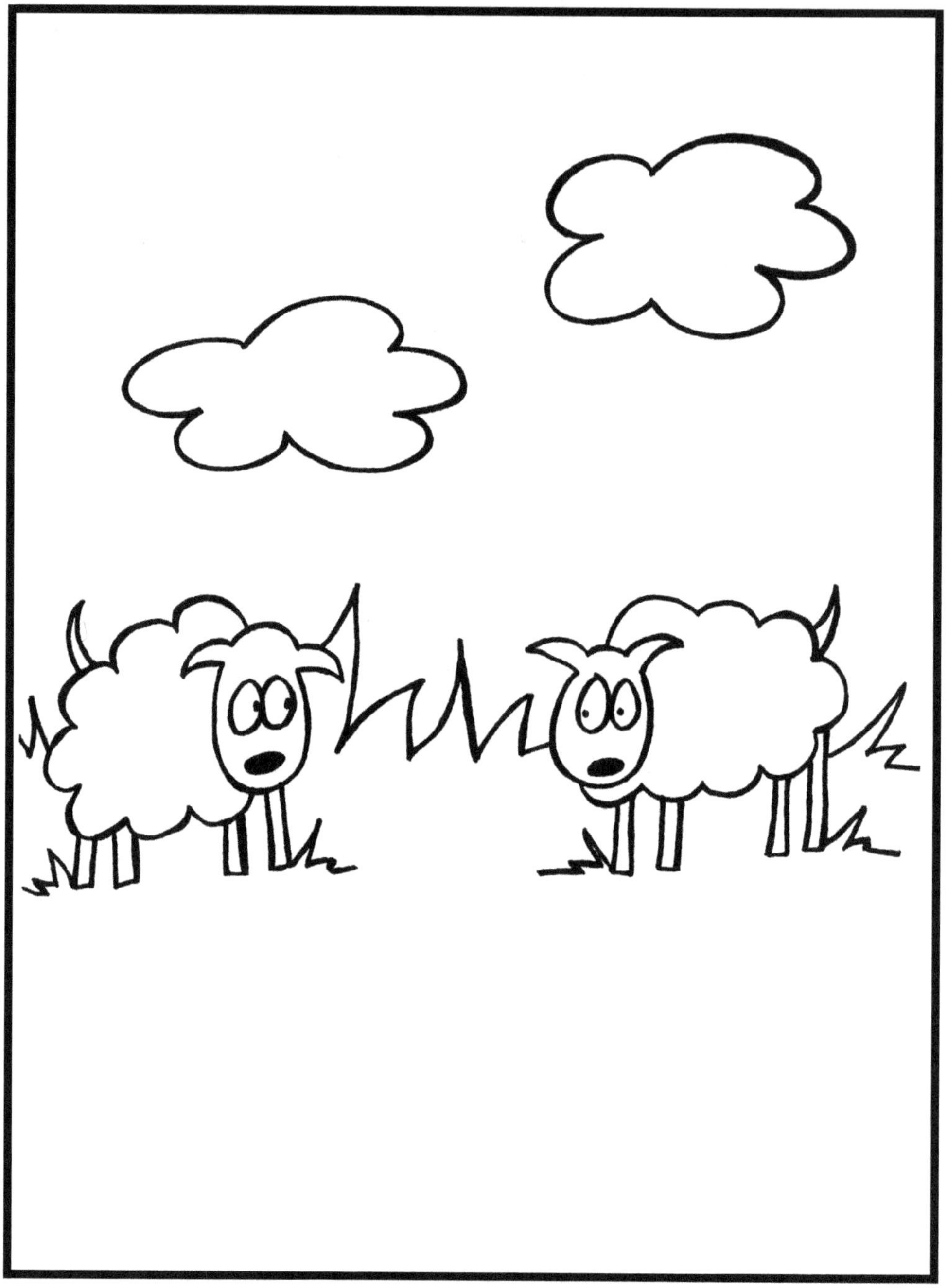

Sheep

sheep

Color the picture, then trace and write the phrase below.

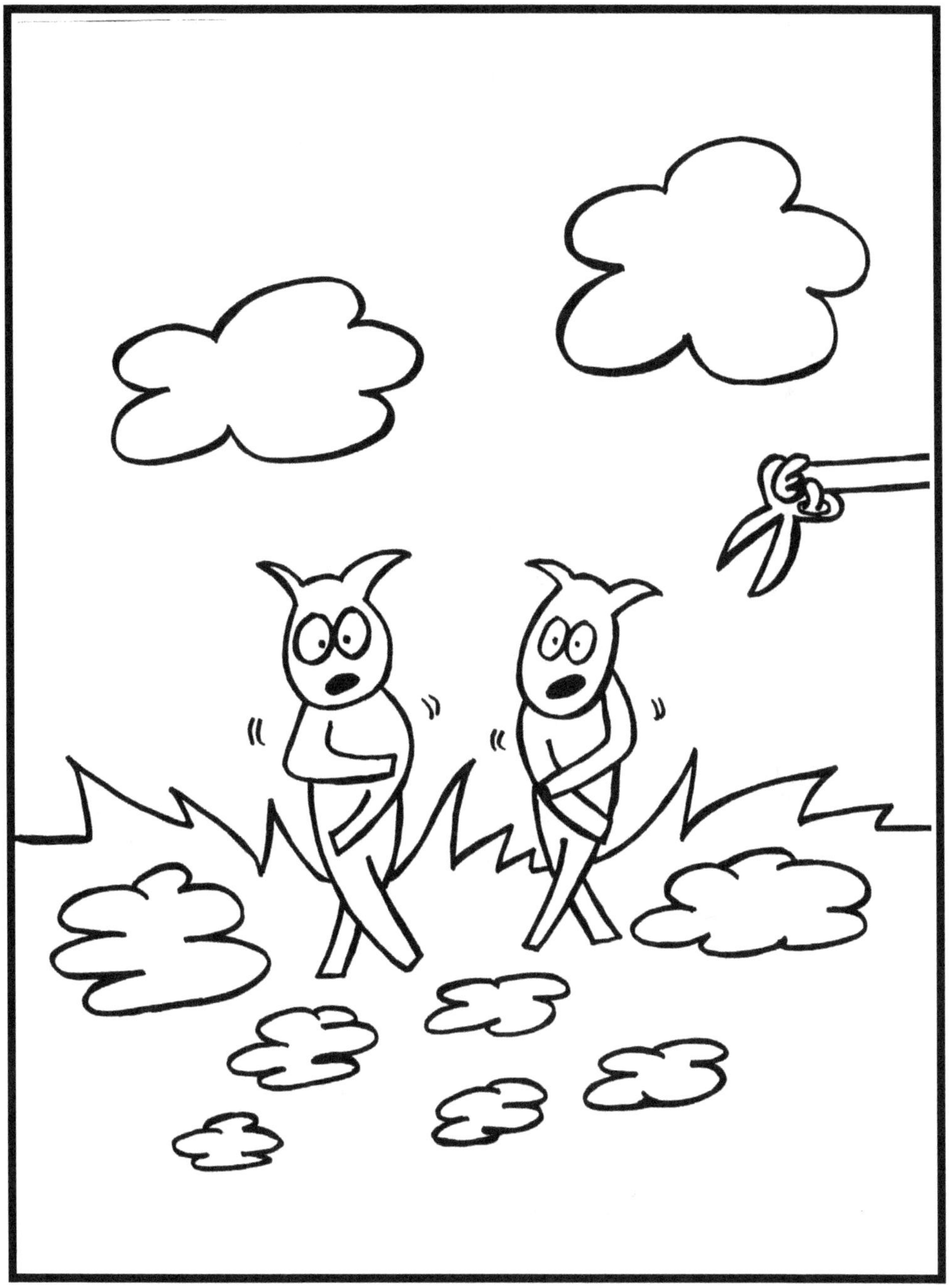

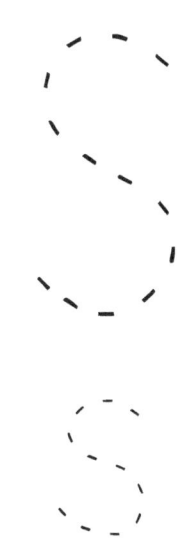

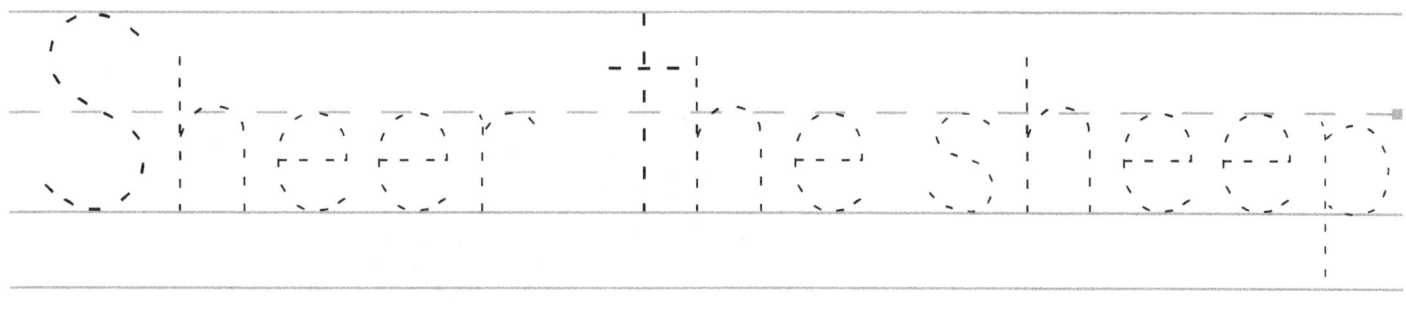

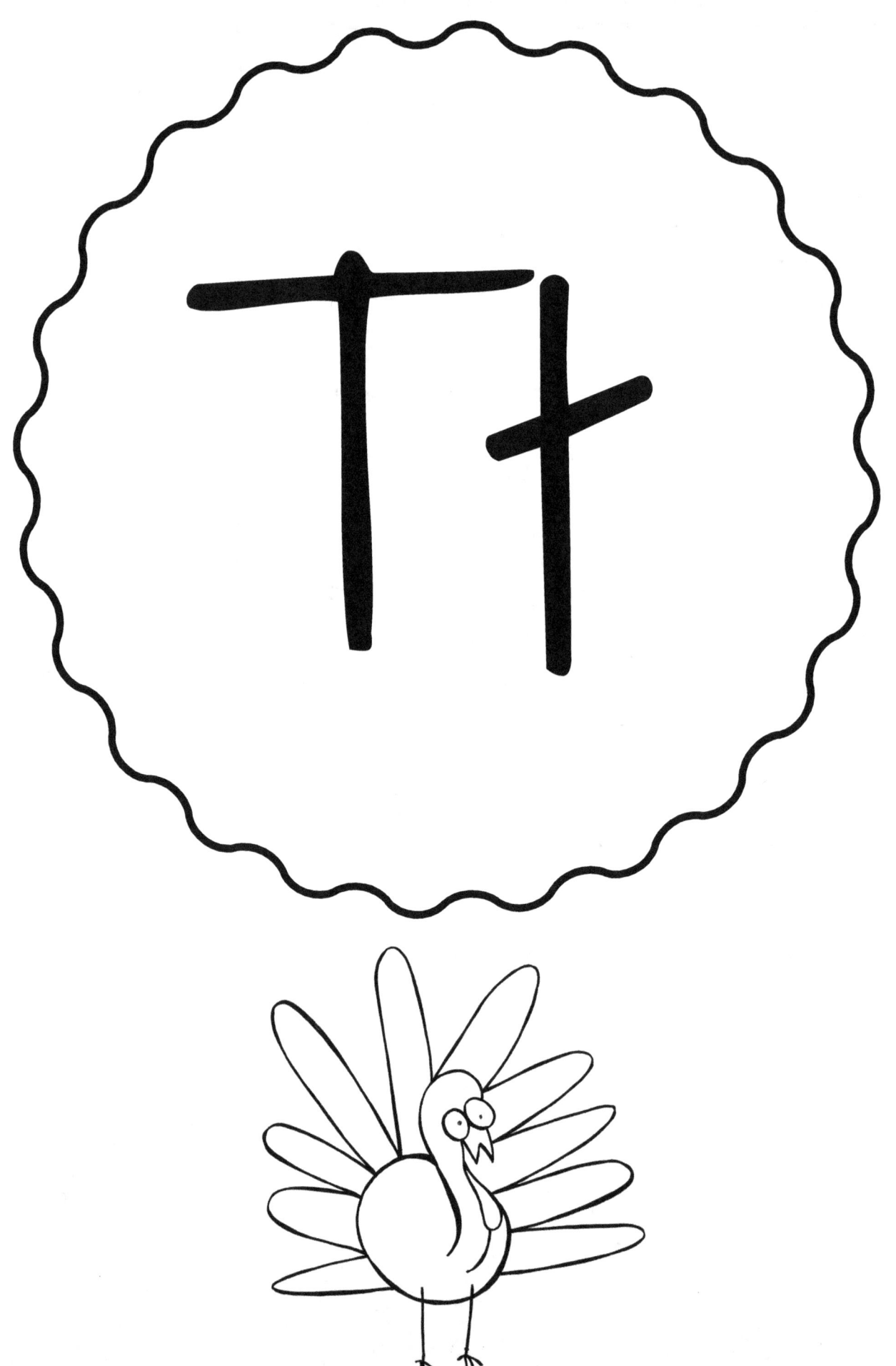

Color the picture, then trace and write the letters below.

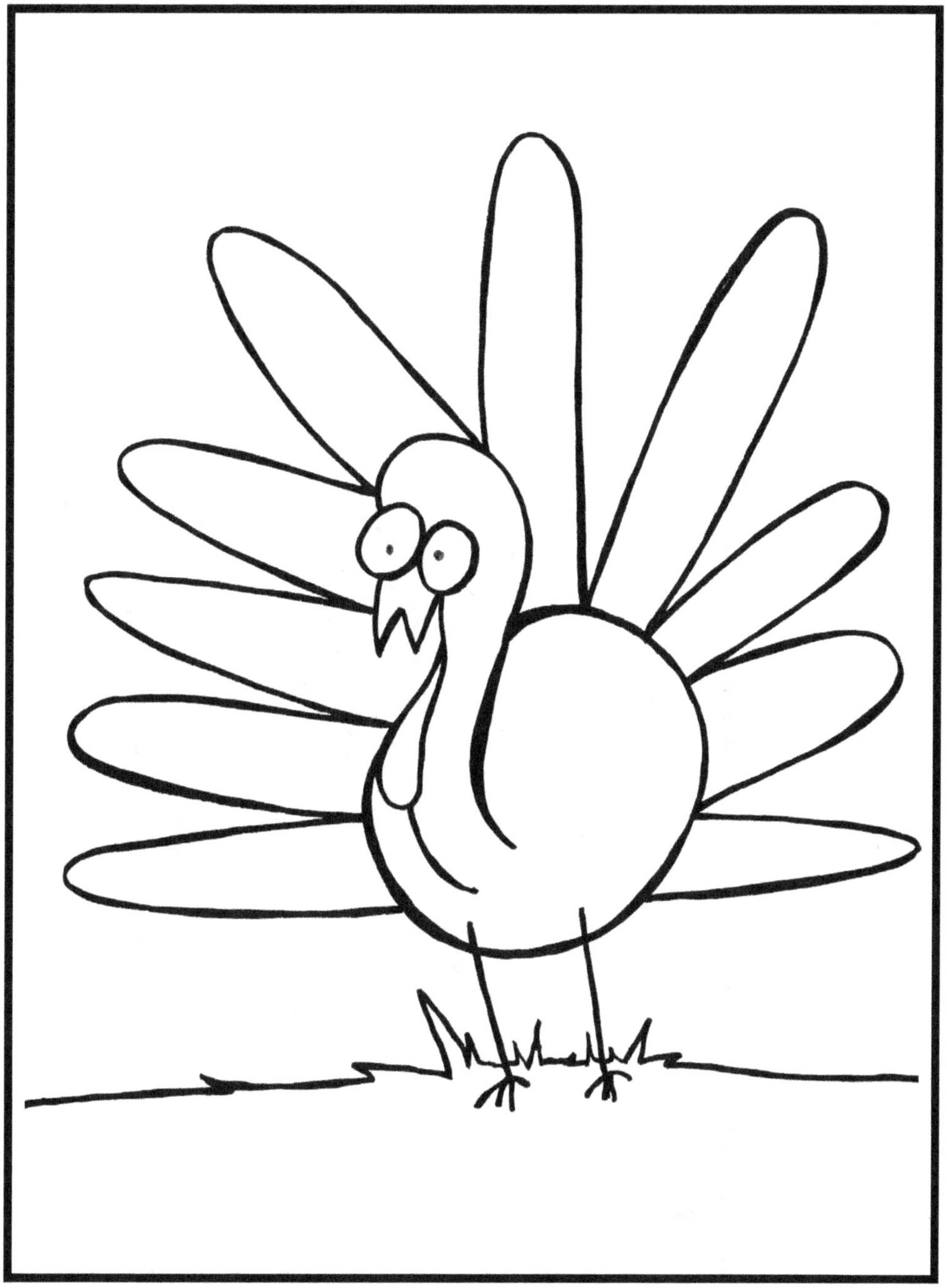

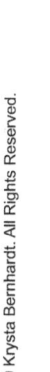

Color the picture, then trace and write the word below.

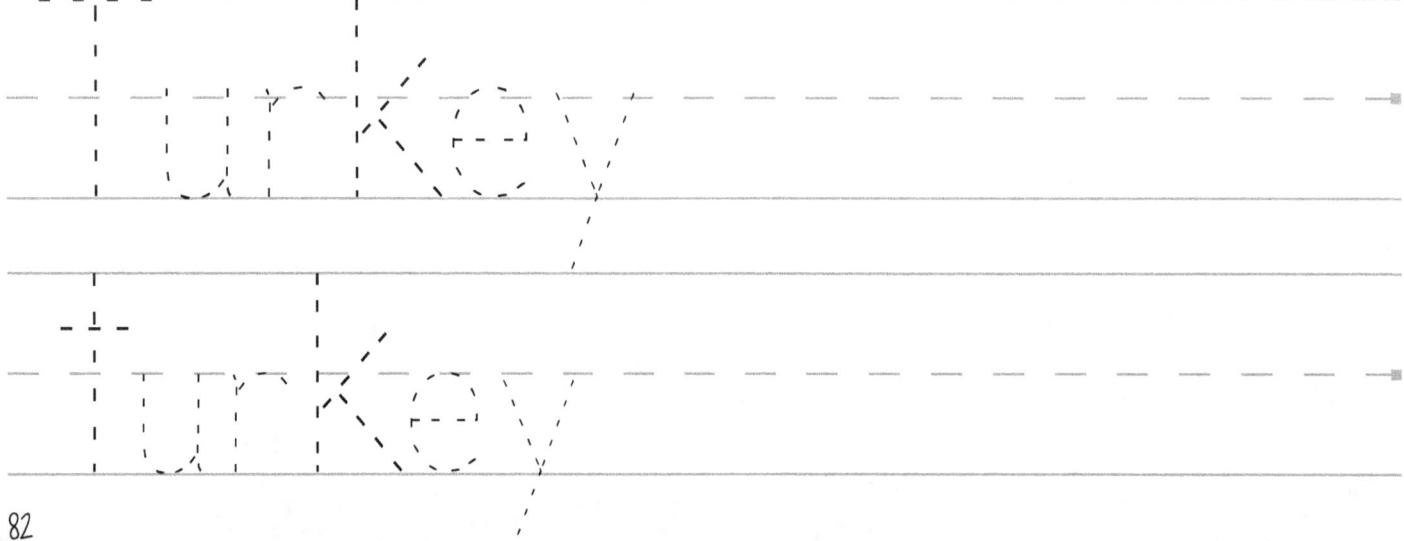

Turkey

turkey

Color the picture, then trace and write the phrase below.

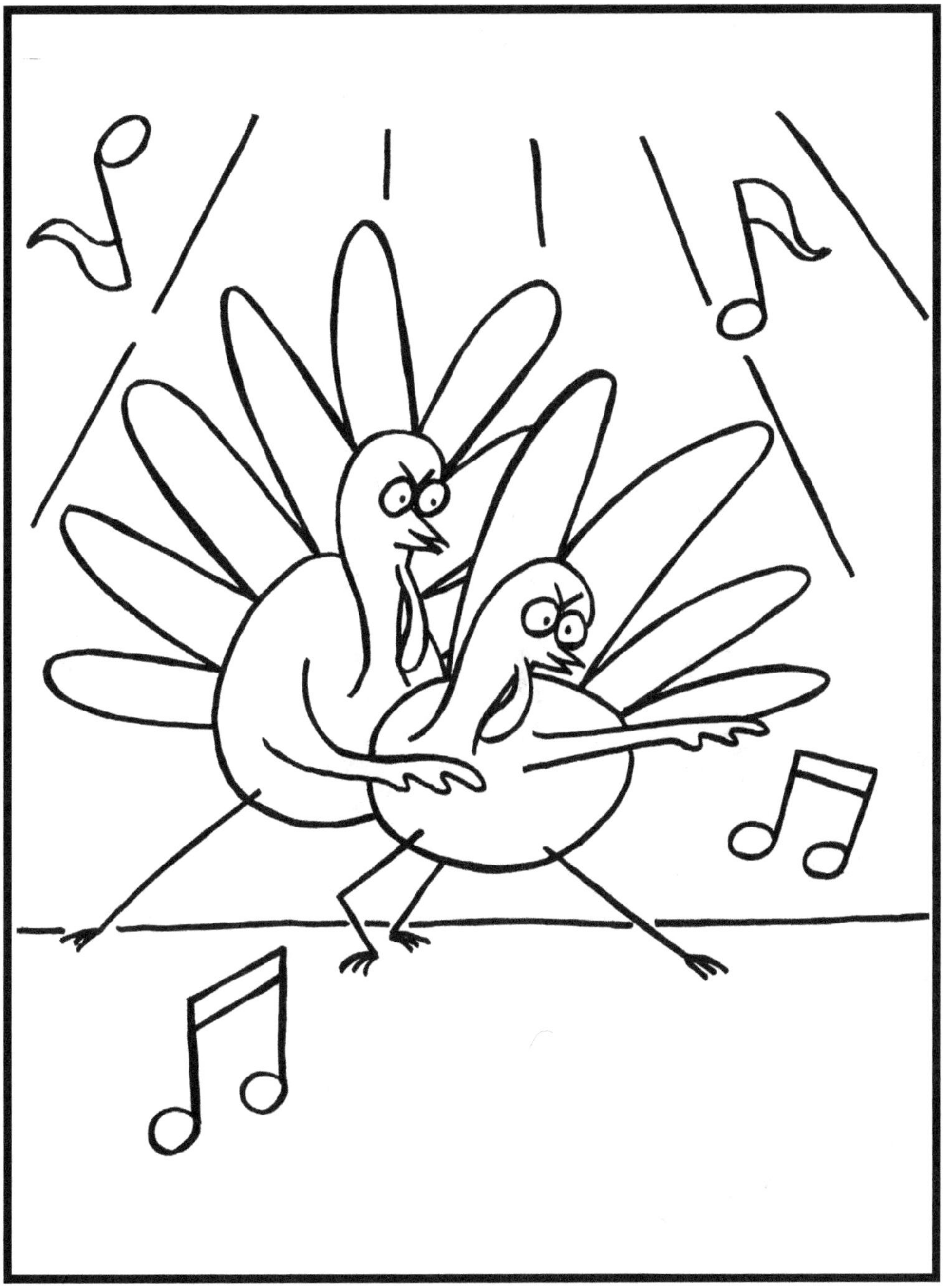

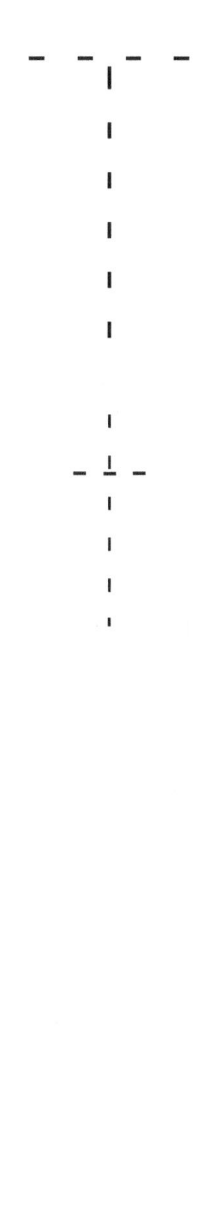

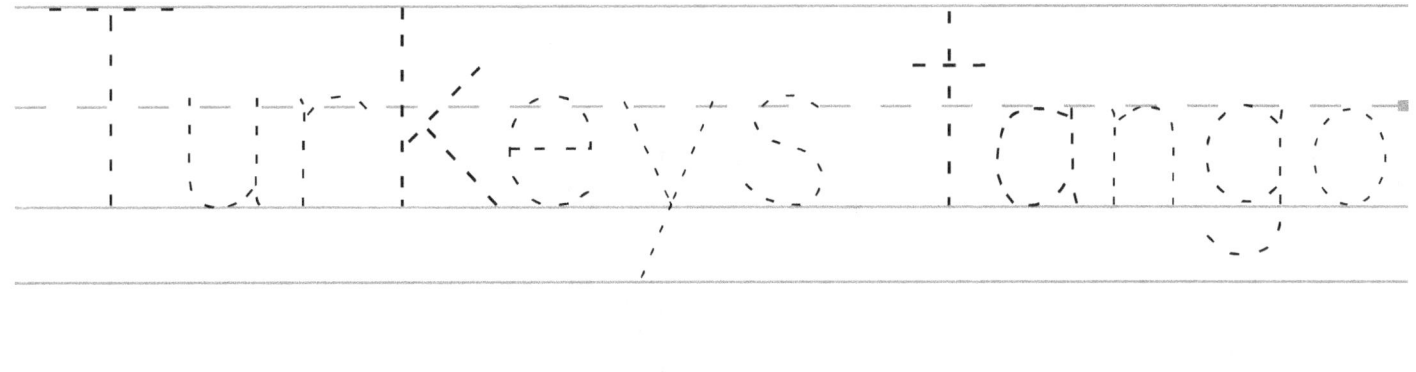

Turkeys tango

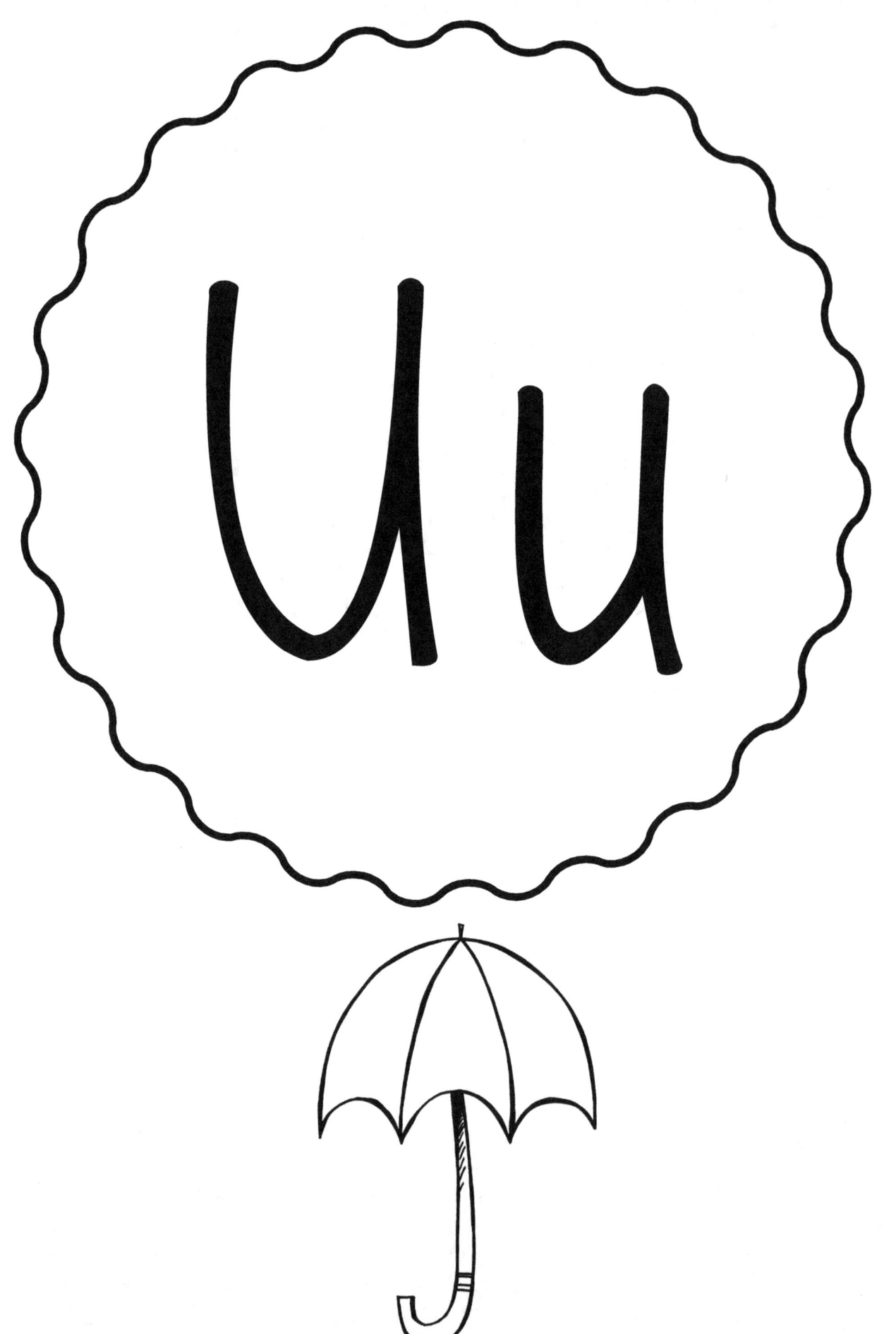

Color the picture, then trace and write the letters below.

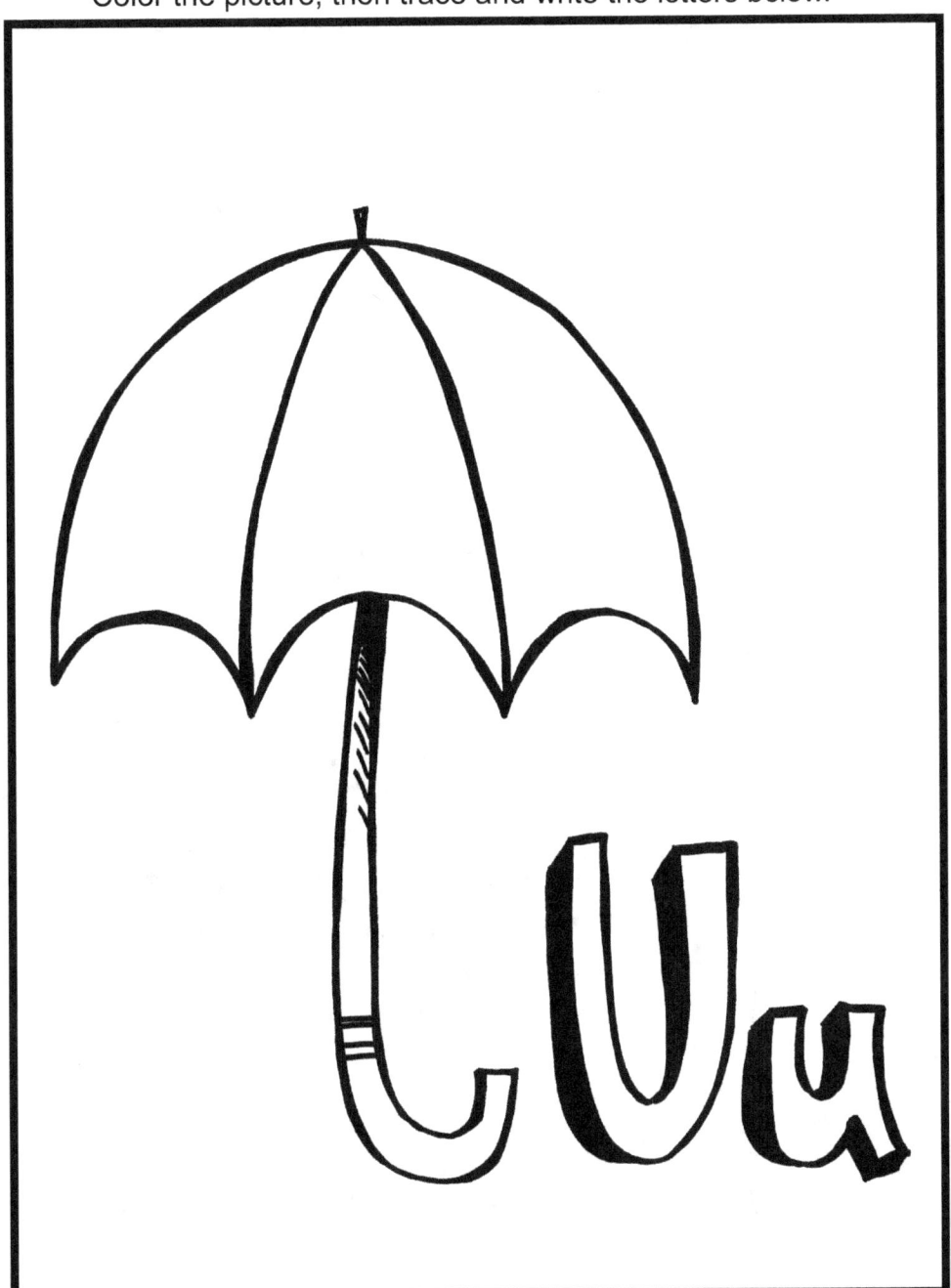

Color the picture, then trace and write the word below.

Umbrella

umbrella

Color the picture, then trace and write the phrase below.

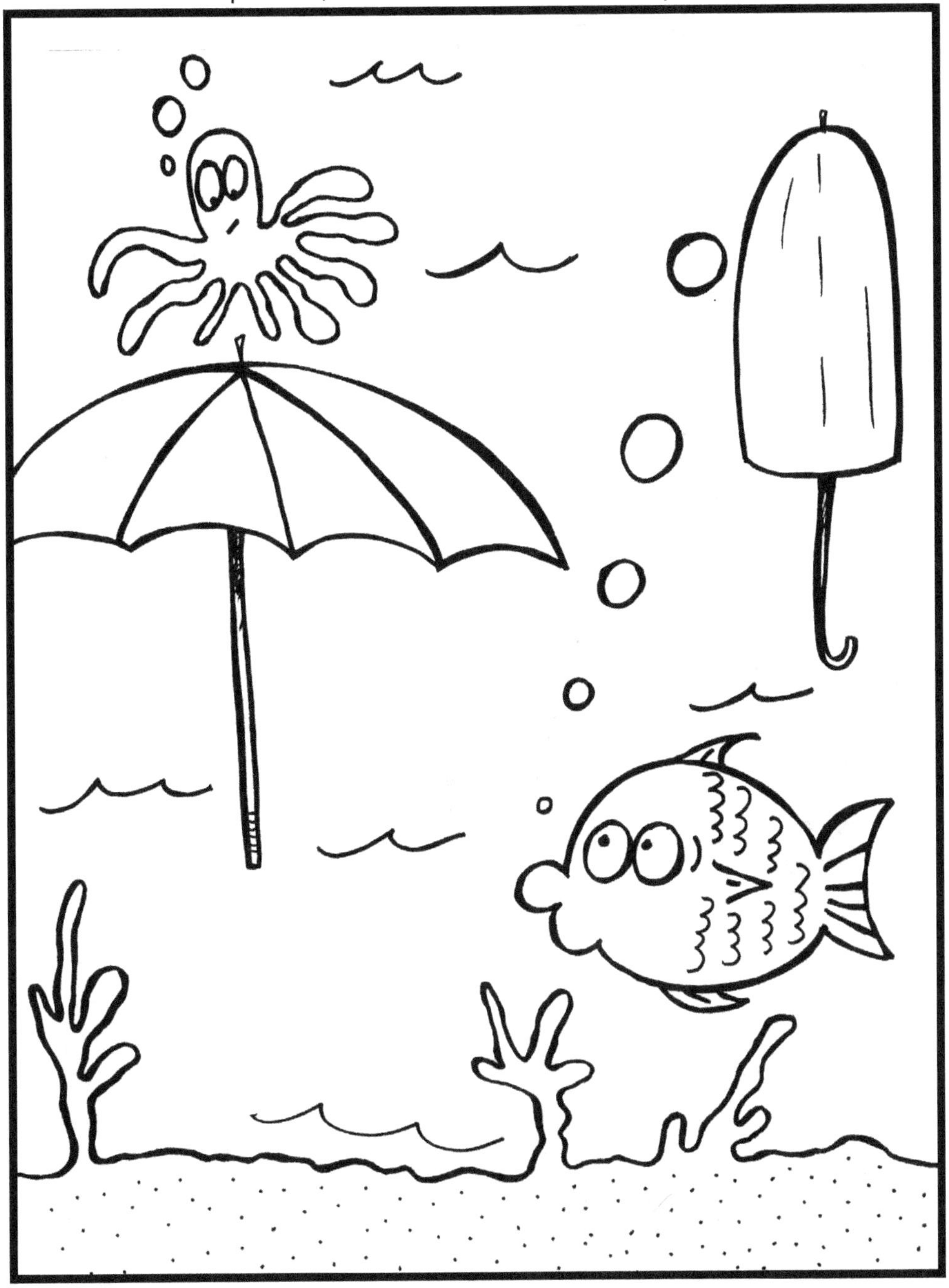

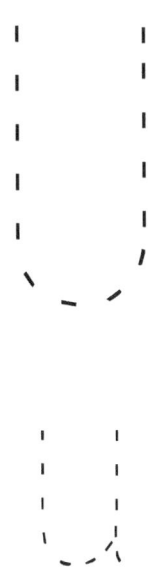

Under sea umbrella

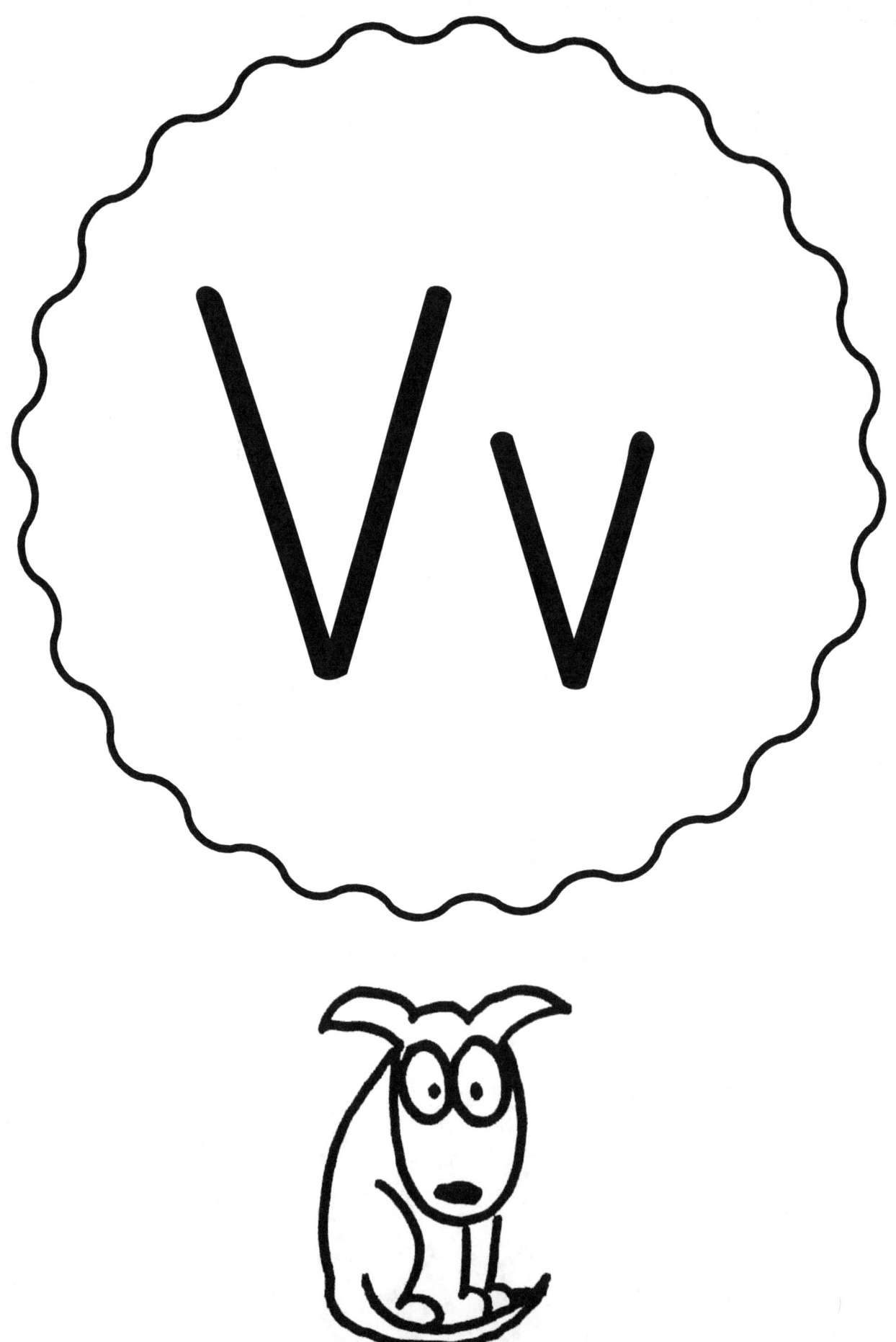

Color in the picture and trace the letters below.

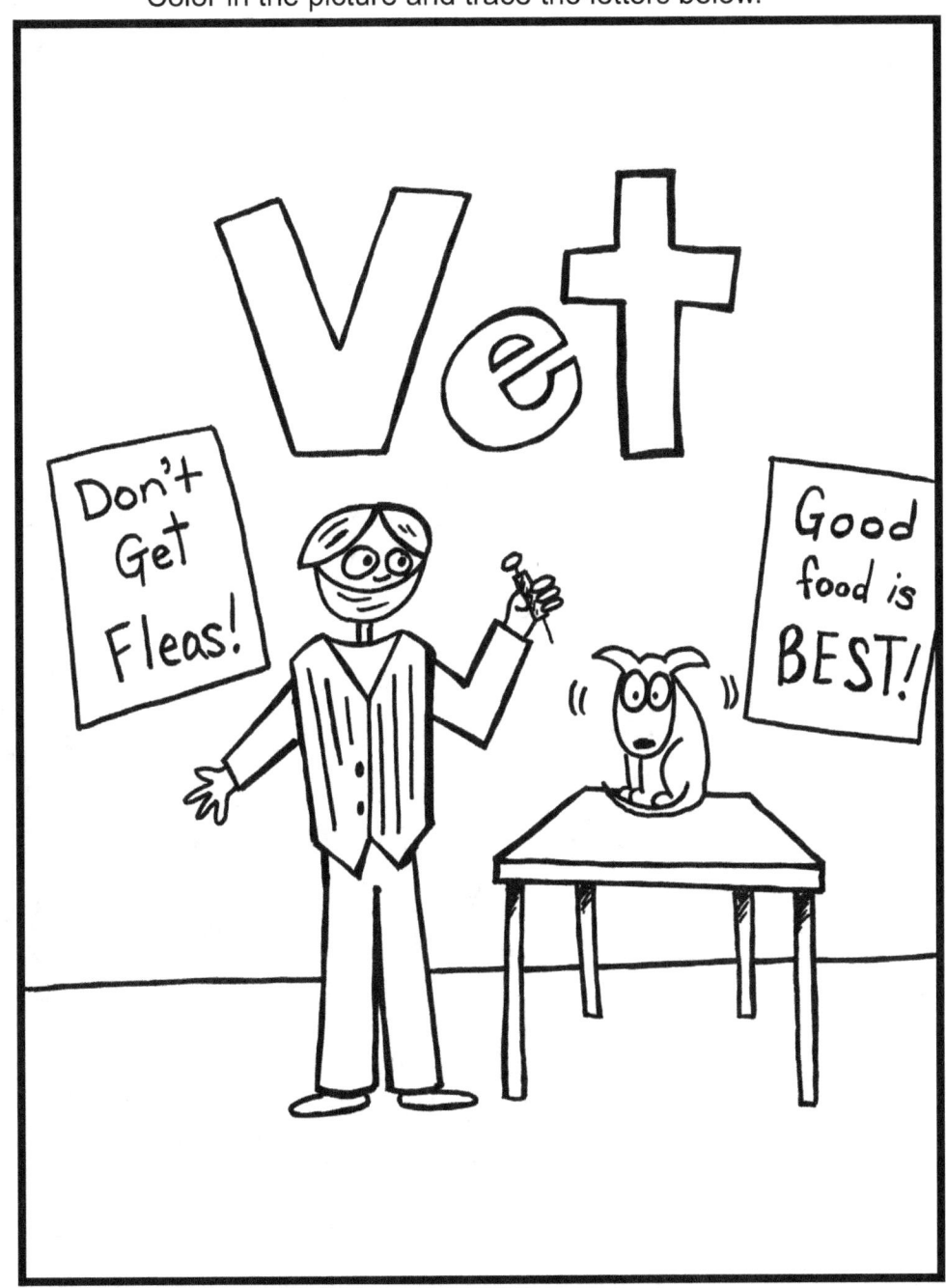

Color in the picture and trace the letters below.

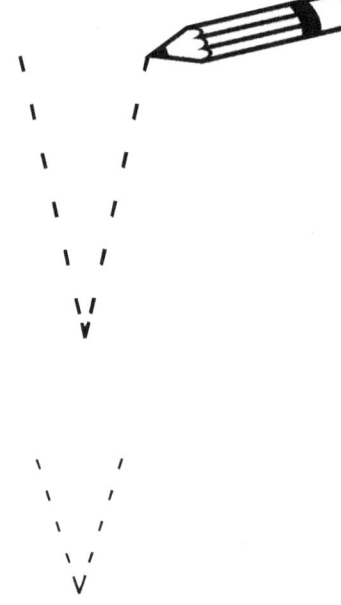

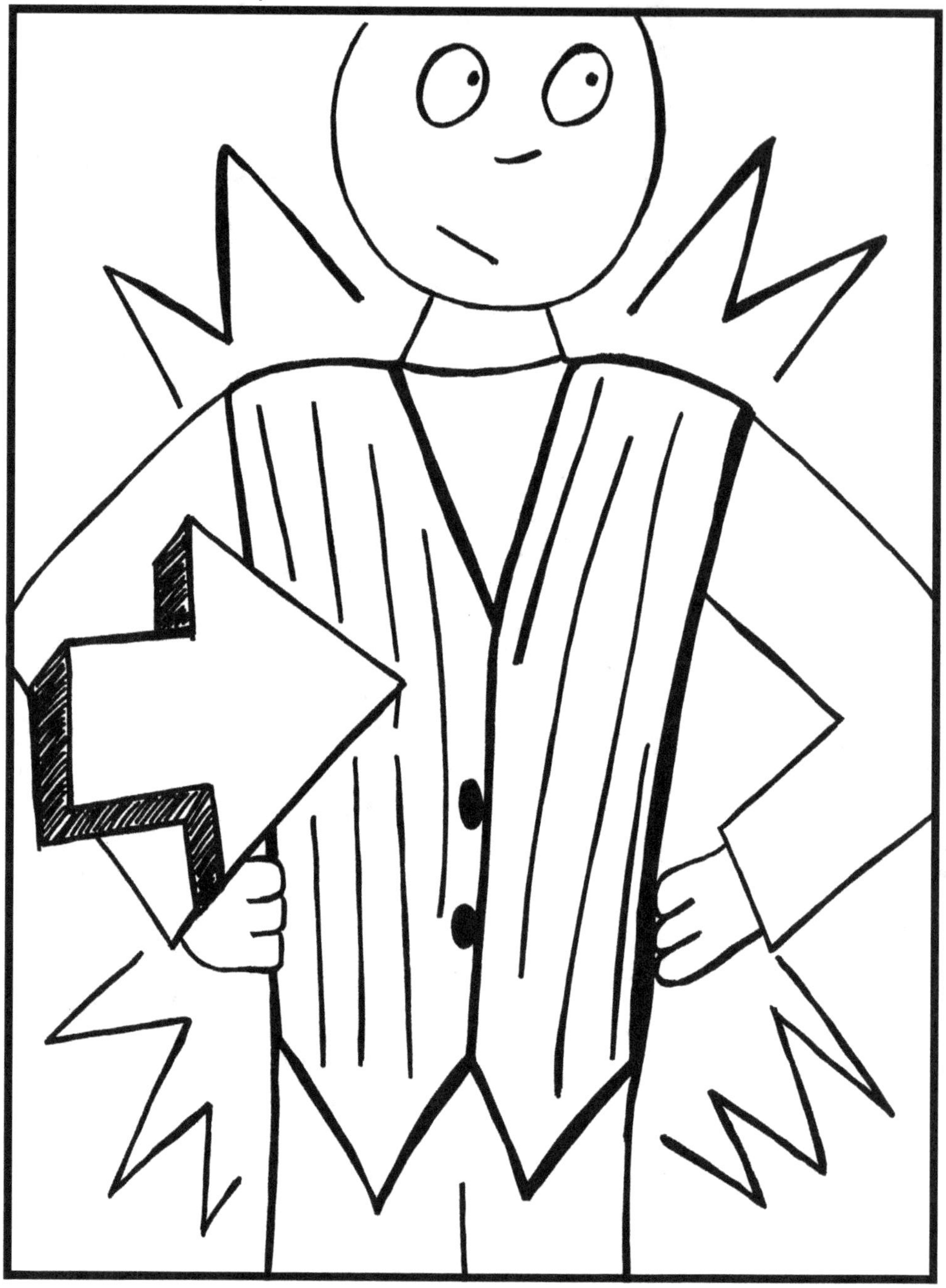

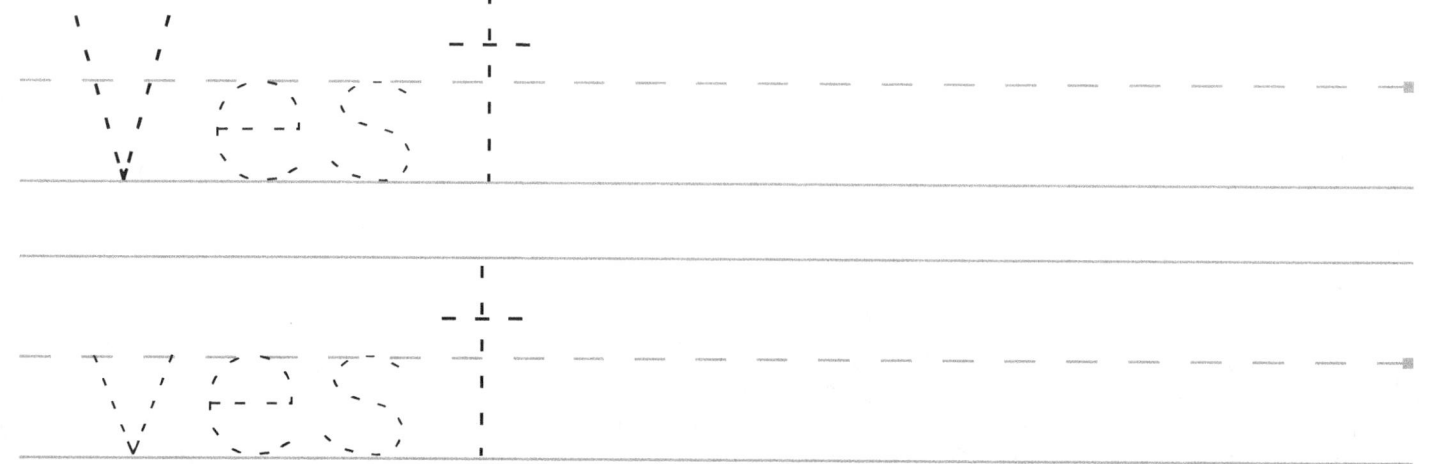

Color the picture, then trace and write the phrase below.

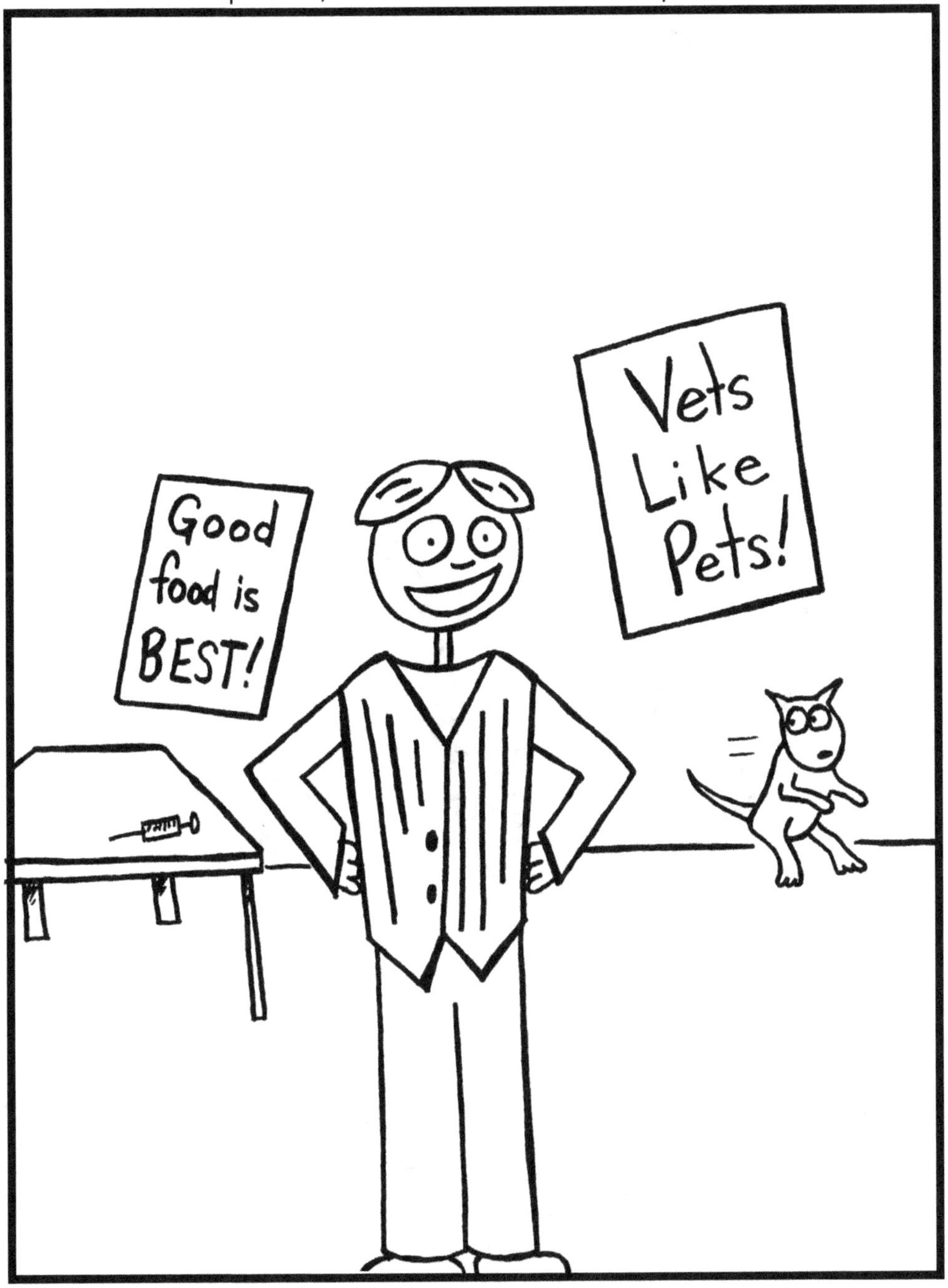

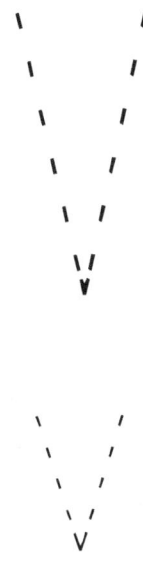

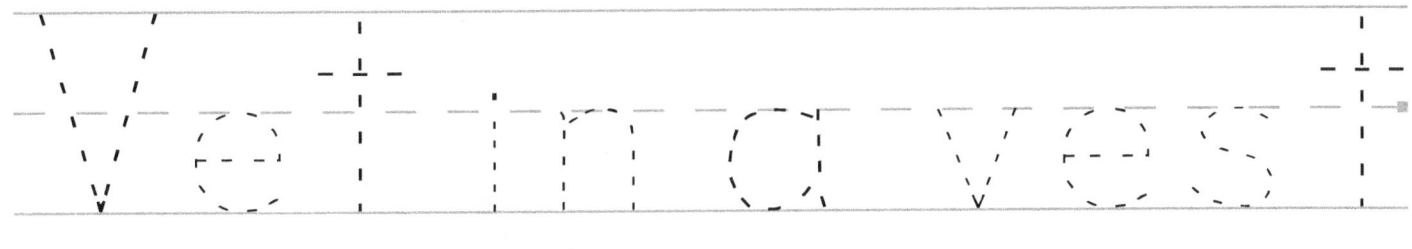

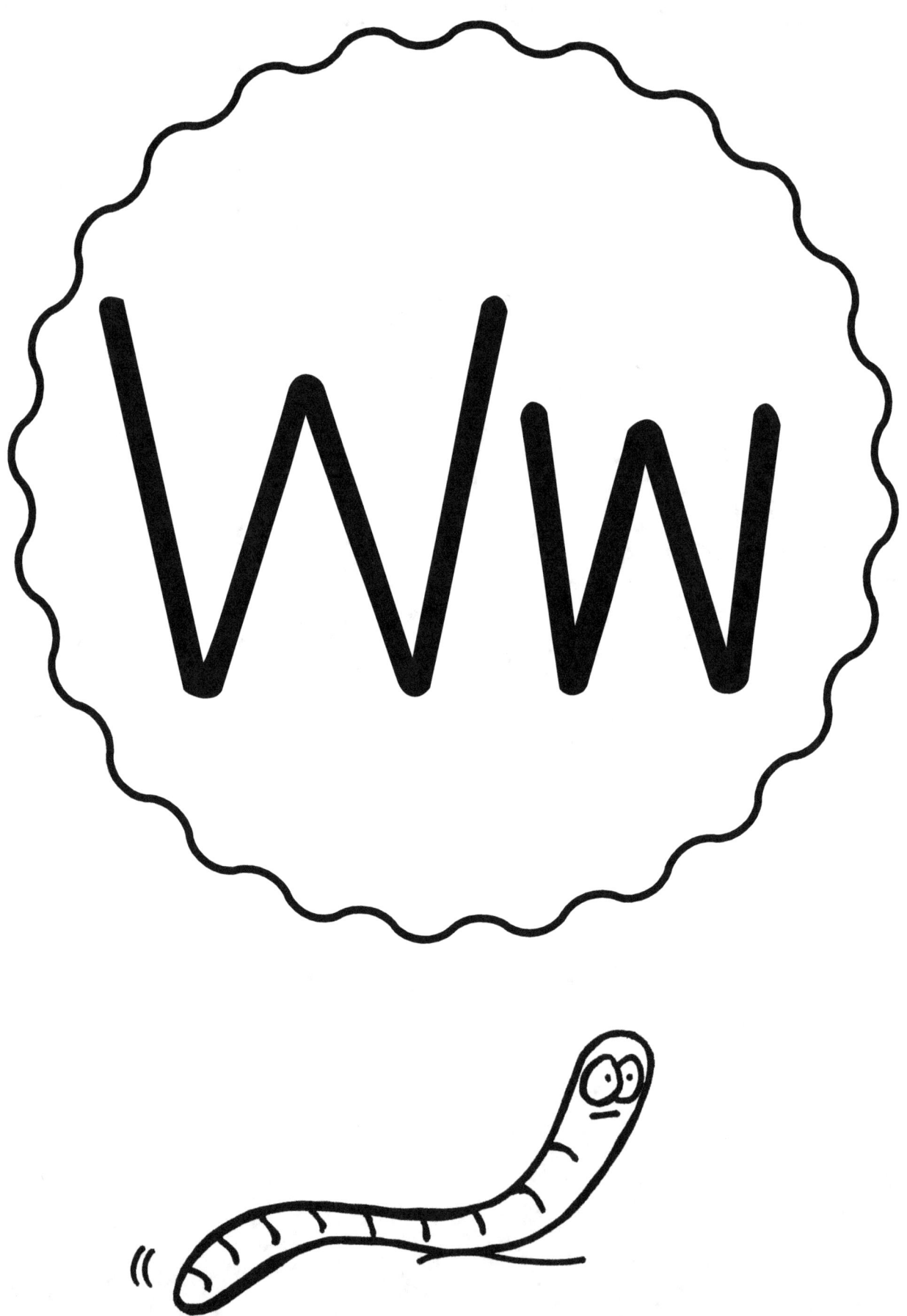

Color the picture, then trace and write the letters below.

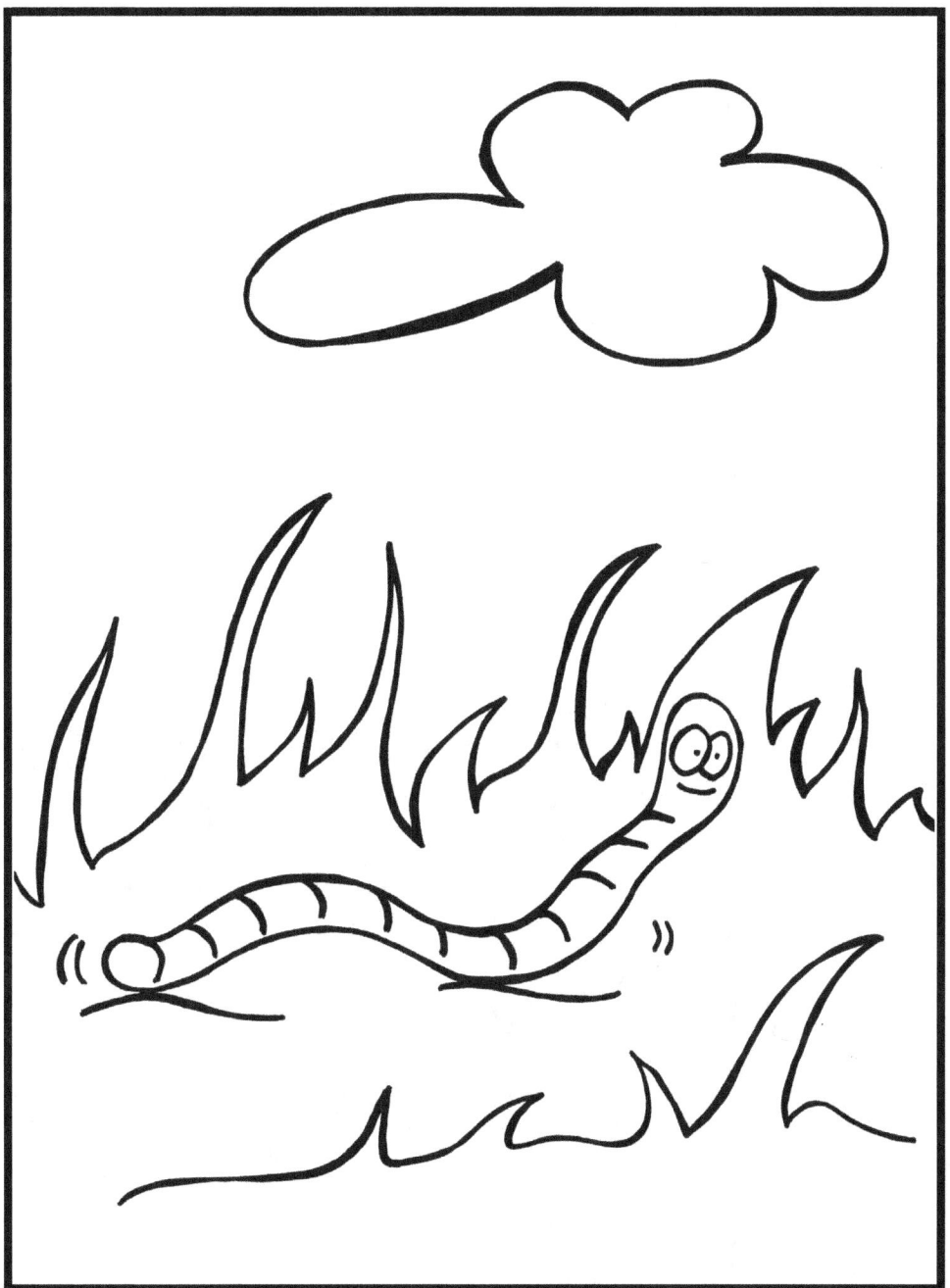

Color in the picture and trace the letters below.

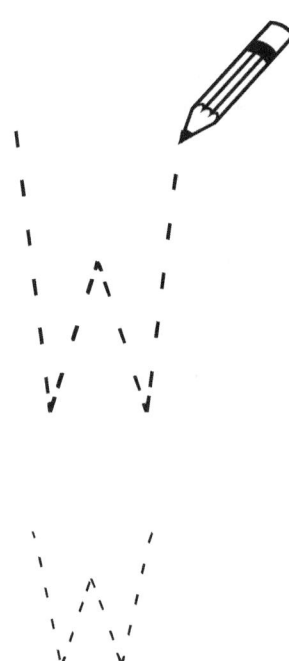

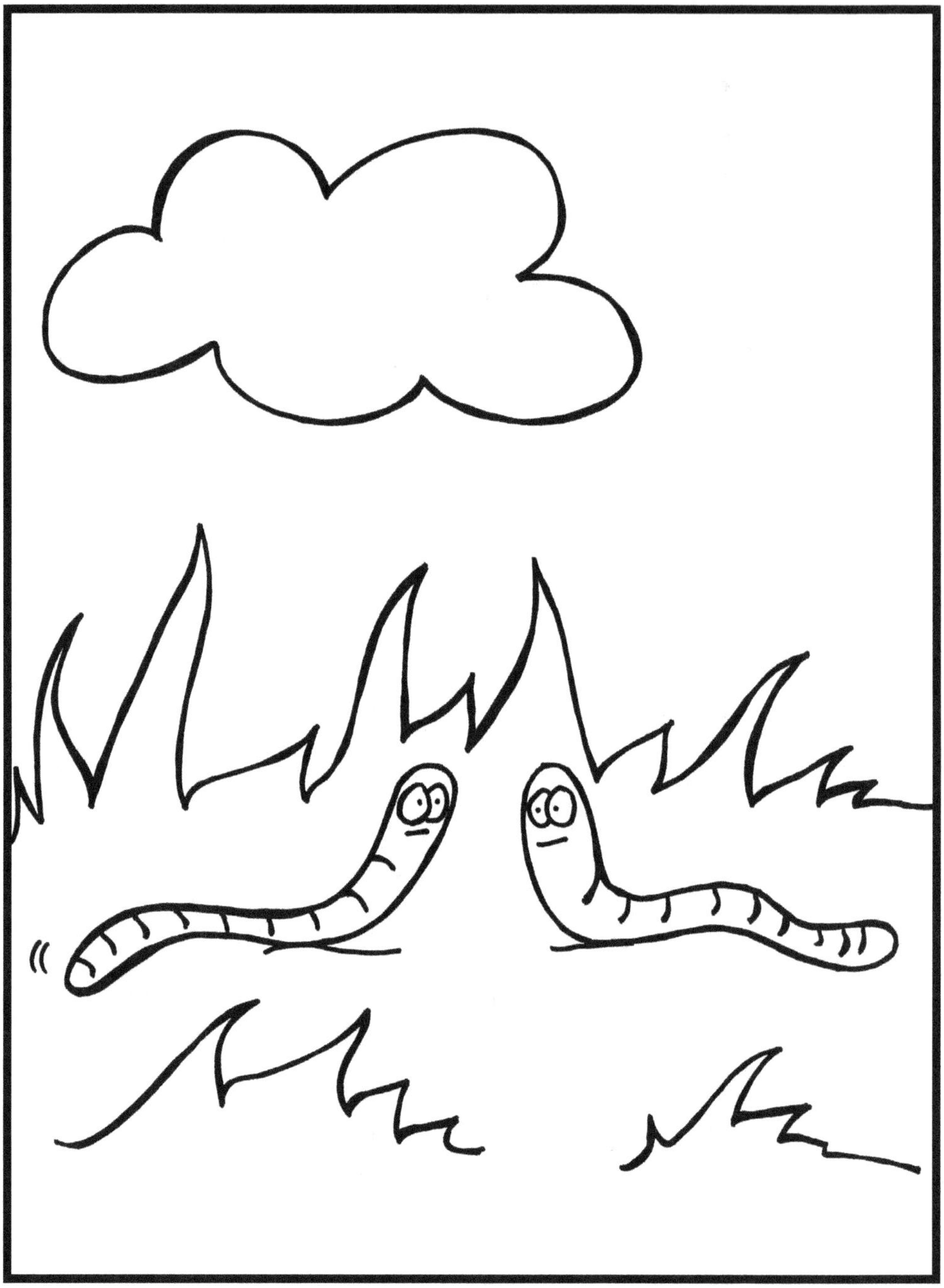

Worm

worm

Color the picture, then trace and write the phrase below.

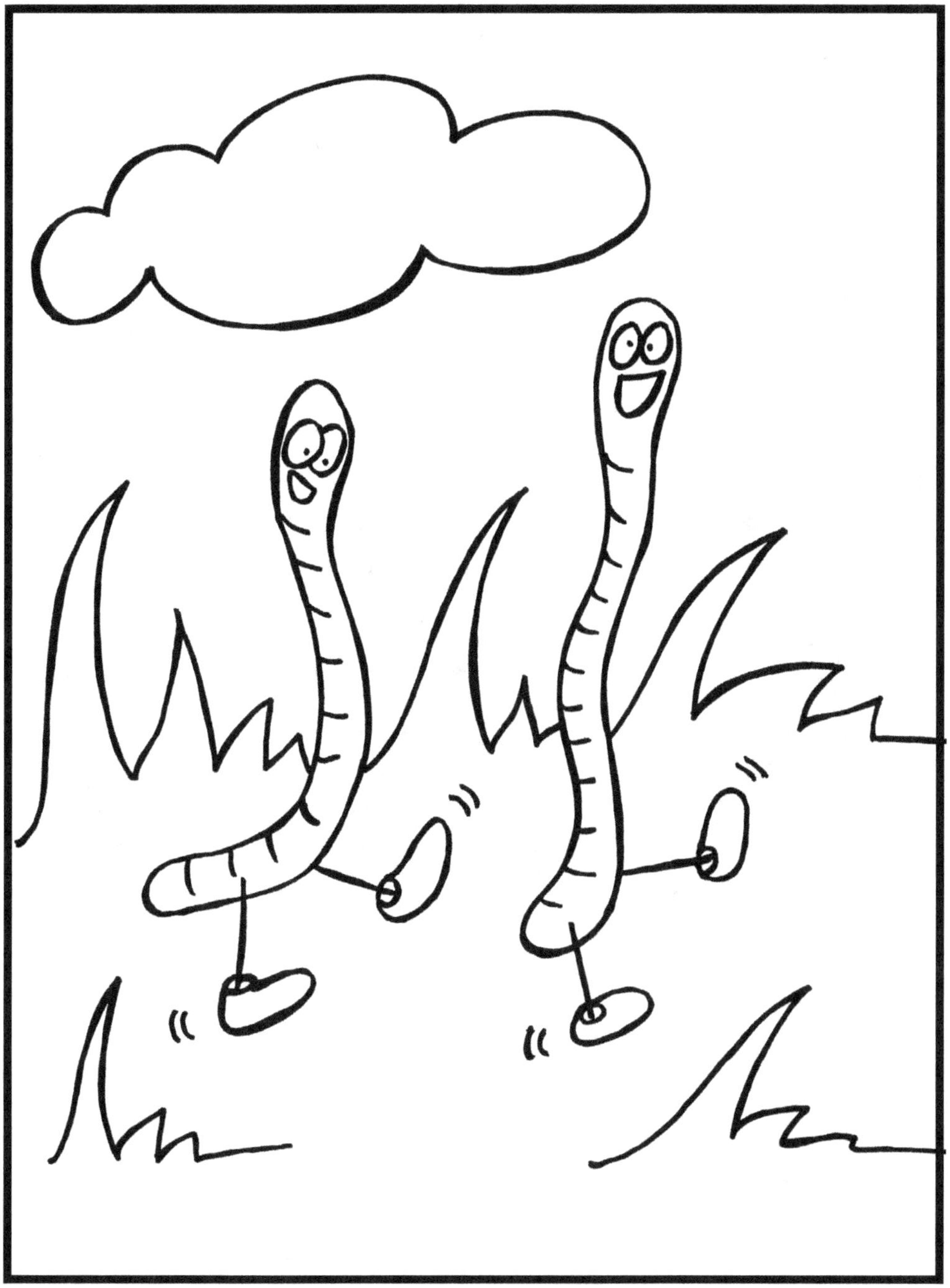

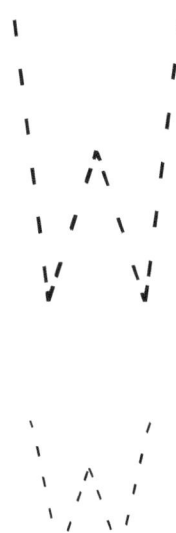

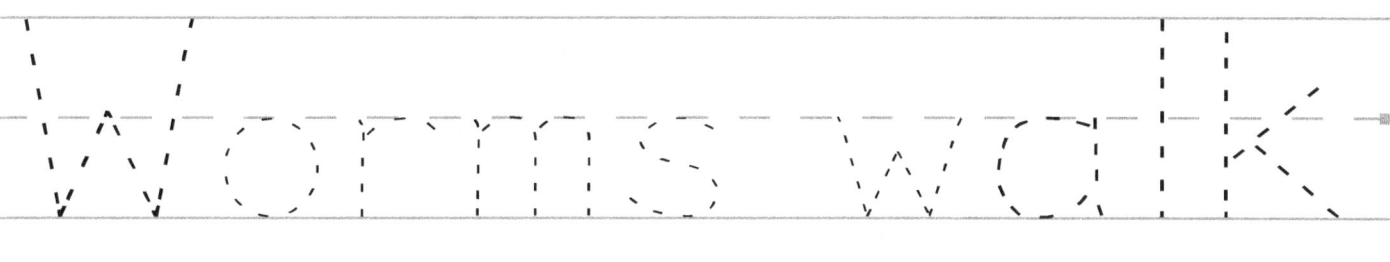

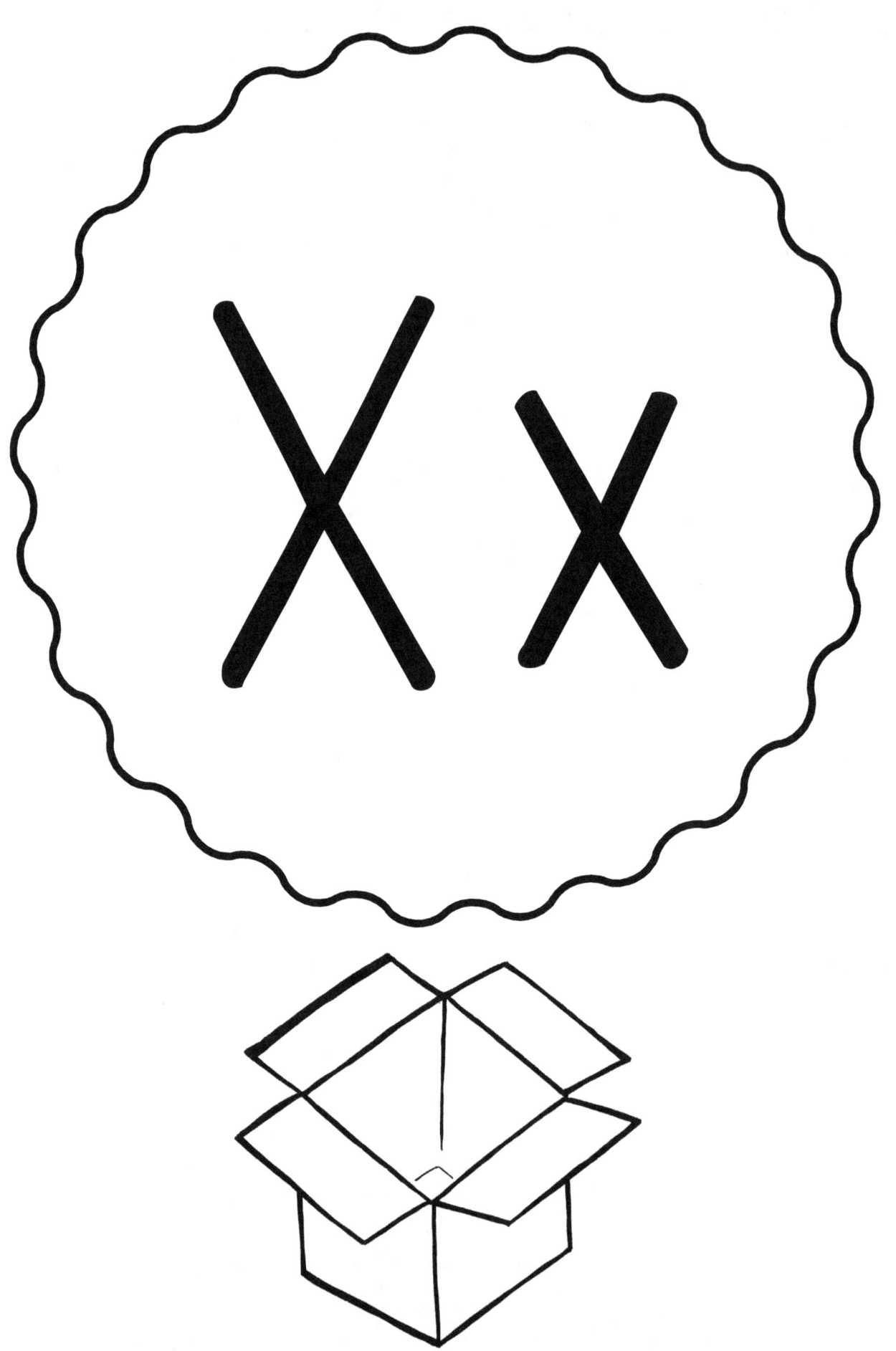

Color the picture, then trace and write the letters below.

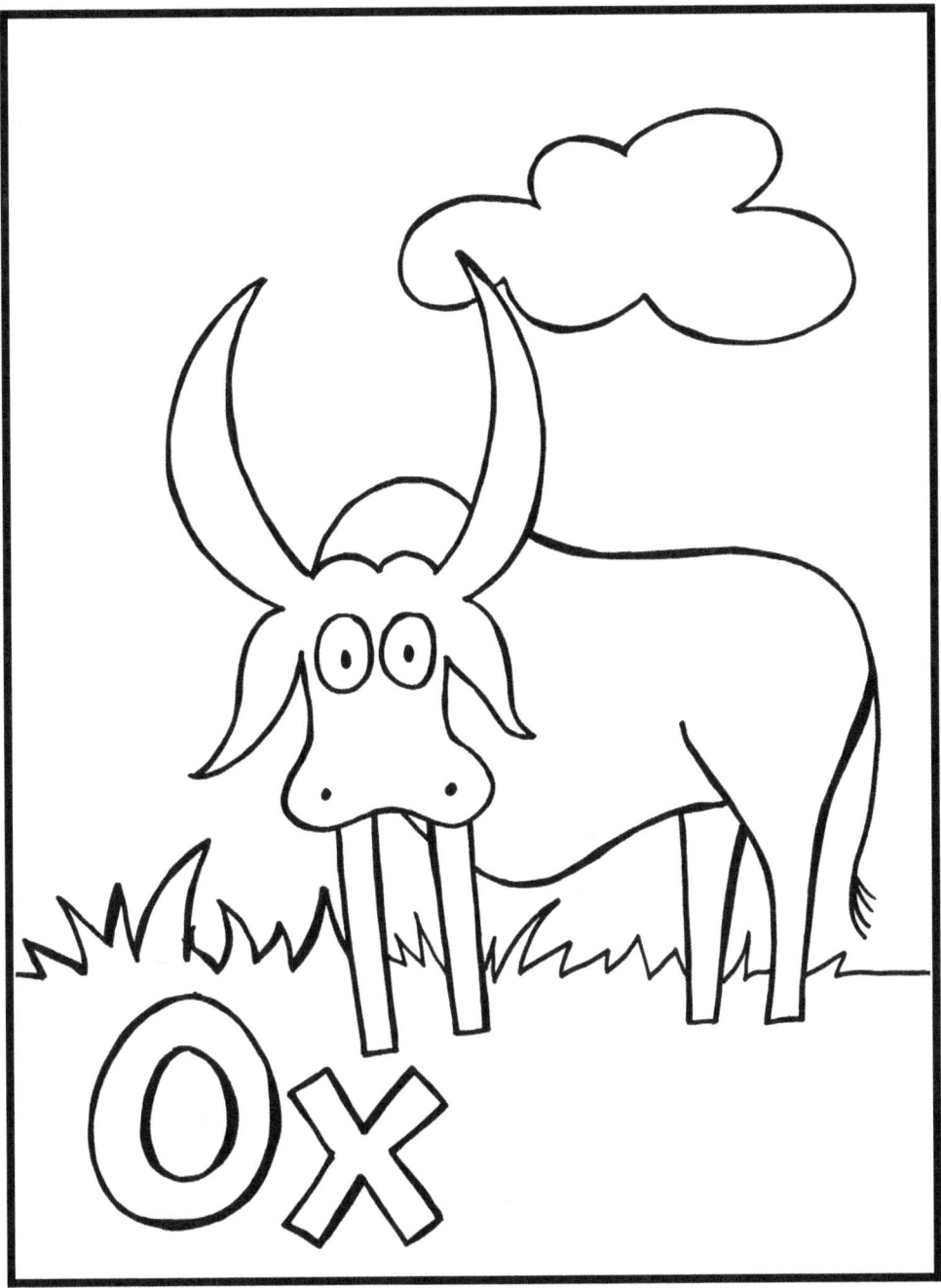

Color the picture, then trace and write the word below.

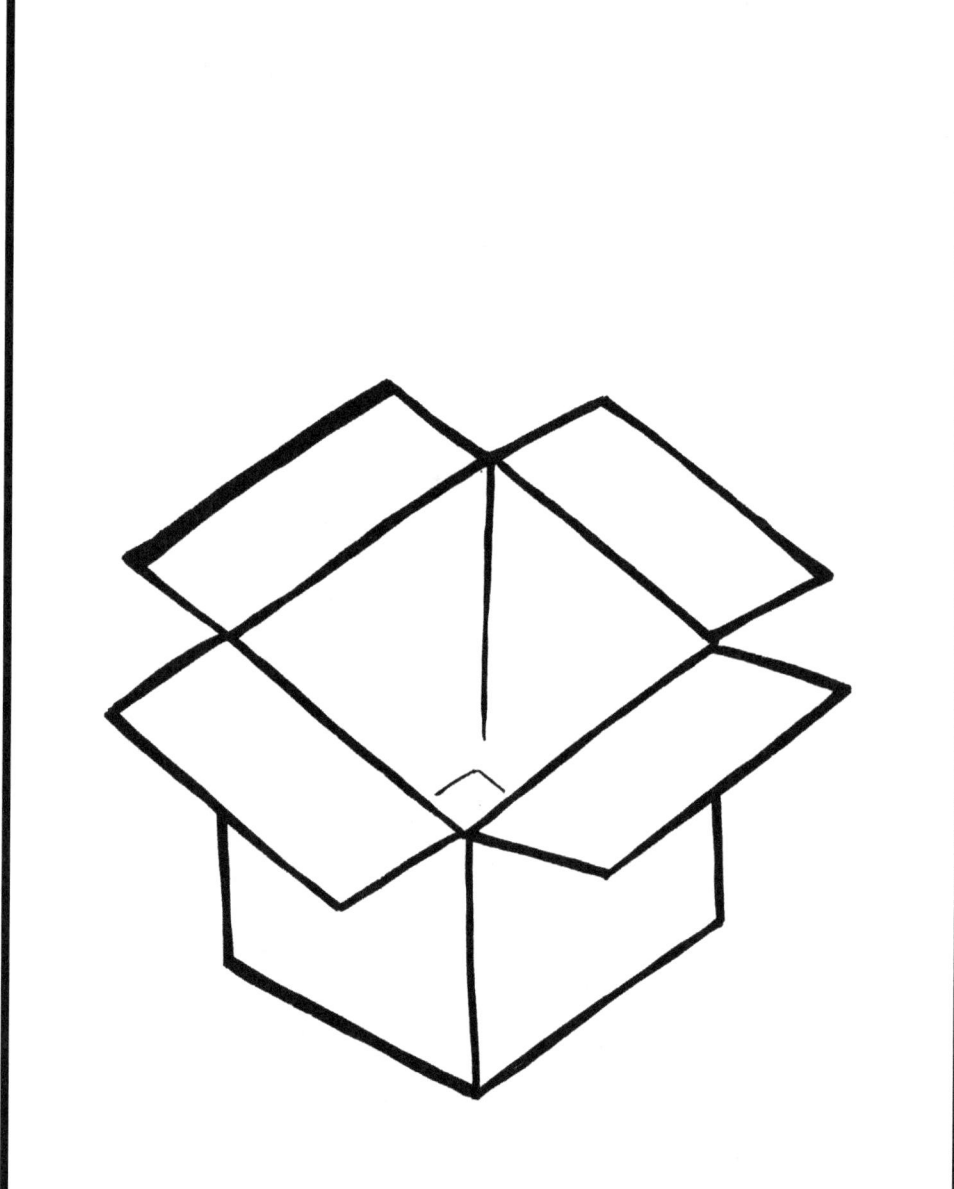

Box

box

Color the picture, then trace and write the phrase below.

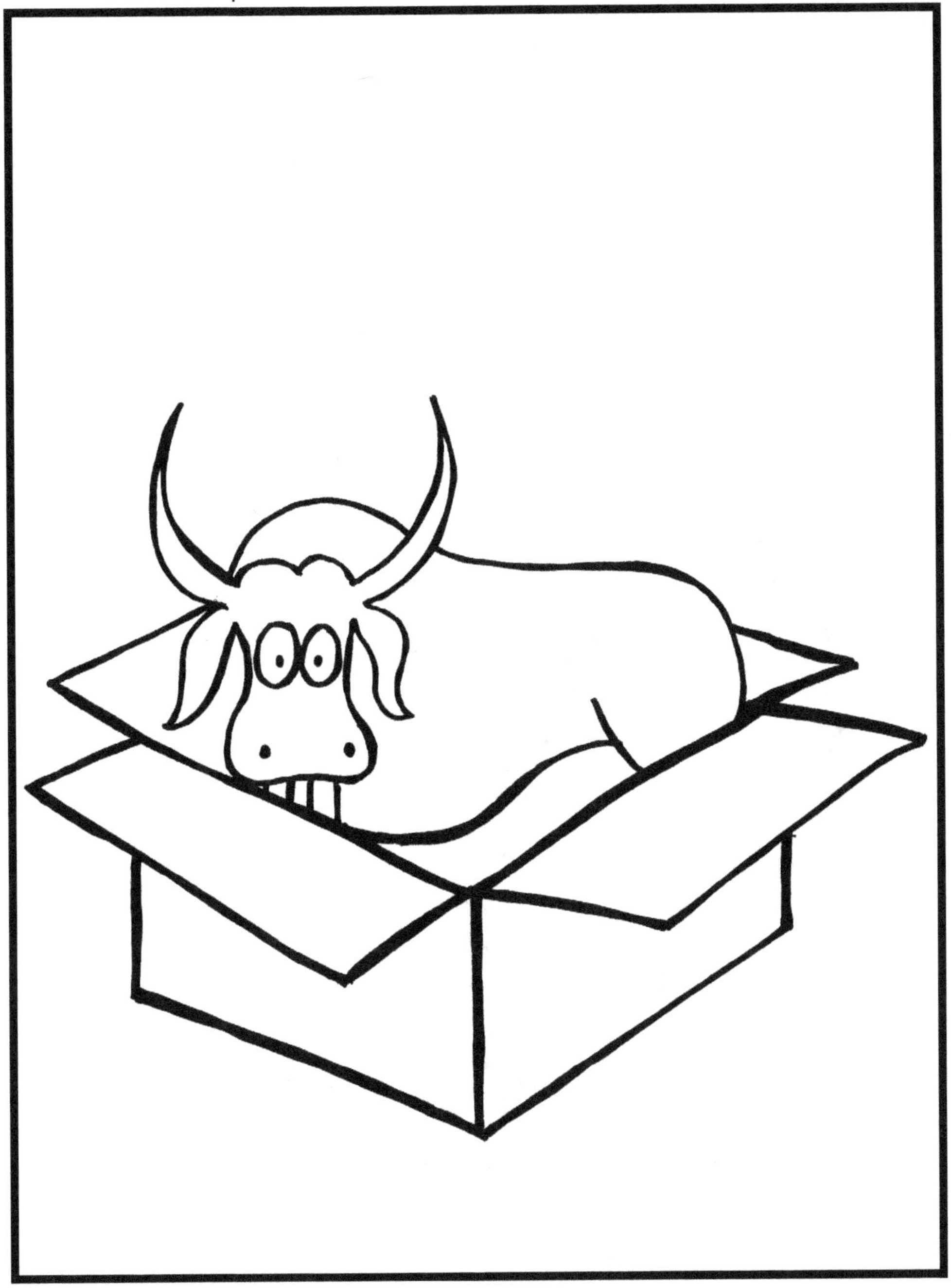

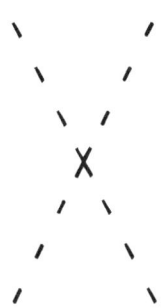

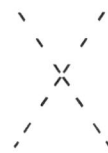

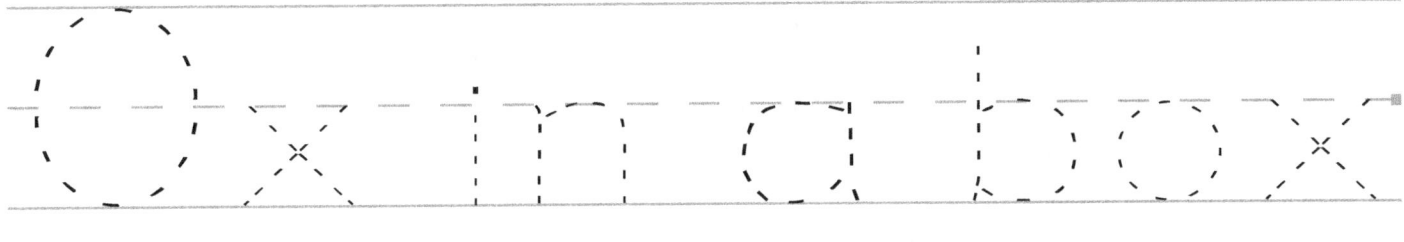

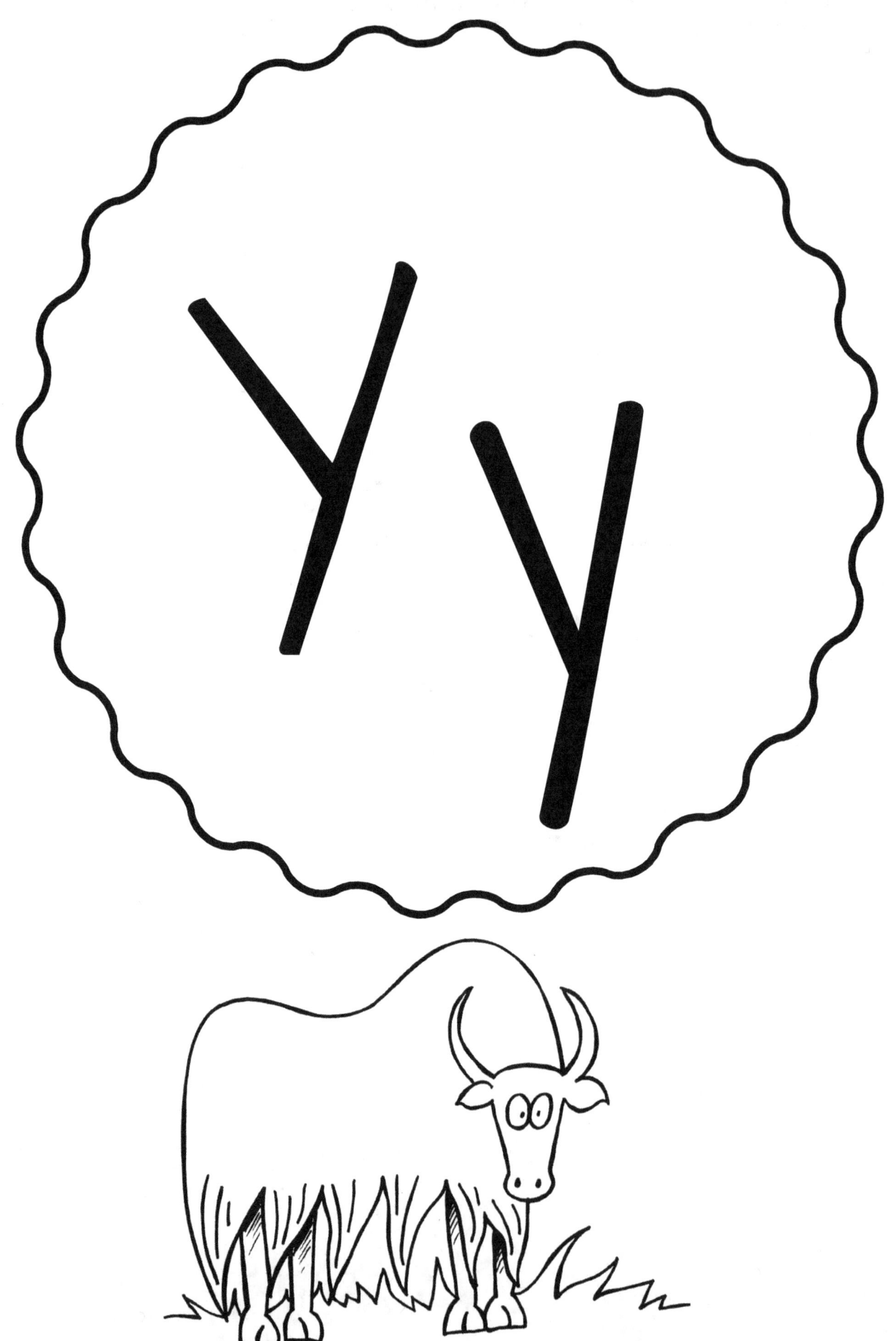

Color the picture, then trace and write the letters below.

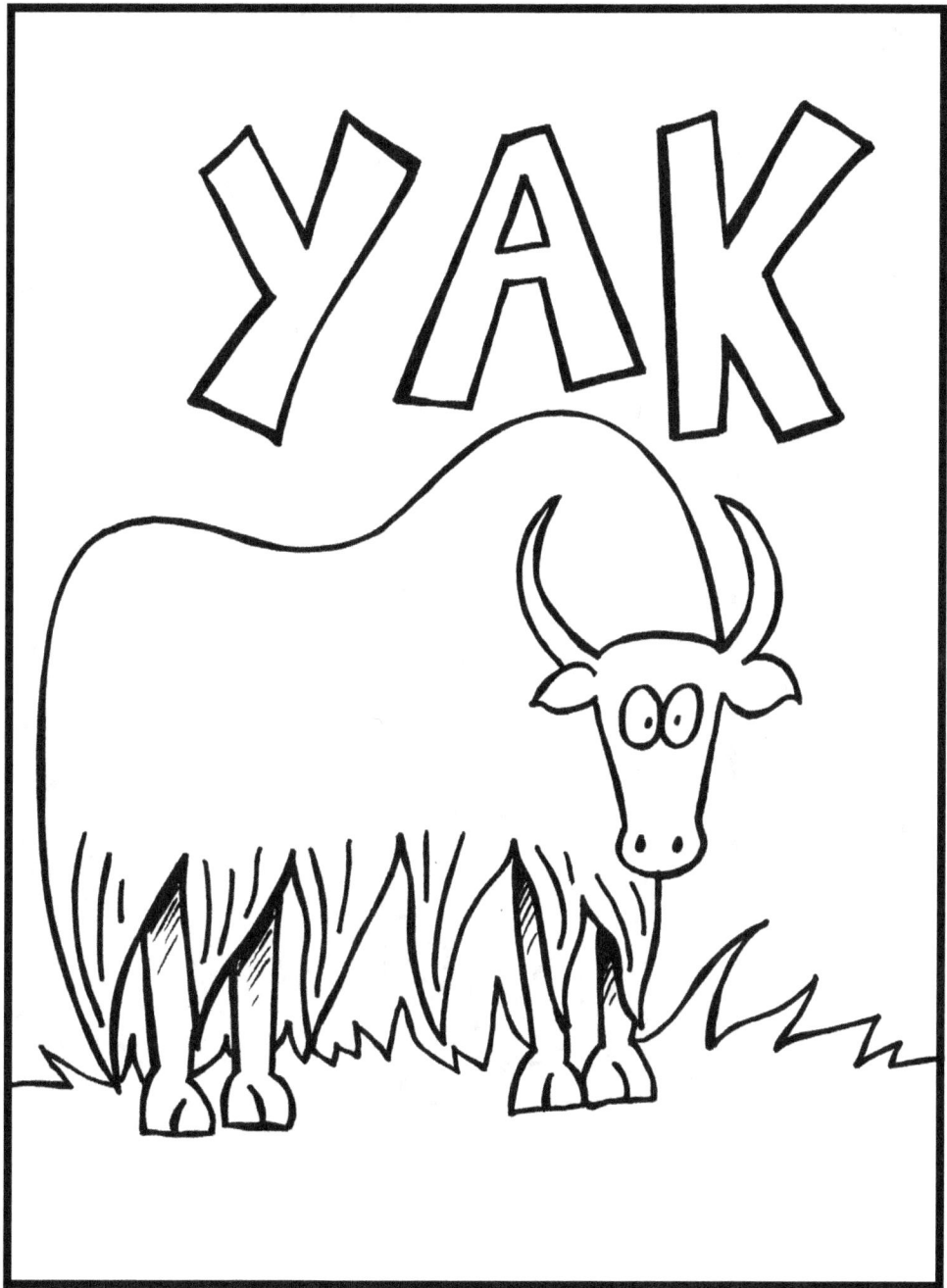

Color the picture, then trace and write the word below.

Y y

Yak

yak

Color the picture, then trace and write the phrase below.

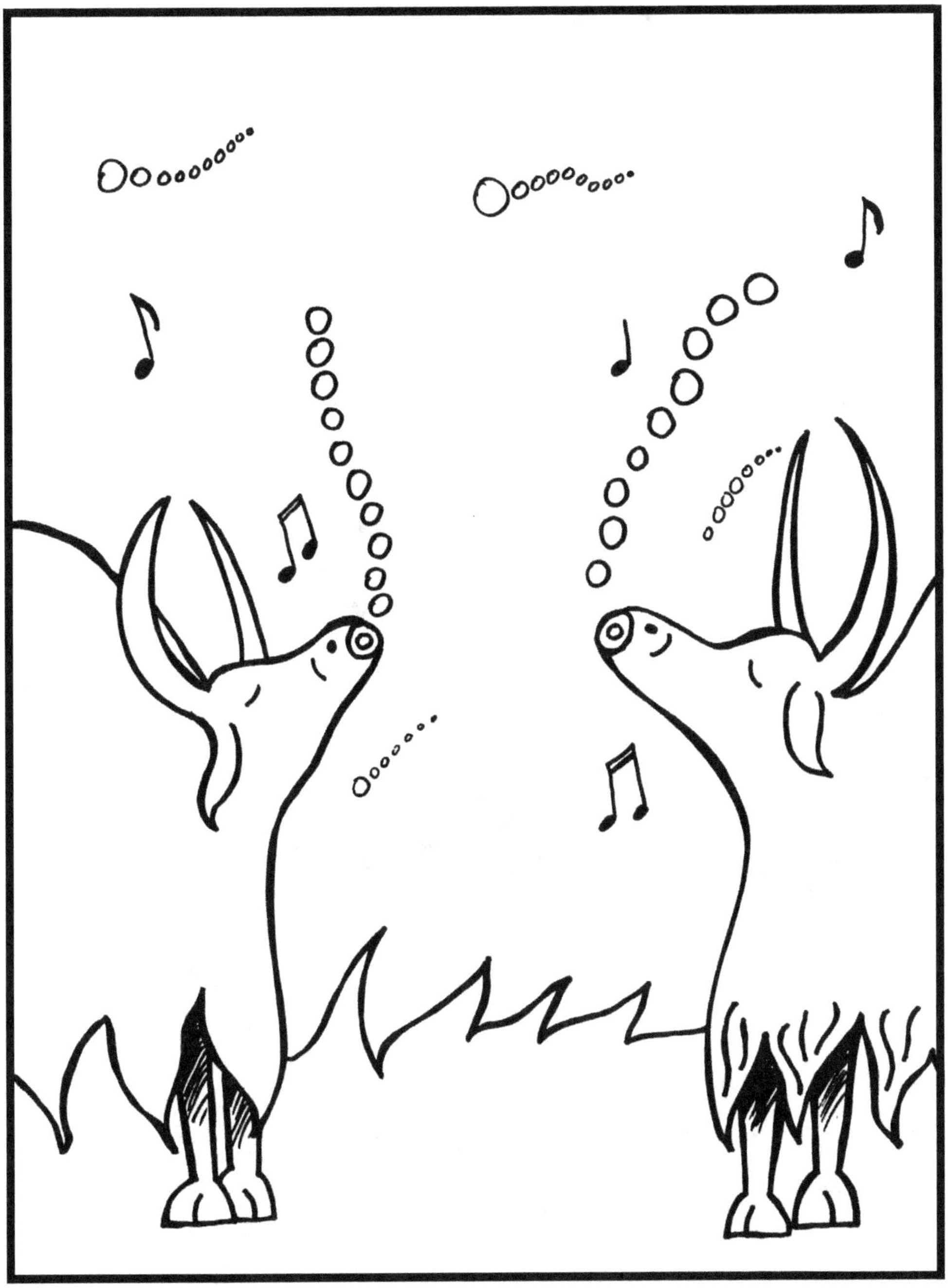

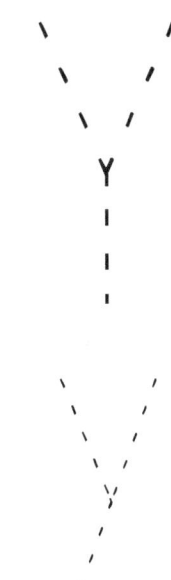

Yaks yodel

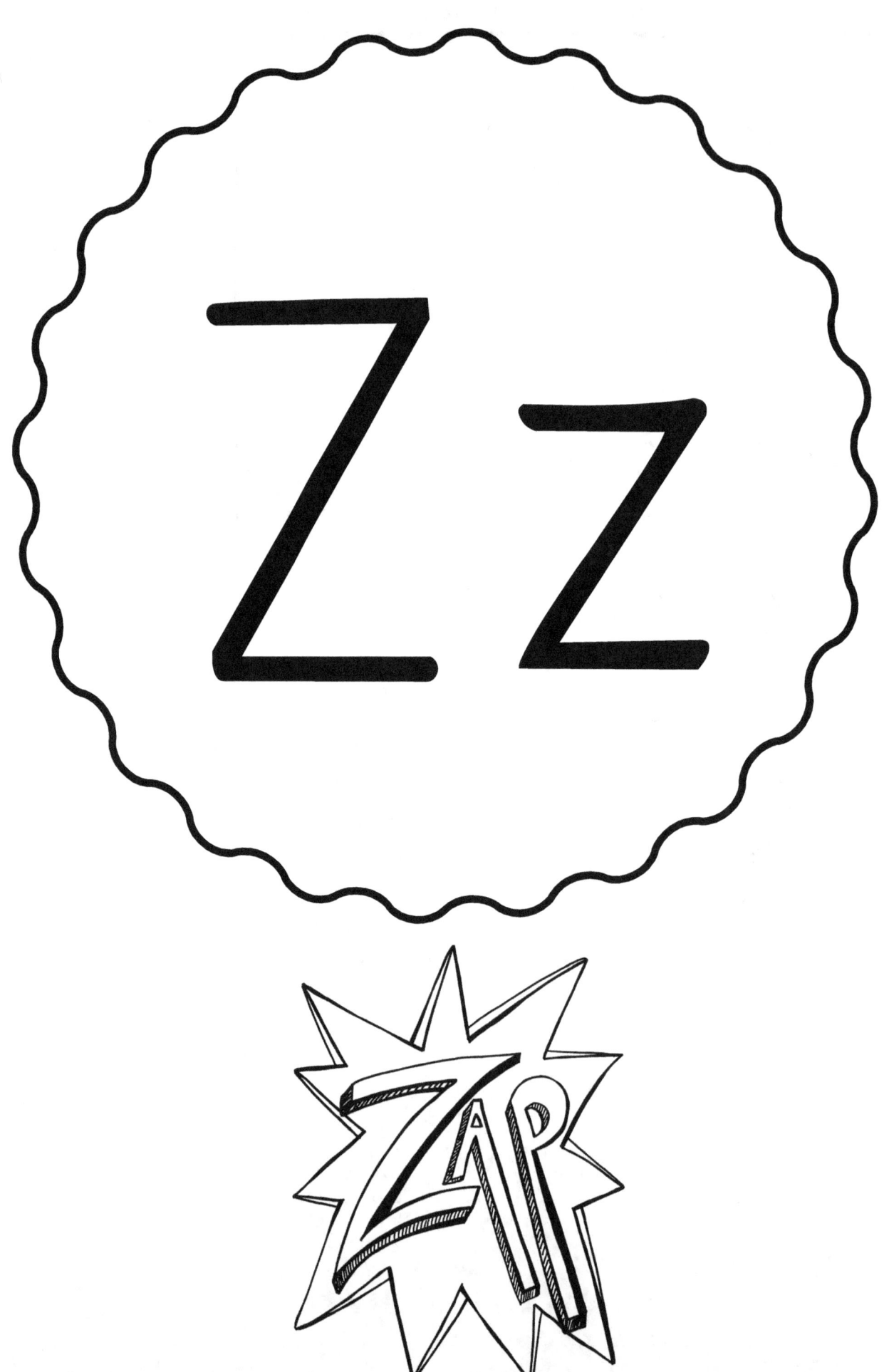

Color the picture, then trace and write the letters below.

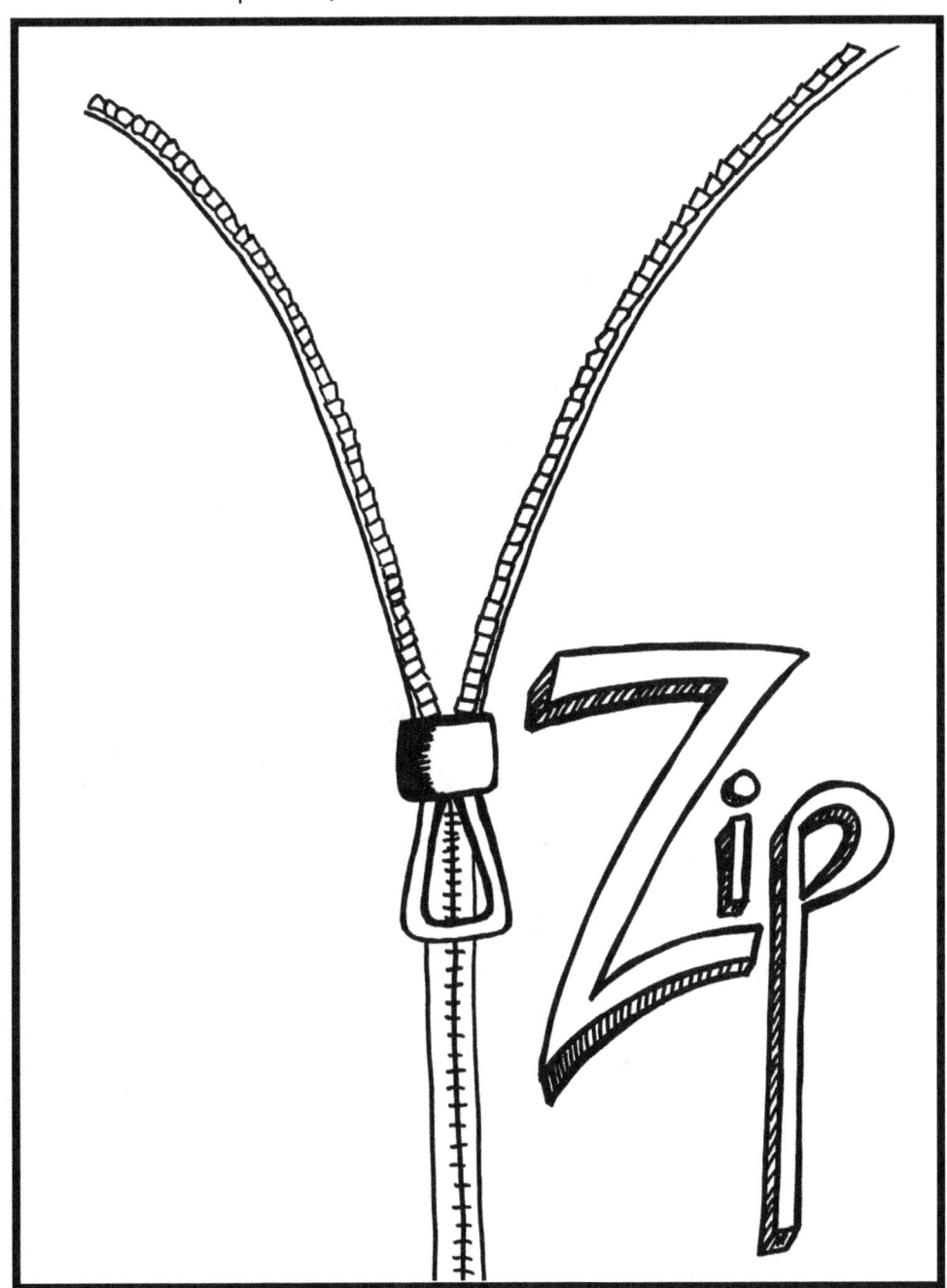

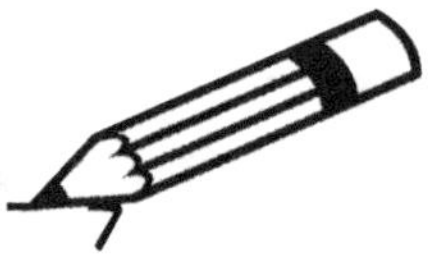

Color the picture, then trace and write the word below.

Z
z

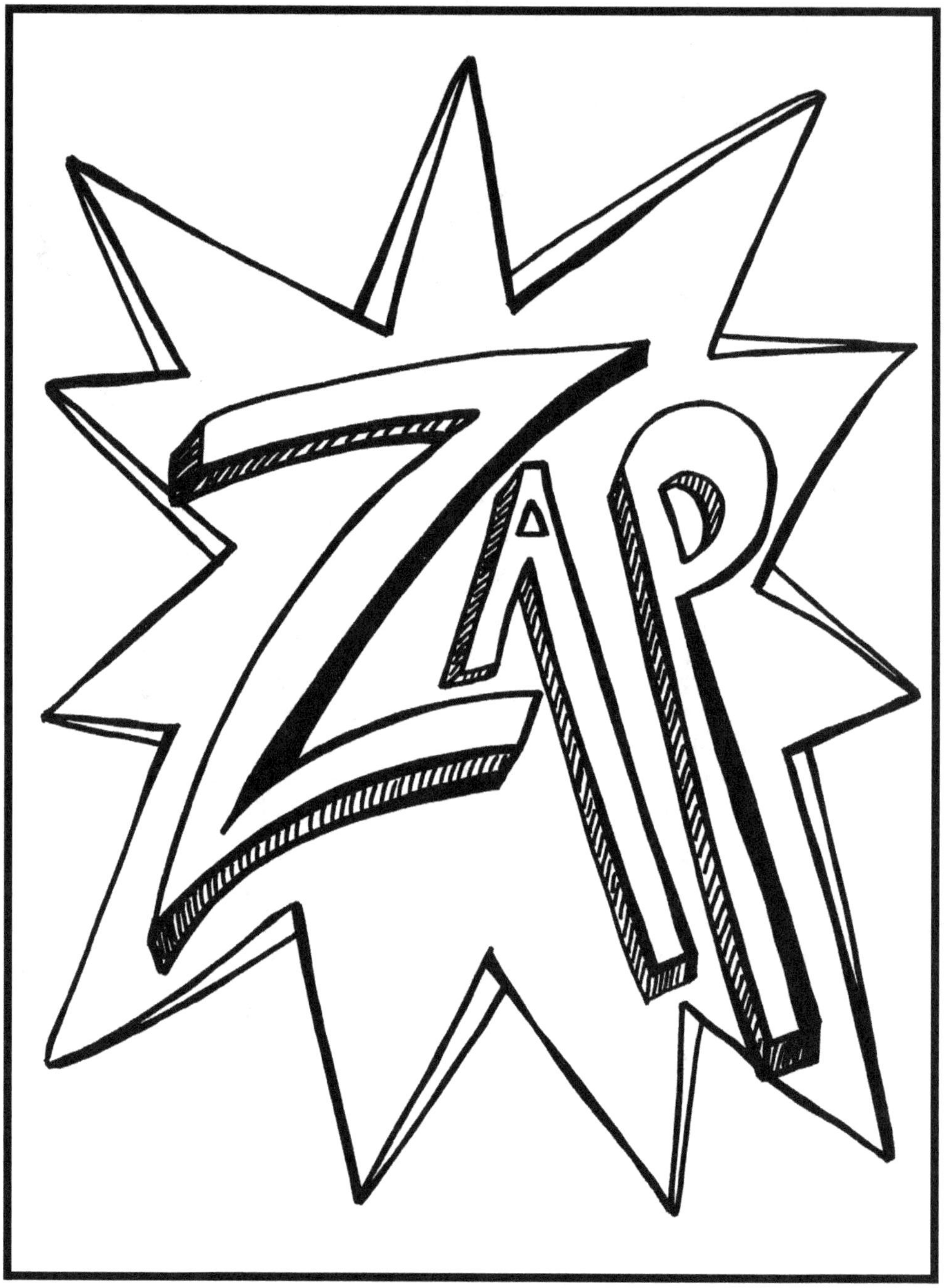

zap
zap

Color the picture, then trace and write the phrase below.

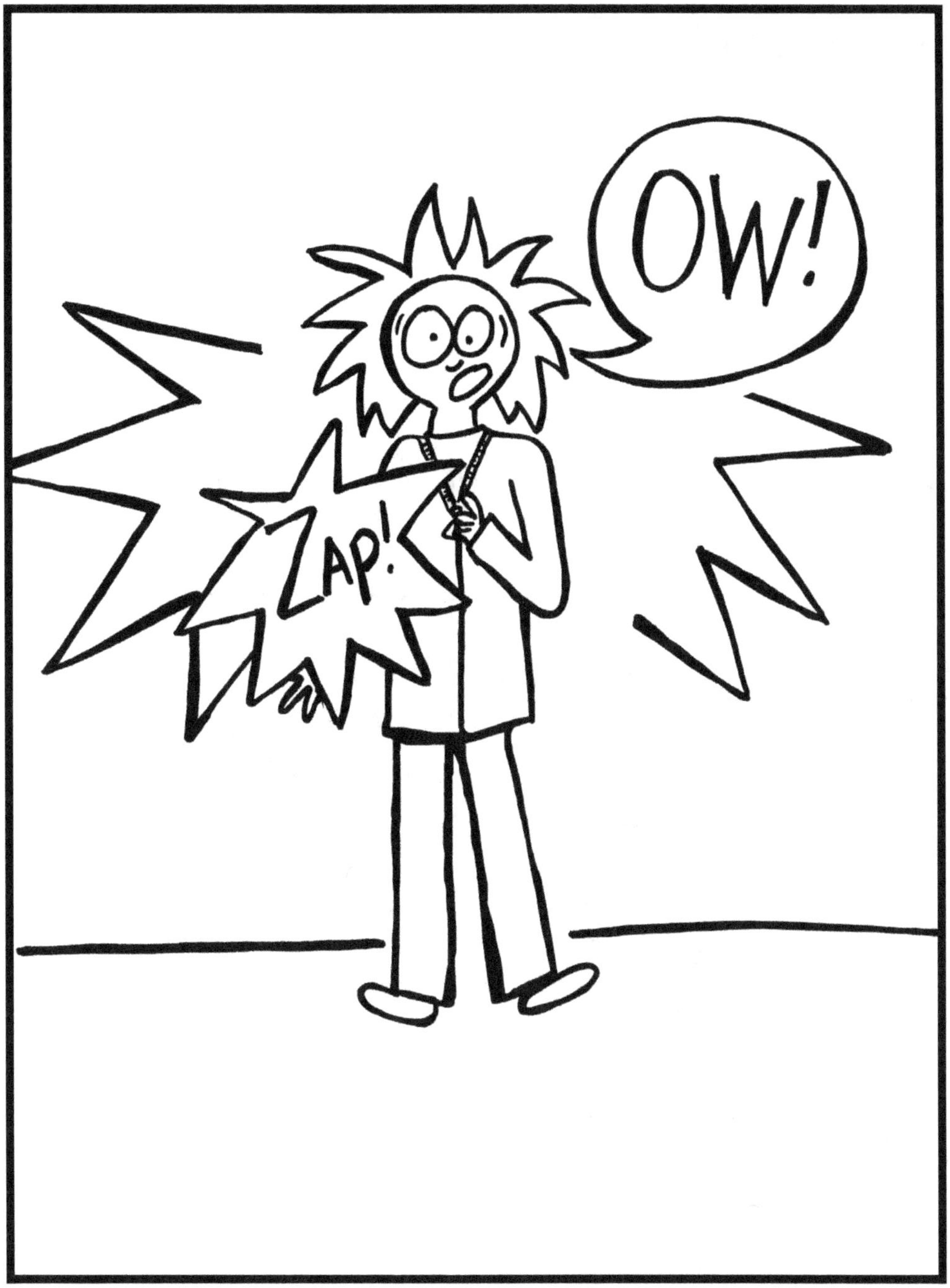

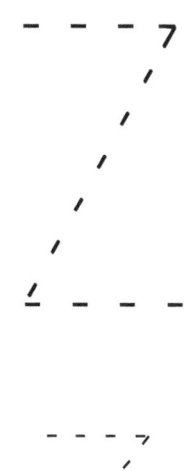

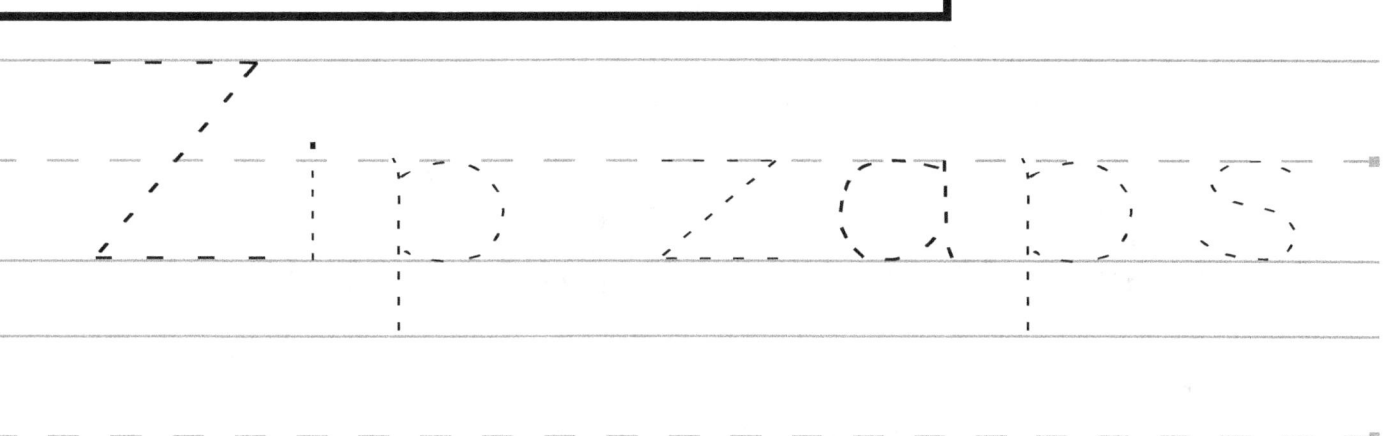

Zip zaps

 # CONGRATULATIONS!

_____
Your name

has completed

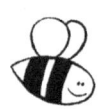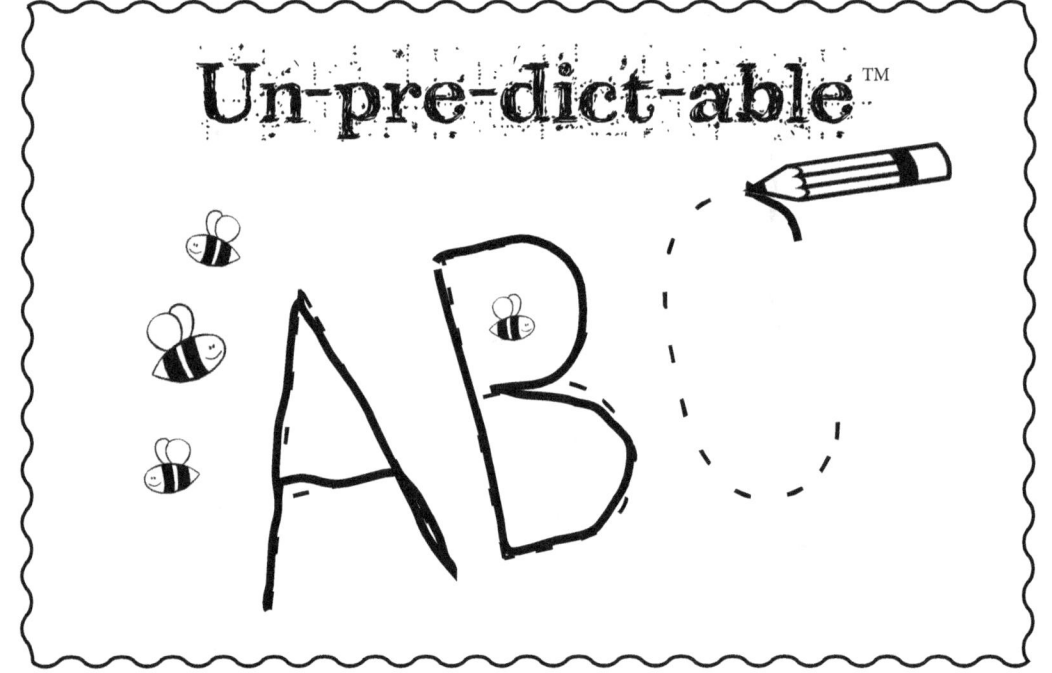

Keep practicing and HAPPY READING!

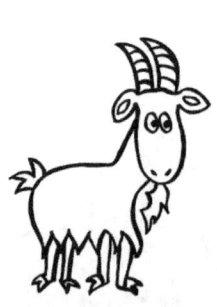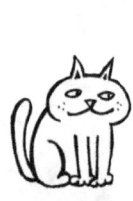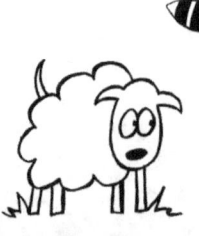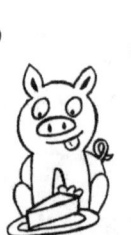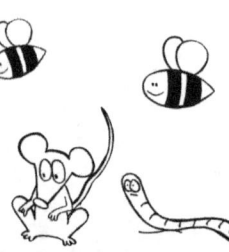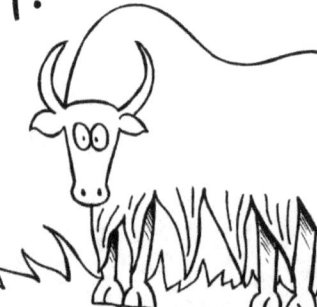

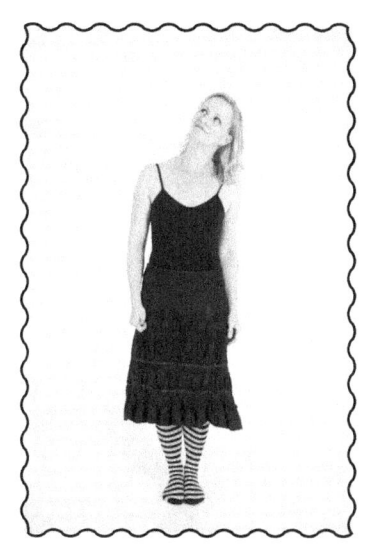

Krysta Bernhardt lives and creates in a little house that she shares with her kids, her husband and her two fat cats. Krysta loves to teach kids, draw, paint, sing, dance, make music and create. Her favorite books have always had big, bold lines and simple, imperfect characters. She believes that if you have an idea, even an imperfect one, it deserves to be created and shared! Keep an eye out for more of Krysta's Un-pre-dict-a-ble and imperfect creations!

Krysta Bernhardt Publishing

If you enjoyed your Un-pre-dict-a-ble adventure, please consider leaving a **review on Amazon** so that other young learners can find out about and enjoy these books! Thank you so much for your support! - Krysta

Find more books at www.KrystaBernhardtPublishing.com

www.ingramcontent.com/pod-product-compliance
Lightning Source LLC
Chambersburg PA
CBHW062330220526
45469CB00008B/2648